Accounting For World Class Operations

A Practical Guide
for Providing Relevant Information
in Support of the Lean Enterprise

ACCOUNTING FOR WORLD CLASS OPERATIONS

A PRACTICAL GUIDE
FOR PROVIDING RELEVANT INFORMATION
IN SUPPORT OF THE LEAN ENTERPRISE

JERROLD M. SOLOMON
AUTHOR OF THE SHINGO PRIZE WINNING BOOK *WHO'S COUNTING?*
AND ROSEMARY FULLERTON

WCM Associates
Fort Wayne, Indiana

Accounting for World Class Operations:
A Practical Guide for Providing Relevant Information in
Support of the Lean Enterprise

By
Jerrold M. Solomon and Rosemary Fullerton

WCM Associates
P.O. Box 8035
Fort Wayne, IN 46898-8035
260-637-8064
www.wcmfg.com

ISBN #978-0-9793331-0-1
      #0-9793331-0-5

Front and rear cover design by:

Robert Howard
Rhoward@bookgraphics.com

Book and text design by WCM Associates
Printed and bound by:
Thomson-Shore, Inc.
Dexter, MI
(734) 426-3939

Layout was completed using Adobe(R) Pagemaker 7.0.

Library of Congress Catalog Card Number:
2007933556

DEDICATIONS

*To my loving parents, Iris and Robert Solomon,
who molded my world to enrich my talents,
making me their center, and teaching through example.
Their support gave me the desire to practice those things I love
and challenge myself with those things of which I dreamed.*

JERRY SOLOMON

*To my children, who bring purpose to my life.
To Shane, Danette & Nathan for their love and encouragement.
To the loving memory of Dustin,
whose warmth and enthusiasm continue to permeate our souls.*

ROSEMARY FULLERTON

ACKNOWLEDGEMENTS

This book became a reality with the help of a number of colleagues. First, I would like to thank Bill Stabler, the Vice President of Finance for the largest group of companies at Barry-Wehmiller. Bill has embraced all of our ideas and supported every step of our Lean accounting transformation at MarquipWardUnited, a division of Barry-Wehmiller Companies, Inc. He has been a tremendous conduit for passing along the message to our corporate accounting team, our other divisions, and our external auditors. Without Bill's support, these real-world examples would never have been possible.

Dennis Hentschel and Bob Switalski, MarquipWardUnited's Plant Controller and Cost Accountant respectively, have also tirelessly supported the accounting transition to Lean. Without their concerted effort to restate all historical costs and embrace new techniques, the applicability of these new principles could not have been proven in the real world.

I would like to thank the staff at the Maryland World Class Manufacturing Consortium, (MWCMC), a unique organization funded by the Maryland Department of Business and Economic Development. The MWCMC is a world class organization in its own right for its groundbreaking efforts assisting Maryland manufacturing companies with their Lean journey. I would also like to express my gratitude to the Consortia for providing me with continual access to world class companies and seasoned Lean practitioners.

And of course, special thanks to my loving wife, Sheila, who has once again learned a great deal about another aspect of Lean. Her patient and supportive nature were a constant source of encouragement. Without her, this book would not have been possible.

JERRY SOLOMON

My thanks are extended to Utah State University (USU), its College of Business and School of Accountancy for granting a sabbatical that has allowed me to gain a practical understanding of the Lean philosophy that I had only experienced previously from an academic perspective. The financial support of a Shingo Prize research grant and the intellectual encouragement of Dr. Ross Robson, long-time Executive Director of the Shingo Prize, were also instrumental in the pursuit of my sabbatical objectives. My informative and rewarding experience as an examiner for USU's prestigious Shingo Prize for Manufacturing Excellence over the past eight years has been helpful in building a better understanding of the need for refocusing accounting practice. The creativity, leadership, and hard work of Shingo applicants are instructive and impressive.

Heartfelt appreciation goes to my most significant Lean mentor, Jerry Solomon. His passion for, understanding of, and commitment to Lean principles regardless of personal career risks demonstrate unusual courage, conviction, and leadership.

I could not have made a meaningful contribution to this book without the expert "real-world" tutelage provided by Brian Maskell and his colleagues, as they played a catalytic role in modifying firms' accounting systems to address the informational needs of their Lean operations. I am also grateful for the controllers and managers who generously welcomed me to their plants during my sabbatical and trusted me with opportunities to participate in Kaizen and other improvement events.

Finally, words are inadequate for expressing my gratitude to my amazing husband, Herb, who is my confidant, editor, and advocate. His love, wisdom, and understanding provide constant inspiration and motivation for all my worthwhile pursuits.

ROSEMARY FULLERTON

TABLE OF CONTENTS

PART III

Lean Accounting and Human Resources Applications

PART IV

Summary

PREFACE

During my 18 years as executive director of the Shingo Prize, manufacturing has experienced a world-wide revolution. Achievements realized via JIT and then Lean have been dramatic and remarkable. Toyota has clearly emerged as the automotive world leader. Today, Toyota is the class of world class business with most of the world striving to copy Toyota's success. Just a few years ago, the revolution was only found on the factory floor. Yet, Lean was described by most commentators and Lean gurus as a total business strategy. Only in the last few years have we begun to pay attention to the role of Lean in the transactional areas of business, such as marketing, sales, human resources, information technology, quality, and particularly accounting. With only a few exceptions, senior leaders have failed to grasp the "power of lean" in terms of total business system improvement and competitiveness.

One major obstacle of Lean business system implementation has been traditional cost accounting systems. Typical standard accounting reports are too complex, difficult for non-accountants to understand, and do not appropriately reflect firm improvements. There has been a disconnect between the accounting office and operations managers, with the latter generating their own internal performance reports that also generally failed to document the financial implications of shop-floor improvements. A system perspective has not existed.

Having an appropriate accounting system in place is especially vital to the Lean process, because firms need performance measurements that reflect the benefits of change made from implementing Lean practices. Too often those benefits are hidden in outdated accounting reports filled with indecipherable, archaic jargon. The need for a clearer, simpler, more strategic performance measurement system in Lean companies is long past due. While many on the shop floor perceive this need, senior leadership, including finance and accounting, has been slow to "see" this need for change in accounting measurement. Leadership needs a practical guide that will provide a roadmap for beneficial accounting change and confidence to achieve global competitiveness.

Solomon and Fullerton present that roadmap in their unique and timely book. Solomon brings a wealth of manufacturing experience in leading accounting change in Lean environments and Fullerton has researched, published, and taught in this area for several years. Their clear and concise writing take the mystery and fear out of a Lean accounting conversion. This book offers encouragement and guidance for moving from a traditional standard cost system to a simple accounting system that provides appropriate information for a Lean manufacturing environment. Their case examples from real-world experiences of successful accounting changes that support Lean conversions are insightful for those wanting reassurance and direction.

The time was yesterday to fully understand and implement a system of performance measurements to support Lean continuous improvement initiatives. The age-old adage that you get what you measure is true and the time to revise your system of performance measurement is now. Understanding the challenges faced when converting your accounting system transactions is clearly analyzed in this book. Solomon and Fullerton's insightful and illustrative book should be required reading for all leadership and a required resource for your Lean library.

Ross E. Robson, Ph.D.
Executive Director
Shingo Prize for Excellence in Manufacturing
College of Business
Utah State University

PART I

LEAN: THE IMPACT ON ACCOUNTING AND THE CASE FOR CHANGE

1
WHY LEAN? SUCCESS STORIES FROM A FEW REMARKABLE, DIVERSE COMPANIES

2
LEAN ACCOUNTING AND ACCOUNTING FOR LEAN: WHAT IS THE DIFFERENCE?

3
WHY A TRADITIONAL STANDARD COST SYSTEM IS INCOMPATIBLE WITH LEAN

4
LEAN BENEFITS CAN BE INVISIBLE

5
GOING LEAN AND THE IMPACT ON EARNINGS

6
DETAILING THE DISTORTIONS CREATED BY STANDARD COST SYSTEM METRICS

1

WHY LEAN?
SUCCESS STORIES
FROM A FEW REMARKABLE,
DIVERSE COMPANIES

The rapidly changing and highly competitive market of the past two decades has pressured manufacturing firms to improve quality, flexibility, and customer response time. They have responded by implementing a variety of practices, including quality circles, statistical process control (SPC), Theory of Constraints (TOC), Just-in-Time inventory management (JIT), Six Sigma, and Total Preventive Maintenance (TPM). While each of these has made a marginal individual contribution to the mindset of continuous process improvement, they have more recently been incorporated into Lean thinking, which is rapidly becoming the dominant paradigm in manufacturing. In addition, Lean thinking has now spread to the non-manufacturing arena, including banking, insurance, distribution, healthcare, the armed forces, and education.

Lean is neither a substitute for a failing business model nor an end in and of itself. Lean is a total business strategy that has the potential to make a good business model great. Like all other business strategies, Lean must be linked to increasing shareholder value; anything else is simply waste!

It is important to understand the impact of Lean on the financial performance of a company. This chapter will illustrate the impact of Lean on the financial results of both public and private companies. Some of these companies are widely published as Lean "poster child" companies. Others might be familiar, yet their utilization of Lean techniques is not fully understood, or even recognized. Finally, Lean may or may not even be a stated strategy of these companies; however, upon investigation of their business strategies, it becomes clear that Lean techniques permeate their entire organization and play a major role in each company's success.

While this chapter does not focus on the accounting aspects of Lean operations, we feel it provides motivational material to those evaluating the cultural-changing commitment to a Lean implementation. It demonstrates Lean as a business strategy that must be interwoven throughout the fabric of the entire company. Accounting is one of those critical threads that connect the fibers together, supplying the right decision-making information for the right environment. So even though we do not discuss specifically the accounting systems of these individual companies, it must be assumed that accounting is an important player in helping to mold, define, guide, and evaluate their successes.

TOYOTA

We will begin our discussion of successful Lean companies with a brief introduction to the "grand daddy" of all Lean companies—Toyota. It is not necessary to spend much time on Toyota, because almost every book written about Lean refers to this tremendously successful automotive company in some fashion. Toyota is perhaps the greatest manufacturing company in the world and has been engaged in Lean for over 50 years. While Ford and General Motors are closing manufacturing plants and laying off tens of thousands of workers, Toyota marches on building plants in North America and increasing market share. Toyota is projected to have the largest share of the automobile market in the very near future, as illustrated in Figure 1.1.

Figure 1.1: Toyota Outlook[1]

Toyota's Lean efforts have led to extraordinary financial results, which are even more impressive when evaluated alongside its competitors in the auto industry. A comparison of Toyota results to those of General Motors is illustrated in Figure 1.2.

Item	Toyota	GM
2005 Net Income	$10.9 B	($10.6 B)
Market share	Growing	Declining
Last layoff	1948	50,000 in process
Quality	Near top	Average

Figure 1.2: Toyota Financial Performance versus General Motors[2]

Lean is literally a way of life at Toyota. This total business strategy, often referred to as the Toyota Production System (TPS), has resulted in extraordinary financial performance, rapid product development, and tremendous customer satisfaction. The TPS culture has given Toyota a tremendous competitive advantage.

WIREMOLD

The Wiremold Company, founded in 1900 and headquartered in West Hartford, Connecticut, provides a complete line of wire and cable management solutions for industrial and retail markets. The Wiremold Company also manufactures power and data quality products, offering a full line of integrated data/communications connectivity. Typical Wiremold products are depicted in Figure 1.3

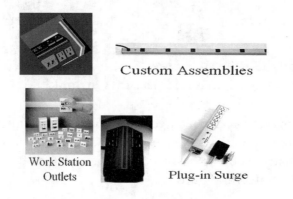

Custom Assemblies

Work Station Outlets

Plug-in Surge

Figure 1.3: Wiremold Products

Before its Lean conversion, "Wiremold was the typical instance of smokestack America: a low tech product made with low tech tools by a unionized, immigrant, aging workforce with limited skills, working in an ancient facility; the type of firm which has had great difficulty in world competition in the past twenty years."[3] Understanding Wiremold's pre-Lean environment makes its post-Lean results all that more extraordinary.

Wiremold began its Lean journey in 1991 with the arrival of Art Byrne, who was committed to Lean principles and the objective of turning the company into a world class organization. Mr. Byrne had previously been an executive at Danaher Corporation, one of the Lean pioneers in North America. At the outset of its Lean journey, Wiremold's performance was deficient in many areas, as depicted in Figure 1.4.

Status as of September 1991:

Market Share	Losing share	Control Systems	MRP mainframe
Sales Growth	Stagnant	Equipment	Old equipment organized in functional departments
Inventory	3 turns per year	Profitability	Low and falling fast
Cash	No cash	Operations	No changes in methods for 40 or 50 years

Figure 1.4: Wiremold at start of Lean Journey[4]

Wiremold's performance was typical of an aging manufacturer of commodity products in a highly competitive marketplace. Over the ensuing ten years, Mr. Byrne and his leadership team led a Lean transformation that resulted in the eventual sale of the company at a price reflecting a twenty-five fold increase in valuation. Operating metric improvements over this timeframe are illustrated in Figures 1.5 – 1.9.

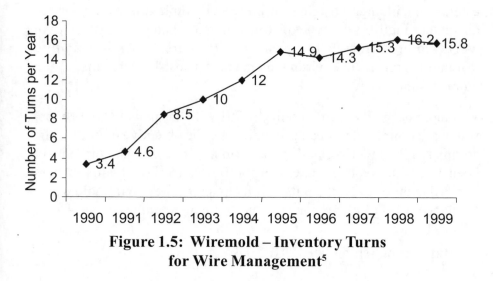

**Figure 1.5: Wiremold – Inventory Turns
for Wire Management[5]**

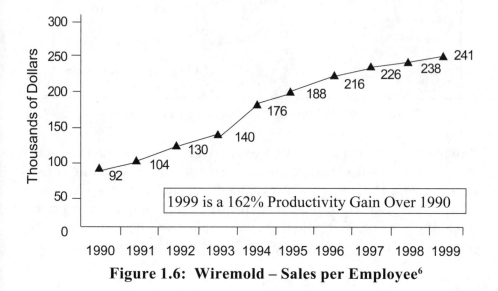

Figure 1.6: Wiremold – Sales per Employee[6]

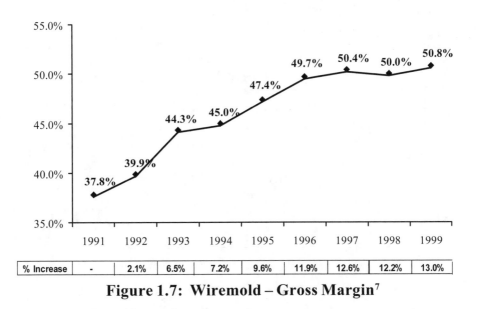

| % Increase | - | 2.1% | 6.5% | 7.2% | 9.6% | 11.9% | 12.6% | 12.2% | 13.0% |

Figure 1.7: Wiremold – Gross Margin[7]

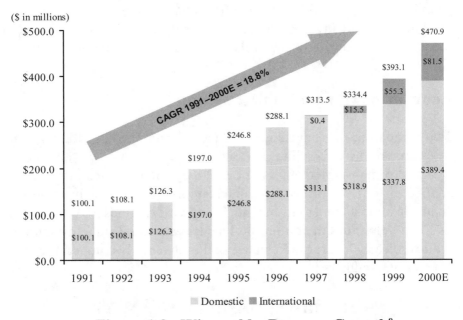

Figure 1.8: Wiremold – Revenue Growth[8]

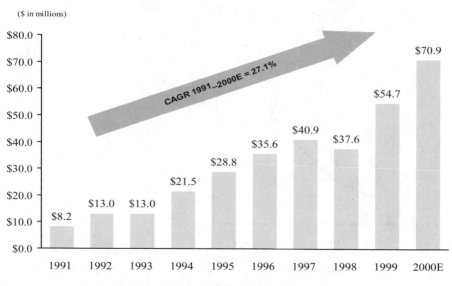

($ in millions)

**Figure 1.9: Wiremold – Earnings Growth
(Before Interest, Taxes, Depreciation and Amortization) [9]**

Wiremold embraced all of the Lean techniques, including respect for people. Every part of the organization was involved in the Lean journey and the resulting performance was truly exceptional. Legrand, a French manufacturing firm, purchased Wiremold in 2000 for $770 million.

Lean in Air Travel and Fashion

Two companies that have enjoyed success from the use of Lean strategies are Southwest Airlines and Inditex. Although not widely recognized as formal implementers of Lean, they each demonstrate how the application of Lean principles can lead to tremendous business performance in almost any environment. Southwest Airlines, (SWA), exhibits Lean behaviors in commercial air travel; and Zara, a division of Inditex, clearly leverages Lean to excel in the highly competitive fashion retailing industry.

SOUTHWEST AIRLINES (SWA)

SWA is the number one U.S. carrier of domestic passengers and the third largest airline in the world by number of passengers transported. While the United States airline industry had losses in excess of $10 billion in 2005, SWA had net income of $548 million.[10] Even more impressive, at the end of 2005, SWA had 33 consecutive years of profitability, a record unmatched in the history of the commercial airline industry.[11] This performance is quite an accomplishment from an airline company that was conceived when Rollin King supposedly doodled the business plan on a cocktail napkin during dinner at San Antonio's St. Anthony's Club for the benefit of his skeptical attorney, Herb Kelleher.[12]

How has SWA accomplished this remarkable feat? One piece of the puzzle appears to be a commitment to Lean practices. Upon close examination, it is apparent that much of what defines SWA's success is rooted in Lean principles, both from a culture and business practice perspective. We will examine some of SWA's impressive business practices.

SWA and Setup Reduction

An airline company has a different environment than a manufacturing company, yet there are many similarities, especially regarding the benefits of quick setups. What could be more important to an airline than the refueling, cleaning, unloading, and boarding of passengers while the plane is sitting idle on the tarmac? The plane is the machine tool, the passengers are the parts, and the flight attendants, crew, and maintenance workers are the operators. SWA takes setups very seriously and has perfected the quick turnaround out of necessity:

> Southwest's industry-leading ability to turn around arriving planes and get them back in the air has been crucial to its successful low-cost operations. SWA invented the "20-minute turn" out of necessity in late 1971, the year it began flying. In order to meet its payroll, the thinly capitalized start-up had to return one of its four leased planes. But by turning its three remaining planes in 20 minutes, it continued operating its full schedule. The idea worked. In the process, Southwest discovered that an intense focus on the highly efficient use of assets—planes, gates, and employees—is a key to its profitability.[13]

The authors have personally timed the setups while waiting in line for Southwest flights, and determined that SWA typically turns a plane around in 25 minutes or less. This is truly remarkable, considering 137 passengers must be unloaded and another similar group loaded during this short window of opportunity. Also, during this short unloading and boarding period, the galleys and restrooms must be cleaned, the baggage moved, the plane refueled, and the main cabin cleaned.

Almost everything that transpires at the gate represents efforts to support SWA's quick turnaround times. Contributing to short setups is the unique boarding process, whereby passengers are assigned general boarding priorities A, B, or C, rather than assigned seating. The boarding classifications are assigned on a first-come, first-served basis per the passengers' check-in times. SWA provides A, B, and C "boarding corrals" adjacent to the terminal gates that encourage passengers to stand in line well in advance of the plane's boarding call. Remarkably, even passengers with "priority A" boarding privileges, who will have ample selection of any type of seat (i.e., window or aisle) and placement in the plane, are agreeable to waiting in line. Having 137 passengers lined up ahead sequentially, with their baggage ready in preparation of boarding the plane, helps to speed up the boarding process. It is amazing that passengers willingly accommodate SWA's unconventional and seemingly inconvenient but efficient boarding process.

Even those SWA passengers that do not join the others in line for a better seat choice are prompted for boarding with the announcement of the plane's imminent arrival. Southwest gate attendants are careful to announce when the plane is ten minutes out, when the plane is approaching the airport, and finally, when the incoming plane has landed. While these announcements appear to be motivated as helpful customer communications, which they certainly are, they also facilitate the efficiency of the boarding system by encouraging passengers to prepare themselves by gathering their belongings and getting in line.

Most of you can probably relate to the author's first experience with Southwest Airlines. I arrived at the gate about 40 minutes before the scheduled departure time and my plane had not yet arrived at the gate. Naturally, I was concerned that my flight would be delayed. I immediately inquired if the flight would be on time, and the gate attendant assured me that it most certainly would. To my surprise, the plane arrived about 15 minutes later and took off exactly on time. After several SWA travel experiences, I have learned to trust in SWA's short turnaround times. Southwest founder, Herb Kelleher, clearly understood that the only time the company was making money was when the planes were flying.

In its continuous improvement efforts, SWA recently conducted an experiment in San Diego to evaluate different boarding methods, including the assigning of seats. This preempted people to assume that SWA is planning to assign seats, similar to other airlines. However, a careful examination of the explanation for the study suggests otherwise, as shown in Figure 1.10, which is a copy of the introduction to the questionnaire given to boarding passengers on San Diego flights. The SWA quote indicates that the company is not moving forward to standard seat assignments, but is simply researching the efficiency of the boarding process. Interestingly, in its May 2006 shareholder's meeting, SWA announced plans to further study the potential of adopting an assigned-seating system in 2008. All of this ongoing research is very much in line with Lean methods, whereby one tests a hypothesis against the current standard process. If the new process has the potential to outperform the current standard process, then it will become the new standard of performance.

Thank you for participating in this boarding test for Southwest Airlines. We appreciate your assisting us in gathering information and helping us determine if a different boarding process is more efficient. As an important part of this process, we would love to hear any feedback that you have.

Please keep in mind that we are researching the boarding process (the way and time that it takes to fill the plane with all of our passengers), and we are not testing the process of assigning seats. How your seats were assigned and distributed on this flight is not the method we would use if we decide to begin assigning seats in the future.

Thank you again for your help. We always appreciate your flying with us and hope to see you back onboard soon.

SOUTHWEST
A SYMBOL OF FREEDOM

Figure 1.10: Southwest Airlines Boarding Process Research

Another more subtle contributor to setup performance is SWA's dress code. As Greg Fields, President of Bridgewright Management Consultants noted, SWA flight attendants are known to "dress for success" by wearing sneakers and cotton shorts or khakis. Since the flight attendants are part of the setup process, it is important that they wear comfortable clothing. Based on our observations, flight attendants on most other airlines often wear more formal attire (such as skirts and heels) that is less suitable for quick clean-up and change-over times. While we are not sure if SWA's dress code was formulated to facilitate quick turnaround times, it certainly has helped the process.

SWA appears to leave no stone unturned when it comes to fast turnaround times. You have probably experienced SWA flights where flight attendants politely ask the departing passengers to clean out the seat pocket in front of them and kindly place the seatbelts in a cross on the seat as they leave. SWA effectively outsources any element of the setup they can, and incorporates the customer as a willing, integral member of the setup crew!

Whether you are in an airport, at a hospital, or on a manufacturing floor, it is easy to spot waste all around. For example, one way to understand the enormous amount of waste present in any manufacturing plant is to walk in any direction on the shop floor and carefully observe the activities of the first twenty people you encounter. Generally, you will find that fewer than five of the twenty associates are involved in value-added work. Then, randomly walk through a machine shop, and watch the machine tools as you pass by to see if they are producing parts or standing idle. You will probably be shocked by your findings. It does not require fancy computer reports to determine the level of productivity, just go to the workplace. Likewise, the next time you are traveling by plane and walking through the terminal to your gate, notice how many planes are sitting idle well in advance of their departure time. However, careful observation will probably confirm that Southwest planes arrive and take-off while idle planes from the other airlines (which probably arrived long before the SWA planes) are still sitting at the gates awaiting departure.

SWA also believes in standardization. Its current fleet is made up entirely of fuel-efficient Boeing 737 aircraft. In fact, SWA has the world's largest fleet of 737's—468 of them as of August, 2006. The average Southwest flight takes one hour and forty-six minutes to travel 619 miles. The daily utilization of each plane is twelve hours and thirty minutes.[14]

How much are quick changeovers worth to SWA? The cost of a Boeing 737 is approximately $50 million.[15] Imagine the impact of utilizing ten percent fewer planes due to standardization and rapid changeovers. At an approximate cost of $50 million per plane, a reduction in the fleet of 47 planes would eliminate the need for over $2 billion in capital and the associated annual interest expense of perhaps $100 to $200 million dollars. Setups are indeed very strategic!

In terms of Lean processes and the elimination of waste, it is much more efficient to train crews and maintain the planes when only one model of aircraft is used. If a crew is stranded in one city and a replacement crew is required, aligning the right pilot with the right type of aircraft is not an issue for SWA. Every pilot can fly every plane in the fleet. The same system efficiencies occur relative to scheduling, maintenance, flight operations, and spare parts. Standardization lowers costs and increases flexibility, resulting in a significant competitive advantage for SWA.

SWA believes in simplification throughout the process, including the customer experience, the route system, and any other area where the company can lower overall system costs. Unlike most other airlines, SWA does not have a hub-and-spoke system, but instead operates a point-to-point travel system to maximize efficiency.[16] SWA does not charge rebooking fees, does not require Saturday night stays, and makes purchasing tickets relatively easy. However, Southwest tickets cannot be purchased through a travel agent or through common online venues like Orbitz or Travelocity. Tickets must be purchased directly from SWA, either over the phone or online at the company's website, which features Web-only fare discounts and is extremely easy to use. Unlike other major airlines, Southwest reservations can be changed at will, without penalty. The only potential additional cost is a change in the price of a new reservation. Southwest also offers significant discounts to senior citizens, with full reimbursement for any senior-citizen fare. All of these rather well designed ticketing policies make SWA a very flexible service for customers. As is evident, everything

SWA does is consistent with its mission of being a low-cost airline targeting business and leisure travelers.

Another area where SWA pursues continuous improvement is the installation of winglets on its aircraft. Used to improve aerodynamics, winglets are curved, eight-foot wing extensions that extend about eight feet skyward from the end of an airplane wing. The Blended Winglet project, which was initiated in 2002, was a proposed technology that cost Southwest Airlines approximately $762,000 per aircraft to install. The winglets promised to provide improved range, greater fuel savings, and reduced noise and emissions. The project was aimed at providing SWA with an additional cost savings over its competitors, an important source of competitive advantage for the company.[17]

When jet fuel prices began climbing in 2003, Southwest Airlines decided the cost of the winglets, including installation, was worth it. The continuing dramatic rise in fuel prices has made the use of winglets more commonplace for other airlines as well. With typical fuel savings of approximately three percent, it takes three to five years to recoup the investment.[18] Southwest initially justified this significant capital investment based on fuel savings of 178,500 gallons of jet fuel per airplane per year. The winglets also extended the range of each flight, which opened up additional nonstop markets for the company.[19] One can only wonder if other benefits may have been considered as well, such as quicker turnarounds due to faster fuel loading.

The required teamwork was a critical element of Southwest's justification process for analyzing the complex winglet capital budgeting project. The winglet project necessitated analyses by the engineering, facilities, and flight operations groups before the economics could be fully assessed. The process lasted approximately one year. The first Blended Winglet technology could be seen on a Southwest flight in early October 2003.

Similar to Toyota in the automobile industry, SWA has ignored many traditional methods utilized in the airline industry. To achieve separation from its competitors, it has deployed techniques that are often referred to as Lean. Certainly a Lean success story, Southwest Airlines has a different business model than any other airline.

INDITEX

Another company that has used Lean concepts to propel itself to an industry leadership position is Inditex. Inditex is one of the world's largest fashion distributors, boasting 2,692 stores in 62 countries.[20] The Inditex Group comprises over 100 companies that are associated with the business of textile design, manufacturing and distribution.[21]

Inditex's financial results versus other leading fashion retailers are depicted in Figure 1.11.

Company	NI %	ROE %
Industry	6%	23%
Zara/Inditex	12%	30%
Aeropostale	7%	28%
American Eagle	13%	24%
Gap	7%	19%
J. Crew	0%	0%
Talbots	5%	16%

Figure 1.11: 2005 Financial Results of Selected Fashion Retailing Companies[22]

From 1991 to 2005, Inditex's sales grew 18 fold and its net income grew 26 fold, a truly remarkable achievement.

Zara is the largest operating division of Inditex. In 2005, Zara had sales of 4,440.8 million Euros, which represented 65.9% of Inditex's total sales.[23] As of January 1, 2006, Zara had 852 stores across 59 countries.[24] Interestingly, Inditex's founder, Amancio Ortega, was number eight on Forbes 2007 list of the world's richest people.[25]

Zara is a complex operation. Each year it creates approximately 40,000 new designs and 300,000 new stock-keeping units.[26]

The company can design, produce, and deliver a new garment and put it on display in its stores worldwide in a mere 15 days. Such a pace is unheard-of in the fashion business, where designers typically spend months planning for the next season. Because Zara can offer a large variety of the latest designs quickly and in limited quantities, it collects 85% of the full ticket price on its retail clothing, while the industry average is 60% - 70%. As a result, it achieves a higher net margin on sales than its competitors.[27]

Figure 1.12 compares Zara's unique industry operating practices to the conventional industry wisdom.

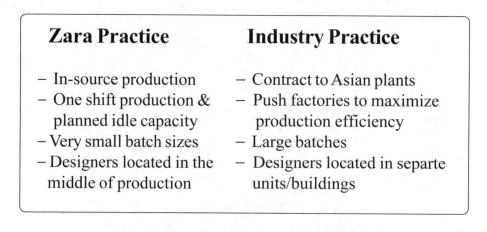

Zara Practice	Industry Practice
– In-source production	– Contract to Asian plants
– One shift production & planned idle capacity	– Push factories to maximize production efficiency
– Very small batch sizes	– Large batches
– Designers located in the middle of production	– Designers located in separte units/buildings

Figure 1.12: Zara Business Practices versus Industry Practices

Zara's practices defy conventional "wisdom" for its industry in the same manner that Southwest Airlines and Toyota practices differ from their competitors. In fact, the list of Zara practices in Figure 1.12 would be considered highly irregular for almost any manufacturing company in any industry, not just fashion retailing. In-sourcing production and planning for idle capacity are counter intuitive to the current rage of offshore outsourcing to the lowest-cost global operation and maximizing the utilization of assets to achieve seemingly lower unit costs.

Mr. Ortega chose vertical integration; owning the factory, the stores, and the distribution network in between. While competitors contracted out manufacturing largely to plants in low-wage countries, notably Asia, Mr. Ortega stocked his stores from his own factories in Spain.[28]

Zara adopted a business model that maximizes performance of the total value stream and astutely recognized that optimizing each separate function is not consistent with total system efficiency.

A review of Zara's practices and their corresponding business impact is critical to understanding how Zara constantly sub-optimizes many industry practices in order to optimize the entire business. This type of approach is virtually impossible in a traditional organization, with functional silos all tasked toward improving local departmental efficiencies.

We will first examine Zara's methods of transporting merchandise from the factory to its worldwide network of retail outlets. Figure 1.13 compares Zara's transportation methods to those of its competitors.

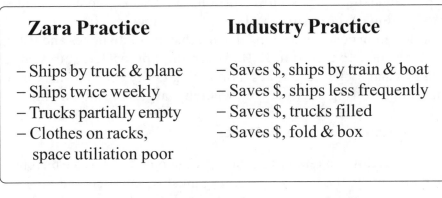

Zara Practice	Industry Practice
– Ships by truck & plane	– Saves $, ships by train & boat
– Ships twice weekly	– Saves $, ships less frequently
– Trucks partially empty	– Saves $, trucks filled
– Clothes on racks, space utiliation poor	– Saves $, fold & box

Figure 1.13: Zara Shipping Practices[29]

While competitors utilize trains and boats to move large lots of merchandise at the lowest cost, Zara transports small lots in planes and partially empty trucks. Consistent with its overall business model, Zara's shipping objectives are based on speed, not transportation cost minimization. Figure 1.14 summarizes Zara's reasons for relying on planes and trucks.

Ship by Plane and Truck

– Can design & deliver around world in 24-72 hours
  vs. months
  • Items on racks
    – Items pre-tagged and priced
    – No need to unpack, tag, and iron at store
    – Accuracy much better
    – Goes from truck to display and sale immediately

**Figure 1.14: Benefits of Utilizing Planes and Trucks
to Ship Merchandise[30]**

Zara's business model is dependent on producing and delivering a steady stream of new designs in small lots to stores twice a week. The mode of transportation and the manner in which the merchandise is packed also plays a significant role in how fast the merchandise gets in front of the customer. Typically, companies aim to minimize transportation costs by packing the merchandise into boxes and filling tractor trailers to their limits. However, this approach requires larger lot sizes and longer lead times, mimicking faulty decision-making in the manufacturing environment, whereby larger lot sizes are mistakenly utilized in an attempt to lower unit costs, regardless of the effects on quality, inventory, and lead times.

At many traditional retail establishments, upon receipt of the merchandise inventory, the boxes of clothing must be emptied and the merchandise must be pressed, tagged, and hung on display racks. These activities add significant waste to the process and delay displaying the merchandise in front of the customer. Zara, on the other hand, simply tags the merchandise and hangs the items on the display rack at the factory, and rolls the racks of clothing onto trucks so the merchandise can move directly from truck to display. This practice is consistent with small lot sizes and speed to market.

Zara also differs from industry norms in the design process and associated advertising methods, as illustrated in Figure 1.15

Zara Practice	**Industry Practice**
– Duplication of design and procurement by product line	– Has central design, purchasing, and sales
– Only in-store advertising	– Significant advertising
– Large areas of store empty	– Fills store with merchandise
– Has frequent stock-outs	– Minimizes stock-outs

**Figure 1.15: Zara Design and Advertising
Versus Industry Norms[31]**

Zara appears to have a value stream organization whereby design and procurement reside in each value stream, rather than in functional silos. The design team is co-located with production to ensure speed in communications and operations.

Zara defies accepted industry wisdom and tolerates, if not encourages, frequent stockouts at its retail establishments. The combination of excess capacity, quick deliveries, and regular flow of new designs all support a business model whereby stockouts become an asset rather than a liability. The benefits of these design and manufacturing practices are further clarified in Figures 1.16 and 1.17.

Design & manufacture in-house, maintain excess capacity

- Small batches, new designs constantly
  - Ship twice a week
    - Deliveries always meet fixed schedule
    - New products all the time
    - Customers frequent store 17 times/annum, industry 4 times
    - High traffic, save 3% advertising
    - Mark-downs way below industry, 15 points
    - Low inventory
    - Can ramp up quickly for a hot item
    - Negative Working Capital

Figure 1.16: Benefits of In-House Design and Excess Capacity[32]

As a result of predictable deliveries of new designs twice a week to Zara stores, customers are conditioned to be on the constant lookout for new merchandise, certainly an important competitive advantage in the highly fashion-conscious women's clothing industry. Zara's rapid replenishment process has resulted in higher and much more frequent store traffic, which in turn has led to huge savings in advertising expenses. In addition to lower advertising costs, Zara's markdowns are significantly below industry norms, a further testament to the benefits of Zara's Lean business model.[33]

Zara management realizes that fast response requires extra capacity:

> This relationship is well demonstrated by queuing theory, which explains that as capacity utilization begins to increase from lower usage levels, waiting times increase gradually. At some point, as the system uses more of the available capacity, waiting times accelerate rapidly. As demand becomes even more variable, this acceleration starts at lower and lower levels of capacity utilization.[34]

Experience has shown that many manufacturing organizations are not well versed in queuing theory. These companies try to reduce costs by operating at, or close to capacity. Contrary to their expectations, these companies often experience poor customer service, long lead times, and high inventories. Zara recognizes how idle capacity enables quick response in support of its business model.

Stores have frequent stock outs and empty racks

– Frequent new products, but limited supply
  - Better buy it now or it might not be here later
    - Empty rack of one item drives sale of other new item
    - Unsold items <10%, industry 17-20%
    - Will come back next week to see the new stuff

Figure 1.17: Benefits of StockOuts and Empty Racks[35]

Empty racks of clothing and stockouts are typically anathema to most fashion retailers. So why does this strategy work well for Zara? There are several reasons that this is a healthy strategy for Zara: (1) Stockouts encourage more frequent store visits and a mindset of, "I better buy it now or it might not be here at a later date." (2) Stockouts are a signal that new merchandise will be arriving shortly, so another store visit in a timely manner would be worthwhile. (3) Stockouts may give the customer the perception that the items are in hot demand. (4) Lower quantities may indicate that the customer owns unique merchandise. They are less likely to run into others wearing the same outfits. (5) Per economic theory, stockouts have the added benefit of significantly reducing the amount of unsold items relative to industry norms.

Ask yourself which business model is more successful—Zara's or the traditional fashion retailer's? It appears that there is no contest here. Zara, and its parent company Inditex, has become a worldwide leader in the fashion retail industry and its financial performance has been consistently stellar. Zara pursues a business model that emphasizes:

· *Innovation*

· *Flexibility*

· *Rapid Response*

· *Quality*

Rather than trying to optimize any one department or function, Zara optimizes the system efficiency, even if it means defying standard industry operating practices.

Zara utilized Lean thinking throughout its operations. (It may be no surprise to learn that Toyota helped Zara with its journey.)[36] Specifically, Zara adopted a value stream organization, created cross-functional teams, focused on one-piece flow and level loading, and understood building to meet customer requirements (takt time). Unlike the majority of its competitors, Zara in-sourced operations when it was appropriate, rather than outsource everything. Zara's actions, evaluated as individual merchandising practices, might not make sense, but appraised from a total system efficiency perspective, they appear to constitute a brilliant strategic scheme that has resulted in outstanding financial performance.

OTHER LEAN SUCCESS STORIES

In addition to Toyota, Wiremold, Southwest Airlines, and Inditex, many other companies have successfully incorporated the Lean philosophy into their core operating practices and culture, thereby achieving superior equity returns for their shareholders over the last five years. Shown below are the most recent five-year stock market performances of four companies who have embraced Lean for many years: Danaher Corporation, Terex Corporation, HNI Corporation, and Eaton Corporation. Figures 1.18 through 1.21 compare the stock market performance of each company to the Standard and Poor's 500 stock market performance for the period January 1, 2002 to December 31, 2006. The top line in each figure is the cumulative performance of each of the respective companies relative to the base stock price on January 1, 2002, while the bottom line is the cumulative performance of the Standard and Poor's market performance for the identical time period.

Figure 1.18: 5 Year Financial Performance of Danaher Corporation[37]

Danaher Corporation is an $8 billion diversified industrial company headquartered in Washington, D.C. The company markets a wide variety of products, including medical and industrial technologies, professional instrumentation, and hand tools. It was one of the earliest North American practitioners of Lean. Danaher attributes its success to the Danaher Business System (DBS), which drives every aspect of Danaher's culture and performance. In the mid-1980s, a Danaher division faced with intensifying competition launched an improvement effort based on the then relatively new principles of Lean manufacturing. The initiative succeeded beyond anyone's expectations, reinforcing the division's industry leadership, as well as spawning its business system. Since this modest beginning, DBS has evolved from a collection of manufacturing improvement tools into a philosophy, set of values, and series of management processes that collectively define the Danaher culture.[38]

It is serendipitous that the origin of "Danaher" goes back to the root "Dana," a pre-700 b.c. Celtic word meaning "swift flowing." In the early 1980s, the vision of a manufacturing company dedicated to continuous improvement and customer satisfaction was conceived during a fishing trip on the Danaher, a tributary to the south fork of the Flat Head River in western Montana. The founders of the company adopted the river's name for their new organization. As Danaher has evolved, the elements of a swift flowing river have been retained. The company has never strayed from the clarity of its initial vision. The flow of the business is ever changing, but the guiding principles of continuous improvement and customer satisfaction remain constant. Over time, the company has grown rapidly in size and success, achieving record levels year after year.[39] In fact, Danaher was recently listed by USA Today as the number two top performing stock over the last 25 years, with an amazing total increase of 47,913 percent.[40]

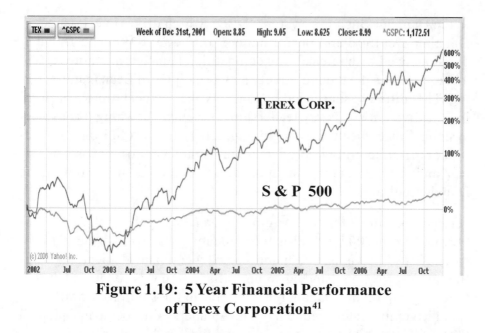

**Figure 1.19: 5 Year Financial Performance
of Terex Corporation**[41]

Terex Corporation is a diversified global manufacturer with 2005 revenue of $6.4 billion. Terex manufactures a broad range of equipment for use in various industries, including the construction, infrastructure, quarrying, surface mining, shipping, transportation, refining, and utility industries.[42] Like Danaher, the Terex Business System incorporates Lean principles in every aspect of the business. The core applications of Lean thinking promote a culture of continuous improvement and the removal of waste at every organizational level of Terex. The company has established Terex learning centers with the purpose of teaching these principles to key personnel throughout the company. Terex's commitment to Lean and its learning centers will serve as the cornerstone of Terex's activities for years to come.[43]

In 2002, Terex acquired Genie Industries, a leading North American Lean producer of aerial lifts. This acquisition paid off handsomely for Terex, as Genie's core competency in Lean was quickly adopted across the entire Terex organization.

**Figure 1.20: 5 Year Financial Performance
of HNI Corporation[44]**

HNI Corporation is the second-largest office furniture manufacturer in the world, and the nation's leading manufacturer and marketer of gas and wood-burning fireplaces. In 2005, HNI had total sales of $2.5 billion.[45]

In 2006, HNI was recognized by Fortune Magazine as one of America's Most Admired Companies in the furniture industry, and was recognized by Forbes Magazine for the eighth consecutive year as one of the 400 Best Big Companies in America. Also in 2006, the Corporation was recognized by IndustryWeek as one of the 50 Best Manufacturing Companies for the fourth consecutive year.[46] Several HNI plants have been awarded the Shingo Prize for excellence in manufacturing.

HNI's culture is built around Rapid Continuous Improvement (RCI) and the notion that every member has something unique and valuable to contribute. At HNI, RCI processes are ingrained across the entire organization; they are part of the fabric of the culture and a tool used for both continuous improvement initiatives and engaging and empowering its people.[47]

Figure 1.21: 5 Year Financial Performance of Eaton[48]

Eaton ($11.1 billion in revenue in 2005) is a premier diversified indus-
trial manufacturer with global leadership in electrical systems and components, fluid power systems and services, intelligent truck drive-train
systems, and automotive engine air management systems.[49]

Similar to Danaher, Terex, and HNI, Eaton utilizes a business system
approach to managing its business. Since its inception, the Eaton Business System (EBS) has increased profitability and helped Eaton achieve
higher levels of performance companywide. Eaton's success can be
attributed directly to EBS encompassing the core values, policies, and
processes that are used to conduct business and continually measure,
assess, and improve performance. EBS permeates everything that
Eaton does, providing the framework for achieving operational excellence. A critical component of Eaton's business system is Eaton's
Lean Six Sigma program, which is deployed across all of the business
units. Eaton Lean Six Sigma combines Lean system initiatives and Six
Sigma quantitative analysis to create a powerful methodology that un-
leashes the true potential of continuous improvement throughout
Eaton.[50]

SUMMARY

Toyota, Southwest Airlines, and Zara all defied conventional wisdom to optimize the performance of their organizations. In the process, they also changed customer expectations and created a Lean culture. In each case, the transformation was led by company leadership. The net result was world class performance!

Danaher, Terex, HNI, and Eaton have incorporated Lean into the fabric of their culture. Lean has become a core strategy of operational excellence that is explicitly stated as such to employees and the investment community. These companies have all achieved extraordinary results with Lean philosophies playing a significant role.

As firms proceed in their Lean journey, time and again financial leadership will be asked to help justify a particular strategy or expenditure. It is important to comprehend the many benefits that can accrue beyond those that are readily observable. Understanding the full gamut of possibilities from the application of Lean strategies will require broad vision, imagination, and leadership. After all, how many companies would have the courage and foresight to fund any of the following strategies: Southwest's vision to eliminate assigned seating and operate a point-to-point route system; Zara's vision to in-source a significant portion of production, eliminate advertising, plan for stockouts, and ship products via plane and truck to partially empty stores; or finally, Toyota's decision to build a variety of models on the same assembly line with one-piece flow?

These strategies were not easy choices and likely unfolded over decades of trial and error. Each organization succeeded primarily due to a dogged allegiance to its own business model. Their unique methods and philosophies were implemented in every facet of their operations; they did not take a piece-meal approach of picking an item from a dinner menu to satisfy their most current appetite. It involved a complete cultural commitment from sales and marketing to accounting and finance to the production floor. Although there is minimal specific information available about the decision-making systems supporting the success of these remarkable companies, it seems obvious that accounting and finance were an integral part of their strategic process, providing information that required a very different approach to analyzing performance. Companies do not achieve world class performance and create separation from their competitors by operating the same as everyone else in their industry. In almost every facet of their operations, these companies all dared to be different!

CHAPTER 1 ENDNOTES

1. "TOYOTA TO PASS GM AS NO. 1," *Detroit Free Press* (December 21, 2005), sec 1, p.1

2. 2005 Toyota Annual Report, *Consolidated Statements of Income*, 78.

   2005 General Motors Annual Report, *Consolidated Statements of Income*, p. 100.

3. Womack and Jones, *Lean Thinking*, 125.

4. Richard Ryan, retired President of Shape Electronics, a Wiremold Subsidiary, *The Wiremold Story Presentation*, (January, 2006), 8.

5. Ibid., p 31.

6. Ibid., p 30.

7. Ibid., p 32.

8. Ibid., p 48.

9. Ibid., p 49.

10. Wikipedia Encyclopedia, http://en.wikipedia.org/wiki/Southwest_Airlines, (December, 2006).

11. 2005 Southwest Airlines Annual Report, p. 2.

12. Joseph Guinto, "Rollin On," Southwest Airlines Spirit (June, 2006), 134 –41.

13. "Southwest Closer to Assigned Seating," *USA Today*, http://www.usatoday.com/money/biztravel/2006-06-21-southwest-usat_x.htm. (June 21, 2006).

14. Southwest Airlines Fact Sheet, Southwest.com, http://www.southwest.com/about_swa/press/factsheet.html#Fleet, (December, 2006).

15. Boeing, Commercial Airplanes, Jet Prices, http://www.boeing.com/commercial/prices/, (April, 2006).

16. 2005 Southwest Airlines Annual Report, p. 2.

17. Betty J. Simkins, Aaron Martin, and Daniel A Rogers, "Southwest Airlines: The Blended Winglets Project", *Social Science Research Network* (July, 2004), 24–26.

18. "The Wonder of Winglets," *The Baltimore Sun*, (September 20, 2005), sec D, p. 1.

19. Betty J. Simkins, Aaron Martin, and Daniel A Rogers, Southwest Airlines: The Blended Winglets Project, p. 24.

20. 2005 Inditex Annual Report, Economic and Financial Performance, p. 25.

21. Inditex Group, http://www.inditex.com/en/who we_are/our_group, (July, 2006).

22. 2005 Inditex Annual Report, *Consolidated Statements of Income*, p. 78.

2005 Aeropostale Annual Report, *Consolidated Balance Sheets and Consolidated State ments of Income*, p. 21 - 22.

2005 American Eagle Outfitters, Inc Annual Report, *Consolidated Balance Sheets and Consolidated Statements of Operations*, p. 27 - 28.

2005 Gap Inc. Annual Report, *Consolidated Balance Sheets and Consolidated Statements of Operations*, p. 37 - 38.

2005 J. Crew, Inc. and Subsidiaries Form 10 – K/A, *Consolidated Balance Sheets and Consolidated Statements of Operations*, p. F3 – F4.

2005 The Talbots, Inc. Annual Report, *Financial Highlights* p. 1.

23. 2005 Inditex Annual Report, Economic and Financial Performance, p. 39.

24. Ibid., p. 40.

25. Forbe's.com, The World's Billionaires, http://www.forbes.com/lists/2007/10/07billionaires_The-Worlds-Billionaires_Rank.html (March 2007).

26. Kasra Ferdows, Michael A. Lewis, and Jose A. D. Machuca, "Rapid-Fire Fulfillment," *Harvard Business Review* (November 2004), p. 107.

27. Ibid., p. 106.

28. John Tagliabue, Spanish Clothing Chain Zara Grows by Being Fast and Flexible, http://www.bc.edu/schools/csom/newsevents/news/2003/gallaugher/ (July 2006).

29. Kasra Ferdows, Michael A. Lewis, and Jose A. D. Machuca, *Harvard Business Review*, p. 109.

30. Ibid.

31. Ibid., p. 107 – 108.

32. Ibid., p. 107 – 110.

33. Ibid.

34. Ibid., p. 110.

35. Ibid., p. 108.

36. Ibid., p. 109.

37. Yahoo!Finance,http://finance.yahoo.com/charts#chart2:symbol=dhr;range=5y;compare=^gspc;charttype=line;crosshair=on;logscale=on;source=undefined (December 2006).

38. Danaher Corporation website, About Danaher Business Ssytem http://www.danaher.com/about/businesssystem.htm (December 2006).

39. Danaher Corporation web site, About History, http://www.danaher.com/about/history.htm (December 2006).

40. "25 Stocks You Should Have Bought", *USA Today* (April 16, 2007), p.8B.

41. Yahoo!Finance,http://finance.yahoo.com/charts#chart2:symbol=tex;range=5y;compare=^gspc;charttype=line;crosshair=on;logscale=on;source=undefined (December 2006).

42. Terex Corporation website, Investor Relations,

http://ir.terex.com/phoenix.zhtml?c=78780&p=irol-irhome (December, 2006).

43. Terex Corporation website, About Terex, Business Strategy,
http://www.terex.com/main.php?action=VIEW&obj=news&id=
e78ba1711f8c2899d5d6b62cf2274f79&nav=content (December, 2006).

44. Yahoo! Finance, http://finance.yahoo.com/
charts#chart4:symbol=etn;range=5y;compare=^gspc;charttype=line;crosshair=
on;logscale=on;source=undefined (December, 2006).

45. 2005 HNI *Corporation Annual Report, Financial Highlights,* p. 12.

46. HNI Corporation web site, Home, http://www.hnicorp.com/index2.htm (December, 2006).

47. HNI Corporation web site, Who We Are, Member Culture,
http://www.hnicorp.com/who/vision/member_culture.htm (December, 2006).

48. Yahoo! Finance, http://finance.yahoo.com/
charts#chart3:symbol=etn;range=5y;compare=^gspc;charttype=line;crosshair=
on;logscale=on;source=undefined (December, 2006).

49. Eaton web site, Our Company, About Us,
http://www.eaton.com/EatonCom/OurCompany/AboutUs/index.htm (December, 2006).

50. Eaton web site, Our Company, About Us, Eaton Business System,
http://www.eaton.com/EatonCom/OurCompany/AboutUs/CorporateInformation/
EatonBusinessSystem/index.htm, (December, 2006).

2

LEAN ACCOUNTING AND ACCOUNTING FOR LEAN

WHAT IS THE DIFFERENCE?

Those of us involved in manufacturing in the Western World realize that, for the most part, we are operating on a burning platform. To compete in the global economy, we must transform our companies to world class status. The operational strategy that has proved most effective in achieving world class performance levels is Lean. According to a 2006 Aberdeen survey, about 90 percent of manufacturing companies are in the midst of implementing Lean or about to begin their Lean conversion, as depicted in Figure 2.1

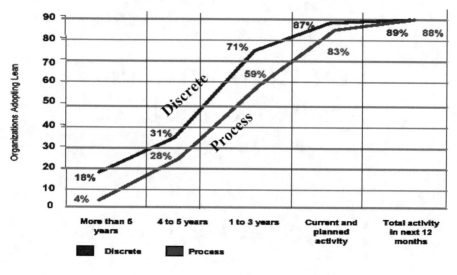

Source: AberdeenGroup, March 2006

Figure 2.1: Lean Philosophy Has Become Mainstream

The seminal book, *The Machine That Changed the World*, by Womack, Jones, and Roos, coined the term Lean as a methodology to eliminate waste in any type of company, functional area, process, or activity.[1] In the last decade, the phrase "Lean Manufacturing" has generally referred to the process of creating a Lean organization. However, using the term "Lean Manufacturing" may have created one of the biggest impediments to the Lean conversion process by advertising Lean as strictly a manufacturing initiative that does not apply to the rest of the company. As a result, the non-manufacturing functional areas of a company have typically adopted a hands-off attitude toward Lean activities.

Early successful Lean practitioners, such as Toyota, Wiremold, Lantech, Zara, Danaher, and HNI, realized a Lean conversion was a total company effort. Other companies have floundered in their Lean implementations by concentrating all of their efforts on the shop floor while having little or no participation by the rest of the company. Lean Manufacturing is now well-entrenched across the world. However, other areas such as Lean Engineering, Lean Accounting, Lean Sales, Lean Customer Service, and Lean Human Resources have a considerable way to go. Only in the last few years have companies realized that Lean is all about a Lean enterprise effort, requiring the full participation and support of the entire organization.

If it is not part of the transformation process, accounting can represent a major obstacle to an effective Lean conversion. Accountants too often are not involved in Lean activities that usually focus exclusively on the shop floor. Thus, they typically do not understand Lean, do not know how to support it, and do not measure Lean improvements. In order to compete successfully on a global basis, the company's accounting and other functional areas must be major contributors and participants in the Lean journey.

Ross Robson, Executive Director of the Shingo Prize, best articulated the definition of Lean as an operational strategy:

• Lean is the organization and empowerment of leaders and associates to *maximize customer value* through the identification and *elimination of waste* throughout the entire business value stream by way of process flow and on demand response to the customer.

• Lean strives to ensure customer value and sustained profitability through the *relentless pursuit of perfection in terms of quality, cost, and delivery* in product design, manufacturing, logistics, supply chain, and all administrative functions.[2]

Lean utilizes a number of tools such as 5S, kanbans, kaizens, value stream mapping, and total productive maintenance to facilitate the elimination of waste and create a world class company. Applying these tools only in the manufacturing arena is the pursuit of Lean Manufacturing and will result in limited success. Likewise, implementing these tools in a single area, such as engineering, might result in a well-regarded Lean Engineering group; however, achievement of a world class company with a leading competitive position will be elusive. Adding the name of a functional area to the word Lean implies using the various Lean tools in isolation to eliminate waste in one functional area. On the other hand, referring to Lean as Lean Enterprise recognizes that success is dependent on a total company commitment across all functional areas, integrated from the top to the bottom of the organization.

LEAN ACCOUNTING

It has become common practice to use the terms Lean accounting and accounting for Lean interchangeably even though there is a significant difference between the two concepts. Lean accounting is no different than Lean manufacturing in that Lean tools are utilized to eliminate waste in the accounting function, whereas accounting for Lean represents an accounting process that captures the benefits of a Lean implementation as well as motivates Lean behavior.

A more expansive definition of Lean accounting is illustrated in Figure 2.2.

LEAN ACCOUNTING IS DEFINED AS:

- An accounting process that utilizes the Lean tool kit to minimize the consumption of resources that add no value to a product or service in the eyes of the customer.

- A discipline focused on providing *actionable information* to users and eliminating transactions, reports, and historical data collection.

- A department of *financial advisors* to a series of focused factories, along with associates who are *involved in the day-to-day activities* of all areas of the company, and are willing to work in the plant and participate in kaizens.

- An accounting department whose lean efforts are fully compliant with GAAP and all internal and external reporting requirements.

Figure 2.2: Definition of Lean Accounting

This definition of Lean accounting includes the elimination of waste by utilizing the Lean tool kit and adds a number of other dimensions as well. Finance departments mainly have focused their efforts on presenting historical information. A Lean accounting organization provides value-added analysis to its customers in a very simple manner so that improvement actions can be taken immediately. Furthermore, accountants actively participating in these improvement activities have a much greater understanding of the underlying processes. This new perspective promotes accountants from strictly historical reporters and clerical bookkeepers to navigators or mini CFO's for the organization's various value streams.

VALUE STREAMS

A value stream contains all of the actions (both value-added and non-value added) currently required to bring a product through the two main flows essential to every product: (1) the production flow from raw material into the arms of the customer; and (2) the design flow from concept to launch.[3] Value streams can encompass an individual product family, entire business units, or subsets of a larger value stream.

It is highly recommended that the process improvements associated with Lean accounting begin very early in the Lean journey so that everyone becomes familiar with the use and application of Lean throughout the company.

ACCOUNTING FOR LEAN

As an organization transitions from traditional manufacturing encompassing batch processing to Lean manufacturing where pull and flow are the norm, traditional cost accounting methods developed in the early twentieth century become irrelevant The old batch and queue environment with large lot sizes, long setups, massive inventories, and a push production system required extensive control points, detailed job tracking, and sophisticated cost allocation routines, which unfortunately were usually incorrect, outdated, and undecipherable for most of the organization.

In a Lean manufacturing environment, product is quickly pulled through the plant via one-piece flow, inventory levels are minimized as well as standardized, skilled labor operates multiple machines simultaneously, water spiders rotate into skilled positions as needed, and generic materials are used to provide greater flexibility and standardization. The overall speed of the operation is many orders of magnitude greater than a batch operation. In this environment, the traditional standard cost system and absorption accounting are not only ineffective, but may become a significant barrier to a successful Lean conversion.

A more expansive definition of accounting for Lean is illustrated in Figure 2.3

ACCOUNTING FOR LEAN IS DEFINED AS:

- An accounting process that provides accurate, timely, and *understandable* information to motivate the Lean transformation throughout the organization and improve decision-making, which leads to increased customer value, growth, profitability, and cash flow.

- An accounting process that supports the Lean transformation by providing relevant leading as well as lagging metrics and actionable information that enables continuous improvement at every level of the organization.

- An accounting process that utilizes value stream costing, "Plain English" profit-and-loss statements, box scores, and other straightforward means to convey performance activity.

- An accounting process that meets the needs of *all* of its customers, including tax authorities, the Board of Directors, creditors, internal and external auditors, and *internal customers such as manufacturing.*

Figure 2.3: Definition of Accounting for Lean

As both the definition of Lean accounting and accounting for Lean demonstrate, under no circumstance will adherence to reporting requirements by regulatory agencies such as the SEC, IRS, and GAAP be compromised.

Accounting for Lean is twenty-first-century cost management in support of world class operations. The accounting department is in the unique position of having to do two things during the Lean conversion process: (1) apply Lean tools to eliminate waste in the accounting department; and more importantly, (2) change the overall method of keeping score for the internal operations of the business. The latter task is daunting, but nevertheless, one that has to be completed for a successful Lean conversion. Given this challenge, it is easy to see why accounting department resources will be stretched during a Lean conversion.

The ideal Lean accounting progression should begin very early in the Lean journey with the accounting staff participating in the events taking place on the manufacturing floor. Enlightened accounting leadership should then immediately deploy the same tools in the accounting department to eliminate waste and all of the non-value added clerical work that is too often all consuming. By following this path, when the time comes to implement accounting for Lean, accountants will not only understand what has taken place in production, but they will also have the knowledge, time, and resources necessary to devote to the change process.

Unfortunately, the finance department typically is not brought into the Lean conversion process until well into the journey. This is generally after significant changes have been made in manufacturing processes but traditional reporting conventions are providing management with confusing signals that contradict the physical gains made to date on the shop floor. At this point, accounting has a very long learning curve which either slows down the Lean journey or derails it completely.

The accounting profession, regrettably, is at least a decade behind the Lean manufacturing movement in North America and faces a rather steep hill to climb. Accountants must decide whether they will be an ally or an obstacle in a company's efforts to successfully navigate the formidable Lean journey.

CHAPTER 2 ENDNOTES

1. James P. Womack, Daniel T. Jones, and Daniel Roos. *The Machine That Changed the World,* (New York: Harper Collins, 1991).

2. Ross Robson, Executive Director, Shingo Prize, Utah State University.

3. Mike Rother and John Shook, *Learning to See* (Brookline, MA: Lean Enterprise Institute, 1999), 3.

3

Why a Traditional Standard Cost System is Incompatible with Lean

HISTORICAL COST STRUCTURES, DIRECT AND INDIRECT LABOR

Without going into an in-depth study of the origins of cost accounting, we should be aware that standard cost systems were originally developed for a totally different type of operating environment. There have been numerous works critical of traditional accounting methods, such as *Relevance Lost, The Rise and Fall of Management Accounting* by H. Thomas Johnson and Robert S. Kaplan;[1] *Real Numbers: Management Accounting in a Lean Organization* by Jean Cunningham and Orest Fiume;[2] and *Practical Lean Accounting* by Brian Maskell and Bruce Baggaley.[3] But perhaps the best depiction of the current state of management accounting can be captured with the two quotes below.

"All of the essentials of modern management accounting were established by 1930 without any significant changes since then."[4]

Brian Maskell

"Accounting is 100% the enemy of productivity."[5]

Eliyahu Goldratt
Author of "The Goal"

Despite the fact that the world has changed significantly, and that cost structures of the typical organization today bear little resemblance to the labor intensive organizations of seventy-plus years ago, we continue to use the same cost management systems.

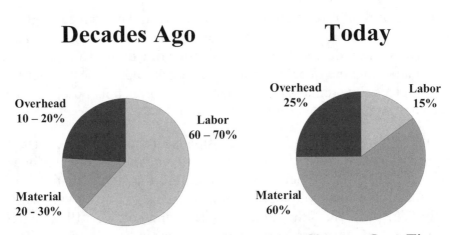

Figure 3.1: A Depiction of Cost Structure Changes Over Time

As shown in Figure 3.1, in the first half of the twentieth century, "labor" was the most significant cost component for manufacturing companies. (It is labeled "labor" rather than "direct labor" because, as you will come to understand during the Lean journey, very little of what we have traditionally called "direct labor" has anything to do with changing the form, fit, or function of the product, i.e., value-adding activities.)

Over time, companies migrated to lower cost labor markets and focused more heavily on substituting capital for labor. As the use of computers became commonplace, labor expenditures shifted from direct labor to overhead, as a greater emphasis was placed on sophisticated MRP and ERP systems to manage more complex internal operations as well as national and global operations.

Use of a traditional standard cost system, where overhead expenses are determined as a multiplier of direct labor costs, was appropriate when overhead was the smallest piece of the cost pie, direct labor was the largest piece, and a batch-and-queue philosophy was universally accepted. Overhead rates of 10, 20, or 30 percent of direct labor were not that significant and did not distort costs a great deal. However, in today's typical cost system, where direct labor has continually declined and overhead has increased dramatically, we typically have overhead rates of 300 to 600 percent of direct labor. The practice of allocating overhead via a multiple of direct labor, or having overhead "ride the back of direct labor" becomes more and more meaningless as the numerator of the ratio grows (or at least remains constant) and the denominator declines. The combination of a diminishing role for direct labor and the transformation from batch-and-queue production to one-piece flow renders the standard cost approach inappropriate or even detrimental in a world class operation.

An interesting offshoot of this discussion is an analysis of the current reports emanating from the finance department and the intense focus on labor analysis. When labor constituted the lion's share of an organization's cost of goods sold, it made sense to track it very carefully. The problem is that in today's environment, we still have the same intense focus on all sorts of direct labor reports, despite the fact that direct labor is usually the smallest component of a firm's production costs. Similarly, firms often try to improve product line margins in response to competitive market pressures by concentrating on cost reduction, and in particular, direct labor cost reductions. Yet this is absolutely the wrong time for this strategy. A Lean company develops products with target costs in mind and establishes competitive direct labor and total cost targets. Focusing on labor reductions after a product has been conceived, developed, and released into the marketplace is not only wasteful, it is usually ineffective and extremely costly. Organizations must establish rigorous cost targets up front in the design of products for manufacture and assembly.

We will conclude this topic by examining what we currently call direct labor in the typical standard cost system. If you have ever participated in a kaizen event for an assembly operation or a setup reduction event in a machining environment, you most likely have observed that about 75 percent of the direct labor effort is waste. Some common activities that require wasted time and effort include: looking for the right material, parts, tools, and fixtures; performing a setup; moving parts within a work cell with pallet jacks, cranes, or other means; transporting the material or completed part from work station to work station; and interpreting work instructions. As we transition to a Lean workplace and eliminate these wastes, the portion of expense that we traditionally call direct labor will decline dramatically while the effort devoted to the in-house logistics system will likely increase.

The in-house logistics system will require an increased emphasis on delivering materials in small batches directly to the point of use throughout the day, as well as kitting materials to both error-proof and eliminate searching for parts. These new activities require tremendous focus and standardization, and are critical to a smooth running Lean operation. In a traditional manufacturing environment, the functions of the in-house logistical system are performed by material handlers, who are classified as indirect labor since they do not alter the form, fit, or function of the parts. Traditional manufacturers typically view material handlers as unnecessary overhead and strive to increase the ratio of direct to indirect labor. During a Lean transformation, the exact opposite will occur, as direct labor will decline per unit of output and indirect labor will likely increase until an efficient material handling system has been implemented. The ratio of indirect labor to direct labor will increase from historical norms (in some cases quite dramatically), and Lean cost management techniques will be required to motivate proper behavior.

Specific Example of Mixed Signals Provided by a Standard Cost System

In order to better understand the mixed signals provided by a standard cost system, we are going to walk through the steps of a Lean simulation, including the typical metrics involved. (This simulation is available at www.wcmfg.com). This simulation, which consists of a four-stage production process, has been performed across North America by thousands of people from all functional areas, with virtually the same outcome every time. The simulation guides a group of people through the assembly of a two-piece Styrofoam box. Step 1 is to affix two adhesive dots to one end of the top of the box. Step 2 is to then place two push pins into the other end of the same side of the box. Step 3 is to tape the two halves of the Styrofoam box together with masking tape. The last step, Step 4, is to insert the completed Styrofoam box into an outer cardboard packing box. The first round of the simulation is laid out as depicted in Figure 3.2, and replicates the traditional manufacturing environment, with poor work flow, haphazard workstations on the plant floor, large inventories, and totally unbalanced production.

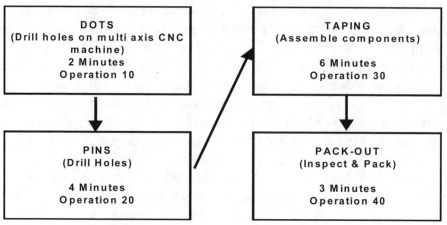

Production Lot Size = 3,000 Pieces

Figure 3.2: Simulation Layout of Traditional Production Process

At the end of this exercise, the group is asked to calculate the cost to produce **one complete foam box** using typical cost accounting methods and the data given in Figure 3.3, in conjunction with the process data shown in Figure 3.2.

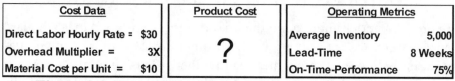

Figure 3.3: Data to Use in Cost Calculations – Round 1

During these simulations, it is made clear that there are no tricks involved in calculating the cost per completed box. The operating metrics are provided as additional information to be used after the game and have no bearing on the cost calculations.

Surprisingly, the author's experience shows that, regardless of the audience's work experience, whether it is a room full of accountants or operations managers, the percentage of correct responses is always about 50 percent, with a very wide range of individual answers from pennies to thousands of dollars.

Test yourself before looking at the correct calculation shown in Figure 3.4. The product cost is calculated by adding up the number of minutes required to make one Styrofoam box, which is 15 minutes, or one-fourth of an hour. Since the direct hourly labor rate is $30, then the cost of direct labor per unit produced is one-fourth of $30, or $7.50. Overhead is three times direct labor, which equals $22.50. Finally, we have to add the $10 for material to arrive at the total cost of a completed foam box, which is $40.

Cost Data		Product Cost		Operating Metrics	
Direct Labor Hourly Rate =	$30	Direct Labor	$7.50	Average Inventory	5,000
Overhead Multiplier =	3X	Overhead	$22.50	Lead-Time	8 Weeks
		Material	$10.00		
Material Cost per Unit =	$10	Total	$40.00	On-Time-Performance	75%

Figure 3.4: Calculation of Product Cost – Round 1

This represents exactly what is happening in the typical standard cost system. The cost accounting program simply adds up all of the time worked at each operation and multiplies the result by the standard   direct labor rate, then applies the pre-determined overhead multiplier, which could be the same across a plant or different for every work center. Finally, material is added and a standard cost is established for the product. This is done over and over for every stock-keeping-unit (SKU) in the business.

During the second round of the simulation, the group forms a U-shaped cell, co-locates the processes, rearranges the sequence into a logical flow, begins to right-size the equipment, and utilizes kanbans to trigger production. These changes significantly reduce the lot size.

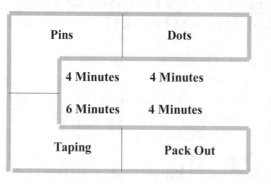

Production Lot Size = 300 Pcs.

Figure 3.5: Production Cell after Kaizen Event

The group is once again asked to calculate the cost to produce **one complete foam box** using the data in Figures 3.5 and 3.6. Again, experience shows that, despite previous instructions on the nature of cost calculations, the number of correct answers does not increase nearly as much as one would expect for an audience that is largely responsible for using the cost system to make decisions.

Cost Data		Product Cost	Operating Metrics	
Direct Labor Hourly Rate =	$30	**?**	Average Inventory	500
Overhead Multiplier =	3X		Lead-Time	2 Weeks
Material Cost per Unit =	$10		On-Time-Performance	5%

Figure 3.6: Data to Use in Cost Calculations – Round 2

The correct cost per unit is $46 as shown in Figure 3.7. The labor component of the product cost is derived by once again adding up the total time required to make the product, which in this case is 18 minutes, or thirty percent of an hour. With a labor rate of $30 per hour, 18 minutes costs $9 per unit. Using the same multiplier for overhead and adding $10 for material yields a total cost of $46, as shown in Figure 3.7.

Cost Data		Product Cost		Operating Metrics	
Direct Labor Hourly Rate =	$30	Direct Labor	$9.00	Average Inventory	500
Overhead Multiplier =	3X	Overhead	$27.00	Lead-Time	2 Weeks
		Material	$10.00		
Material Cost per Unit =	$10	Total	$46.00	On-Time-Performance	95%

Figure 3.7: Calculation of Product Cost – Round 2

Herein lies one of the problems of using a traditional cost system as a company progresses down the Lean conversion path. While shop-floor personnel are doing all the right things, such as improving lead times and on time performance (OTP), and reducing production lot sizes, the cost system is reporting that costs have increased. See Figure 3.8 below for a summary comparison of Round 1 and Round 2 simulation results before and after the Lean improvements.

Metric	Before	After	% Improvement
Inventory	5,000	500	90%
Lead Time	8 Weeks	2 Weeks	75%
On Time Performance	75%	95%	27%
Batch Size	3,000	300	90%
Sq. Footage	8,000	3,000	63%
Quality	50 PPM	15 PPM	70%
# of Transactions	Many	Few	Dramatic
Throughput	?	?	?
Flexibility & Teamwork	Poor	Improved	Dramatic
Unit Cost per Cost Acctg.	$40	$46	(15%)

**Figure 3.8: Comparison of Performance
Before and After Lean Improvement**

The production cell experienced tremendous improvements in all of the metrics that matter to the customer, such as quality, lead time, and on-time performance. Internal performance also has improved, as the space utilized has significantly decreased, inventory has declined dramatically, cash flow has increased, and the workforce is more engaged. In fact, when one questions the simulation participants, they all mention that their work has become less stressful, they can communicate better with their upstream and downstream teammates, and they are more inclined to offer suggestions to each other. The change in their work environment, along with reduced lot sizes, noticeably improves quality.

However, Figure 3.8 shows that the internal cost reports will report that the cost of this product increased by 15%. This demonstrates the problem with a traditional cost system. The focus is on the departmental statement or area profit-and-loss statement, which incorrectly broadcasts to everyone that performance is deteriorating.

It is necessary to distinguish actual outcomes from the results expressed by the traditional cost reports. While the cost reports erroneously indicate a 15% cost increase, it is also incorrect to imply that unit costs would immediately decrease as a result of Lean improvements. Unless staffing levels were immediately reduced, (rather than redeployed elsewhere in the company), the total cost structure would remain the same for this one improvement exercise. However, as the Lean journey accelerates, and similar improvements take place in other areas, the firm will find that overall productivity improves, much of the infrastructure required to keep track of very complex operations becomes unnecessary, and inventory and storage requirements are vastly reduced. Costs will decline as a result of personnel losses through normal attrition, reductions in scrap, simplified computer systems, and other cost-reduction improvements. Eventually, these cost savings would be reflected in a traditional cost system if, and only if, overhead rates were re-examined and adjusted on a regular basis, which is usually not the case. Until overhead rates are adjusted, the traditional cost system will continue to send confusing local signals indicating that costs are increasing despite improvements on the shop-floor. These misleading signals have the potential of derailing a Lean transformation.

Another example will clarify the distortions of a traditional cost system. In Figure 3.8, the throughput results of the two simulations are left unanswered. Yet, this is a critical measure for both the customer and the business. From a customer perspective, knowledge of capacity and throughput allows the company to accurately respond to the market and provide accurate lead times. From a business perspective, the only way to achieve sales is to ship product and invoice the customer, and that means all manufacturing operations have to be completed.

How do we determine the before and after throughput numbers? Since the taping operation is the constraint in both simulations, total output is limited by the ability of the taping operation, which is six minutes. Therefore, regardless of what happens at the three other operations, the maximum output of taping is 10 units per hour, which in turn limits the output (and associated revenue) of finished product to 10 units per hour. The process is not in balance, and this becomes much more visible when the operations are all located in one area.

Metric	Before	After	% Improvement
Inventory	5,000	500	90%
Lead Time	8 Weeks	2 Weeks	75%
On Time Performance	75%	95%	27%
Batch Size	3,000	300	90%
Sq. Footage	8,000	3,000	63%
Quality	50 PPM	15 PPM	70%
# of Transactions	Many	Few	Dramatic
Throughput	10/hour	10/hour	No Change
Flexibility & Teamwork	Poor	Improved	Dramatic
Unit Cost per Cost Acctg.	$40	$46	(15%)

**Figure 3.9: Comparison of Performance
Before and After Lean Improvement**

The business would be better off by slowing down all operations completed in less than six minutes until the cell is "leaned" out by either eliminating waste in the six minute operation and therefore reducing cycle time, combining operations, or redesigning the product. But slowing down an operation is totally at odds with everything we have learned in the past, because the cost system will indicate further erosion in unit costs. In fact, a traditional standard cost system encourages faster production in all operations in order to absorb more overhead and generate healthier month-end numbers. Because a traditional factory usually has its work centers spread throughout the plant according to functionality (e.g., all like equipment is located together such as drill presses and lathes), it is virtually impossible to "see" the flow until one relocates and right-sizes the equipment into a cell that contains all of the necessary equipment to complete the process from start to finish.

To illustrate this, I will share a true story with you about a traditional factory and the associated cost system. A number of years ago I took my teammates on a benchmarking trip to a truly world class company. My teammates had never been exposed to a world class company and were skeptical about everything to do with Lean. Participating in this venture was our machine shop manager who had almost thirty years of experience, as well as our plant manager who had twenty years of experience. During our visit the host company showed us a new cell it had set up to produce a new, smaller-scale product, intended to penetrate a market segment where cost was paramount. The tour guide escorted our group to the first operation of the new production cell, the sawing operation. As soon as our machine shop manager observed this operation, he could not contain himself. I overheard him asking our plant manager why I brought them 3,000 miles to see such a poorly run operation. The unpretentious saw was cutting a two inch channel and the process took almost five minutes to accomplish this simple sawing task. The machine shop manager joked that he could almost count the teeth on the saw because it was going so slow. Boy, were my teammates in for an education!

At this point, our host explained that the takt time of the operation was five minutes. He also explained that the batch size of the operation was one piece at a time. The saw in use was the slowest and least expensive saw the company could find that could accomplish the task within takt time. (Actually, the sawing operation took four minutes and forty seconds, which allowed a safety factor in the event of any problems.)

Takt Time

"Takt" is a German word meaning either clock or musical meter. Takt time is the rate at which each product needs to be completed to meet customer requirements and is expressed in seconds (or other time unit) per part. It is the beat or pulse at which each item leaves the process. Takt time is determined by taking the available production time and dividing it by the rate of customer demand.[7] Producing any faster than takt time is wasteful as it creates inventory. Producing slower than takt time results in order backlogs, poor customer service, and lost orders.

Besides the obvious cost considerations, the advantages of using such a slow, simple saw were: a) the saw required hardly any lubrication because of the slower speeds; b) setups were extremely simple; c) deburring of the metal was all but eliminated; and d) the Total Productive Maintenance (TPM) program consisted of an identical spare saw located on a shelf over the work area. In the event of a malfunction, the spare saw could be exchanged for the operating saw in less than half a minute.

Total Productive Maintenance (TPM)

TPM is an equipment maintenance system that proactively addresses maintenance issues before they become major problems and cause equipment downtime. TPM engages machine operators and staff in the routine maintenance of equipment so machines are constantly maintained on a basic level. More advanced maintenance procedures are still performed by skilled maintenance professionals. TPM efforts include putting machines on a schedule so that all of their maintenance needs are addressed on a regular basis without overlooking essential steps and processes.[8] A good TPM program will free up maintenance workers so they can address urgent and critical repairs that result in immediate downtime. Maintenance staff also will have additional time to allot to more proactive and preventative maintenance activities. Operators and production staff generally wait less for maintenance department assistance and learn some new ways they can resolve minor machine issues without need for further maintenance support. Truly, everyone wins when a TPM program is functioning as it should.

The host continued to explain the rest of the unique characteristics of this truly world class cell, but by now my two co-workers were deep in thought. Everything about the sawing operation was counter to all of their previous experiences. They had been taught to buy big, fast equipment that could do almost everything. Then they would run that equipment around the clock, minimize the number of setups to save time by processing large batches of material, and occasionally shut down the operation for maintenance when there was no other choice. The traditional cost system rewarded my teammates for these large batches, even though the downstream operations could never process these batches of parts all at once, leaving a large percentage of each day's production in inventory.

In this exemplary lean cell, the standard cost system will provide erroneous information relative to the improved performance taking place. As the cell intentionally slows down the non-bottleneck operations to balance the line, the direct labor and overhead absorbed will also decline. As the output of some of the operations temporarily declines, the departmental statements, or local profit-and-loss statements, will be adversely impacted. Absorption of both direct labor and overhead will be reduced, thereby generating unfavorable direct labor and overhead variances, sending another false signal that the Lean improvement efforts are a waste of time.

THE ADDED BENEFITS OF CELLULAR MANUFACTURING AS IT RELATES TO COST MANAGEMENT AND CUSTOMER SATISFACTION

From an accounting and financial perspective, there are some tremendous advantages of organizing in cells and value streams at the plant level. In traditional production environments, chaos is often the order of the day. It becomes virtually impossible to predict when product will be available to ship unless there is a huge finished goods warehouse from which to pull product. Our sympathies are extended to the production managers and supervisors who have to provide a completion date for those all-important, special orders that have to snake their way through multiple operations in the plant, with each operation having different processing times, work-in-process inventory levels, and large batch sizes. Despite the proliferation of sophisticated computer systems, providing a reliable completion date is almost impossible.

PULL SYSTEM

A Pull System is characterized when the flow of parts, products, and information occurs as a result of the consumption of that item at the immediate downstream operation. A signal is provided to the upstream operation to replace what has been consumed.

On the other hand, if custom sales orders must be filled from production without the benefit of an inventory buffer, utilizing cells with balanced work flows allows for much more predictable results, which in turn leads to better forecasting of cash flows and avoidance of late-delivery penalties. This is the added benefit of pull systems.

Another benefit resulting from the formation of cells is a much improved capital investment process. When operations are disconnected and spread haphazardly around a plant, then capital investment decisions are based on local optimization. If the first operation in Figure 3.5 could be improved by buying another piece of equipment that would process the dots in half the time, it is probable that such an investment would be approved. But in reality, not one more product would be produced each hour with the enhanced equipment, because the process is constrained by a downstream operation that may not be visible in a traditional operation. In fact, speeding up any process in front of a bottleneck is always a poor investment, as it will result in "feeding" the system with more inventory. Value streams, if measured correctly, will become the Finance Department's "best friends," because they allow for a huge magnifying glass to be held over the area. With this structure, one can fully understand and appreciate the system, and consequently work with the team to continuously improve it.

SUMMARY

As illustrated in the previous examples, it is imperative to change the cost management system in concert with the physical changes occurring in the plant; otherwise, traditional accounting practices will send misleading signals to management that just might derail the entire Lean effort.

In the end, one must ask which cost system will allow for more accurate reporting of results, enhance the ability to analyze and improve operations, as well as provide proper incentive to continuously improve customer service, quality, overall cost, and inventory turns. The only answer is a Lean cost management system supporting a Lean operation.

CHAPTER 3 ENDNOTES

1. H. Thomas Johnson and Robert S. Kaplan, *Relevance Lost: The Rise and Fall of Management Accounting* (Boston, MA: Harvard Business School Press, 1987).

2. Jean E. Cunningham and Orest J. Fiume, *Real Numbers: Management Accounting in a Lean Organization* (Durham, NC: Managing Times Press, 2003).

3. Brian Maskell and Bruce Baggaley, *Practical Lean Accounting* (New York, NY: Productivity Press, 2004).

4. Brian Maskell, *Making the Numbers Count* (New York: Productivity Press, 1996), 16.

5. Eliyahu Goldratt, "Cost Accounting: The Number One Enemy of Productivity." American and Inventory Control Society 26th Annual International Conference Proceedings, New Orleans, LA (November, 1983), 433-35.

6. Larry Rubrich and Mattie Watson, *Implementing World Class Manufacturing* (Fort Wayne, Indiana: WCM Associates, 2004), p.351.

7. Stephen Cimorelli, *Kanban for the Supply Chain* (New York:Productivity Press, 2005), 10.

8. TPS Throughput Solutions, http://www.tpslean.com/glossary/tpmdef.htm, (April, 2007).

4

LEAN BENEFITS
CAN BE INVISIBLE

One of the biggest mistakes is thinking of Lean as simply a cost reduction program. While truly world class companies such as Toyota, Wiremold, Lantech, and Danaher have favorable, if not industry leading cost structures, cost reduction as a long-term objective is vital, but it does not drive their Lean implementations. The primary goal of a Lean transformation is to eliminate waste and thereby improve customer service. This goal is accomplished by developing people and establishing an empowered culture where trust, honesty, and integrity are paramount. Costs are reduced as an outcome of achieving this goal.

A successful Lean transformation will generate cash, improve customer service, create capacity, and perhaps most importantly, create a learning organization. The true benefits of the transformation will be determined by how these operating improvements are utilized.

Below is an example which illustrates why Lean is generally invisible to accounting and is not focused exclusively on cost reduction.

Setup Time	Machine Run Time	Lot Size	Number of Different Part Numbers Produced
2 Hours	6 Hours	512	1
1 Hour	6 Hours	256	2
30 Minutes	6 Hours	128	4
15 Minutes	6 Hours	64	8
7.5 Minutes	6 Hours	32	16
3.75 Minutes	6 Hours	16	32
113 Seconds	6 Hours	8	64
56 Seconds	6 Hours	4	128
28 Seconds	6 Hours	2	256
14 Seconds	6 Hours	1	512

Figure 4.1:
Daily Operating Profile Options of a Molding Machine[1]

Figure 4.1 illustrates the operating profile options of a molding machine at a consumer products company. For the purposes of this discussion, assume that the incumbent company, referred to as the Old

Style Company, operates according to the first row of the chart. Old Style produces 512 widgets daily over a continuous six-hour run. Old Style also performs one setup per day, which takes two hours. The setup is usually done at the beginning of the first shift of this one-shift operation. Finally, its widgets are sold in four different colors.

The current production rate of 512 finished units per day is sufficient to meet Old Style's current demand. Although there are a number of other competitors in the market, Old Style's market share has been relatively constant during the last few years.

About a year ago, John, a new manufacturing engineer, joined Old Style with the hopes of utilizing his knowledge of Lean to move Old Style's operational philosophy into the twenty-first century. John just received his master's degree from a progressive engineering school that had an extensive Lean curriculum. He was anxious to put his Lean education to good use and improve Old Style's antiquated methods.

At the end of his first six months, John had made little headway convincing management that they could significantly improve the molding operation if they started a 5S program and setup reduction activities. John, still a rookie, had limited influence over operations, and the most senior people had little patience for his new ideas.

5S

"5S" is a methodology to improve safety, housekeeping, and organization by bringing order to the workplace and eliminating searching, hunting, looking, motion, and transportation waste. While there are many different definitions for each "S", they generally are as follows:

    Sort
    Straighten
    Sweep
    Schedule
    Sustain

A properly implemented 5S program will pay dividends by helping to change the culture of an organization.

Steve, a new salesman, had also joined Old Style six months ago. Steve and John lived in the same neighborhood and carpooled together. During the course of their commute, John frequently complained to Steve about the resistance he encountered toward implementing Lean techniques. Likewise, Steve was getting frustrated because his customers were constantly complaining about poor lead times and lack of product variety. Evidently, Old Style's competitors were starting to offer additional colors and shorter delivery times. Steve was fascinated by John's Lean ideas and the potential impact they might have on the business. During the following three months, Steve and John mulled over the idea of starting their own widget business based on Lean principles. After much contemplation, both gave their notice to Old Style when it became abundantly clear that the company would never adopt Lean.

Shortly thereafter, John and Steve formed New Style Company and purchased, at a significant discount in the used equipment market, the exact same molding equipment as was used by Old Style. During the first few months of operation, John adopted the same methodology as was practiced at Old Style, and the results were similar: two hour setups and six hours of run time, yielding 512 widgets. Before embarking on any new methods, John established a minimum performance level. Fortunately, demand had grown for the product, and Steve was able to sell the entire output.

During this time, Steve also spent a great deal of time with current and prospective customers to better understand their requirements. It became obvious that they wanted a greater choice of colors, shorter product lead times, and improved on-time deliveries. They were growing frustrated with the long lead times and the poor on-time delivery performance of all of the suppliers. This was exactly what Steve had hoped to hear, as he knew John's Lean techniques would address these issues.

Over the course of the next three weeks, John and his production team 5S'd the molding operation. The results were astounding. Since all the necessary tools and materials were now located exactly where needed, a tremendous amount of wasted time looking for tools was eliminated. Also, since the work area used was compressed by about

50 percent, operator walking time was reduced. The net result was that setups were reduced from the original two hours to one hour. See Figure 4.2 for the operating data.

Setup Time	Machine Run Time	Lot Size	Number of Different Part Numbers Produced
1 Hour	6 Hours	256	2

Figure 4.2: Setups Reduced to One Hour

At this point, a decision needed to be made as to how to take advantage of the setup gains. John and Steve agreed that they would now run two batches each shift and therefore produce two different colors each day. In effect, the daily operation would still be in the setup and run mode for two hours and six hours, respectively, but it would now be spread across two batches of different colored product. Based on this improvement, New Style introduced some new colors, which were well received by the marketplace.

John then decided to conduct a setup reduction event. He had learned that by video-taping an operation, engaging the team, and focusing on separating internal setup activities from external activities, setup times could be cut in half. New Style conducted a week-long event, which resulted in new setup times of thirty minutes—another fifty percent setup reduction. Once again, John and Steve decided to change the operating model by running four daily batches of 128 pieces of various colored product. New Style was producing the same number of finished widgets each day in a much more efficient operating profile, as depicted in Figure 4.3.

Setup Time	Machine Run Time	Lot Size	Number of Different Part Numbers Produced
30 Minutes	6 Hours	128	4

Figure 4.3: Setups Reduced to Thirty Minutes

Each time New Style reduced the time for setups, it expanded the number of colors offered. Sales were brisk as customers appreciated the variety and were pleasantly surprised that lead times had not been sacrificed. New Style was now offering variety packs of widgets that commanded a premium price. Customers were getting used to continuously improving performance and started to ask for even more colors. Rather than add capacity or build inventory to preserve lead times, John conducted two more setup reduction events over the ensuing three months. With each effort, the team was able to cut setup times in half. New Style was now achieving single digit setup times,as shown in Figure 4.4.

Setup Time	Machine Run Time	Lot Size	Number of Different Part Numbers Produced
7.5 Minutes	6 Hours	32	16

Figure 4.4: Setups Reduced to Single Digits

New Style's business had never been better, with customers excited about the ever-increasing variety packs, shorter lead times, and competitive pricing. It was clear that New Style would soon need to add capacity to keep up with sales growth.

During this same time period, Joe, the most senior sales person at Old Style, was getting hammered by his long-time customers. The new competition had placed an inordinate amount of pressure on Joe, with Old Style having difficulty meeting customer demands of more colors and shorter lead times. Joe was forced to offer price concessions and promised to deliver new colors soon.

In addition, the cost accounting team at Old Style headquarters was publishing reports illustrating declining margins for their mainstay product line. A meeting was called to discuss the situation and it was agreed that Old Style must come out with new colors quickly. Since Old Style needed to meet current demand, as well as start to build an inventory of new colors, additional capacity was required. After debating the issue, it was decided to add some new equipment as well as extend the shift to ten hours a day for the next few months. To accommodate the increased inventory levels, additional finished-goods racking was ordered.

Finally, in order to compete with New Style, who now had 24-color variety packs, Old Style needed to forecast demand by color, since it could only produce one color per day. It will take Old Style more than a month to cycle through all of the colors, so forecast accuracy was critical. In the meantime, Old Style's only customer-retention strategy was to continue to offer price concessions.

Observe what has happened to Old Style as it tries to compete with a company that is successfully implementing Lean. In the absence of world class methods, Old Style continues to repeat the same mistakes of the past by replicating existing practices and adding even more waste throughout the organization. Figure 4.5 outlines many of the cost-increasing competitive responses that Old Style is compelled to implement.

All else equal, a traditionally run company can never compete effectively head-to-head with a Lean company unless the traditional company has a unique market position resulting from proprietary products.

Old Style Company Competitive Responses

Lower Prices

Add Capacity

    New Equipment

    Extended Hours

    Added Staff

Add Inventory

    Warehouse Space and Racks

    Forecasting

      Increased Excess & Obsolete Inventory

Figure 4.5: Additional Costs Incurred by Old Style Company to Compete without Lean Methods

If New Style had looked at Lean as just another cost-cutting program for capturing the benefits resulting from setup reduction, it might have reacted in an entirely different manner. For instance, New Style could have been satisfied with a one-hour reduction in setup times and started each day with the one-hour setup, operating the equipment six hours to produce the 512 pieces, and then shutting down the line after a total of seven hours to save one hour of payroll expense. Or New Style could have achieved the same weekly output by operating eight-and-one-half hours each day and working a four-day week. Finally, New Style could have increased production by working all five days. However, these strategies would not reach the same level of benefits achieved by focusing instead on the customer value proposition.

In contrast to Old Style, New Style is better equipped to improve quality, lower inventory levels, shorten lead times, increase flexibility, and benefit from the virtuous learning cycle of further setup reduction activities. In this particular case, all of New Style's advantages were the result of simply focusing on reducing the two hours of waste associated with the long setups.

In analyzing operations strictly from the traditional cost accounting perspective, does the operating profile really make any difference to the cost reports as long as the company selects any of the choices depicted in Figure 4.1? Regardless of which combination of setup time and lot size is performed per Figure 4.1, the cost reports will indicate that each day 512 pieces were produced, two hours were devoted to set-ups, and six hours were devoted to run time. Whether one is reporting productivity, efficiency, or utilization, all reports will be the same, regardless if the lot size was 512 pieces or 1 piece. The results are identical because the cost accountants only examine the number of pieces produced over a given time frame compared to a standard. There is no incentive in traditional accounting systems to reduce lot sizes. Cost accountants typically do not understand and are not involved in the operational improvements that are being made. Thus, there is no mechanism to report or make visible the impact from implementing Lean practices.

Unless accountants are involved in improvement events and fully recognize the competitive benefits of Lean, they will join the chorus of naysayers that resist change and do not appreciate the value of Lean. Even worse, they will present distorted reports that do not illustrate any improvements.

If you were an owner of a business, which operating profile would you prefer? It is obvious that we need a new way to account for operations so that the financial reports not only motivate people to do the right things, but also make the improved results obvious to everyone.

CHAPTER 4 ENDNOTES

1. Larry Rubrich and Mattie Watson, *Implementing World Class Manufacturing* (Fort Wayne, IN:WCM Associates, 2004), 312.

5

GOING LEAN
AND THE IMPACT
ON EARNINGS

As explained in Chapter 3, a traditional cost system will result in misleading signals during a Lean conversion. Adding fuel to the fire, a successful Lean implementation will often result in depressed earnings at either the local level, or for the entire business unit. The greater the success with Lean, the greater the potential initial "hit" to earnings. This effect should not be a surprise, and in fact can be planned and calculated well in advance. Unfortunately, Lean leaders generally do not understand this phenomenon.

A successful Lean conversion will result in improved inventory turns and improved throughput (sometimes referred to as velocity) in a manufacturing facility. These improvements can have a negative impact on earnings in three ways: (1) labor and overhead expenses are moved from the balance sheet to the profit-and-loss statement; (2) lead times are reduced, potentially delaying new customer orders; and (3) additional excess and obsolete inventory is exposed. The reasons for each of these effects will be examined.

INVENTORY TURNS AND EARNINGS

As stated above, implementing Lean correctly will improve inventory turns. If inventory turns improve and everything else stays the same (i.e., sales, gross margins, and the cost structures), earnings will decline. It is critical to understand this concept because it has the potential to undermine all the other successes resulting from the Lean journey.

Inventory Turns

Inventory turns is a frequently used metric to measure the speed at which a company can convert its production inputs—raw materials, purchased components, direct labor, and overhead—into sales. The higher the turns, the faster this conversion process occurs, resulting in less capital tied up in the business. Inventory turns is calculated by dividing the annual cost of goods sold by the average month end inventory. Inventory turns will differ by industry, and generally ranges from 3 turns up to 20 turns.

Part 1: Impact of Increased Inventory Turns on Labor and Overhead

So how does improving inventory turns penalize the income statement? While the answer is relatively simple, most people, including many accountants, do not understand the related accounting methods well enough to grasp this concept. During a company's existence, it cumulatively produces more product than it ships. (If this were not the case, there would be no inventory on the balance sheet.) Typically, excess production is accounted for on the balance sheet by extending the year-end inventory quantity of each SKU times the standard material, direct labor, and overhead cost per item to arrive at the total inventory value. For many companies, inventory is one of their largest assets.

Another way of looking at this phenomenon is to realize that each year, a percentage of a firm's direct labor and overhead is capitalized on the balance sheet rather than expensed when incurred. This is done to comply with the matching principle of Generally Accepted Accounting Principles, (GAAP). Capitalizing product costs, rather than expensing them in the period incurred, results in higher reported earnings for a company.

Matching Principle

The Matching Principle is a fundamental concept of basic accounting. In any one given accounting period, a company must match the revenue it is reporting with the expenses required to generate that revenue in the same period, or over the periods in which the company will be receiving benefits from that expenditure. A simple example is depreciation expense. If you buy a building that will last for many years, you do not write off the cost of that building all at once. Instead, you take depreciation deductions over the building's estimated useful life. Thus, you have "matched" the expense, or cost, of the building with the benefits it produces, over the course of the years it will be in service.[1] Direct production expenses incurred in a period, but not associated with the revenue generated in that period, are capitalized, which means they are placed on the Balance Sheet as inventory to be charged against income in some future period when those products are sold.

The amount of product produced in excess of the amount shipped is inventory, and often this inventory has built up over many years. As a company improves inventory turns, by definition it will be producing at a level *below* the shipping level. The company then meets its shipping requirements by drawing down inventory. It is this process of reducing inventory during the Lean journey that can negatively impact earnings. As a company builds inventory, it capitalizes a portion of its costs onto the balance sheet, and the reverse happens as inventories are reduced. The company must take those capitalized costs from the balance sheet and charge them to the income statement, along with the current period expenses. Thus, there is a period of time when the company is incurring a "double hit" on some product costs.

As inventory turns improve, manufacturing managers are often victimized by the additional direct labor, overhead, and fixed product costs released from inventory. Managers are confused and at a loss to explain the decline in operating results, since as far as they are concerned, operations have not changed. Yet, the double hit of some product costs manifests itself in larger than usual unfavorable direct labor and overhead variances. It is critical for operations executives and accountants to grasp the reasons for these unfavorable results and isolate their impact.

The easiest way to explain this complex concept is to look at the notion of inventory turns in the most extreme case. Imagine that a company turns its inventory just one time per annum. This leaves the company with twelve months of inventory on hand. Also, assume that in the coming year, sales will equal that of the current year. If the mix of products stays the same, this company would not have to produce one single item to satisfy its needs in the coming year. Finally, assume this company is confident that it will become fully world class in a year, so it will be in position to produce according to demand in the subsequent year. As a result, this fictional company will use its entire inventory to meet demand in the coming year and will not need to produce anything to provide a beginning inventory position in the following year when the entire demand will be accommodated from production.

What will be the impact on the profit-and-loss statement of going from one inventory turn to virtually infinite turns during one calendar year? As each unit ships, the cost system automatically charges to cost of goods sold the standard amount of material, direct labor, and overhead for every end item. The related accounting transactions decrease inventory and increase cost of goods sold at standard. By the end of the year, every single dollar of inventory is removed from the balance sheet and charged to the profit-and-loss statement. In total, cost of sales at standard remains the same as the prior year. But this is where the similarity ends.

In this extreme example, what has happened at the company during the year when there has not been any production? Relative to manufacturing labor, has the direct labor force been furloughed, have all manufacturing salaried personnel been laid off, have all support positions, such as purchasing, planning, and manufacturing engineering, been eliminated? Most likely, overtime and temporary positions would be eliminated, but it is doubtful that the company would eliminate all manufacturing personnel. Since it is a going concern, it would need experienced production personnel to be ready to build sufficient product to meet demand the following year.

Now consider overhead expenses. The company would continue to incur property taxes, insurance, depreciation, and utility costs. It will still have lease expenses on equipment and the building. So even though there was no production during the entire year, all of the current year's direct labor and overhead costs will be charged directly to the profit-and-loss statement. Since there was no inventory, these costs will not be deferred and capitalized on the balance sheet. This, of course, assumes that all of the costs were fixed, rather than variable in the short-term. So in addition to what constitutes a full year's expense for material, direct labor, and overhead embedded in the standard cost that is being charged to cost of goods sold at standard for items that were produced in prior periods (and shipped in the current year), the company will have to charge the income statement with the current year's expenses for direct labor and overhead costs as well. For this one-year period, the company will have almost two years worth of direct labor and overhead expenses. The word "almost" is used because through attrition and other cost avoidance techniques, some costs will be marginally reduced, but nothing of significance. The company's profit-and-loss statement will likely show a significant decline, or even a loss, for that one-year period.

The increase in direct labor and overhead expenses will appear as large unfavorable variances, assuming accounting continues to use standard costs and tracks variances. In this particular example, the "hit" to the profit-and-loss statement would happen just for the one year in which the company transitioned from a traditional, low-inventory-turn production process, to a world class organization that produced product on demand. However, in more realistic circumstances, this inventory transition would take several years, and the profit-and-loss statement would be burdened with extra costs every year until a steady state was reached, all else remaining equal. This phenomenon can, in effect, neutralize (and mask) many of the gains resulting from Lean improvements.

There is one caveat that should be mentioned that may offset the usual negative impact from inventory reductions. Companies that use the last-in-first-out (LIFO) method for their inventory costing often have layers that are valued at lower, older costs. If these LIFO layers are invaded as inventory is reduced, the standard unit cost of goods sold can be significantly lower. Under this situation, there may be a dramatic increase in bottom-line figures due to the lower standard product costs. This effect will continue as long as those old LIFO inventory layers are reduced and not replaced with more current costs. This is not the venue to discuss this phenomenon in depth, but it would be helpful to discuss it with your accountants and be aware of other false signals that may arise from inventory reductions.

Graphically, Figure 5.1 illustrates the buildup of inventory over time. All product cost elements (material, direct labor, and overhead) will reside on the balance sheet in relative proportion to each company's cost structure.

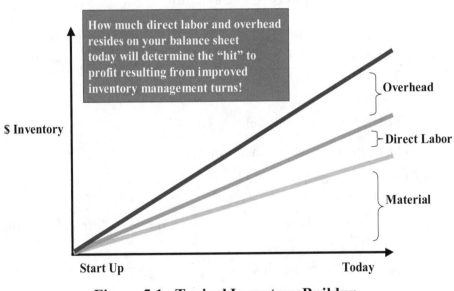

Figure 5.1: Typical Inventory Buildup Over Time at any Company

Once a company begins to implement Lean techniques and improves inventory turns, the historical process of building inventory is reversed, as depicted in Figure 5.2.

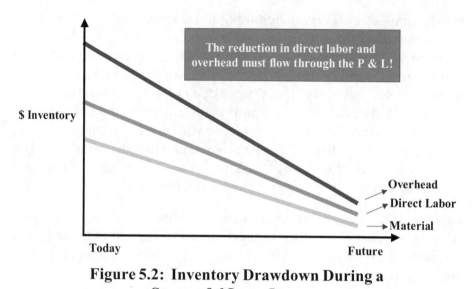

**Figure 5.2: Inventory Drawdown During a
Successful Lean Journey**

In general, and assuming sales, margins, and cost structures remain stable, the after-tax earnings impact of improving inventory turns will be determined by:

1. The current level of inventory turns

2. The projected level of inventory turns

3. The projected time frame over which inventory turns improvements are made

4. The proportion of inventory value comprised of direct labor and overhead

5. The current earnings level

6. The firm's tax rate

Knowing the values of the six items above will allow you to calculate, in advance, the after-tax earnings impact resulting from improvements to inventory turns and avoid any surprises.

A CRITICAL CONCEPT RELATIVE TO CALCULATING THE IMPACT OF LOWERING INVENTORY

A company's proportion of annual expenditures for material, direct labor, and overhead will likely be different than the proportion of material, direct labor, and overhead carried in inventory at the end of any reporting period. This difference arises because direct labor and overhead are applied to material in stages throughout the manufacturing process, while the material content is fairly fixed at each stage of production. In order to properly calculate the impact of an improvement in inventory turns and its affect on earnings, the ratio of cost components on the balance sheet is critical as opposed to the ratio of these components based on annual expenditures. This topic will be expanded upon in Chapter 9.

Perhaps the most critical factor in determining the financial impact of improved inventory turns is the current level of a compnay's inventory turns, as shown in Figure 5.3

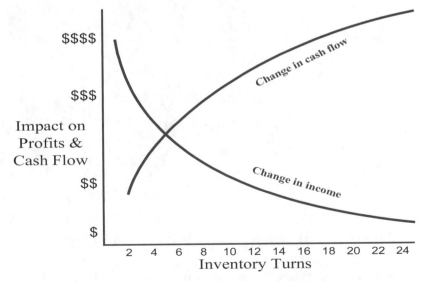

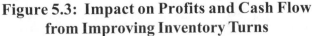

Figure 5.3: Impact on Profits and Cash Flow from Improving Inventory Turns

Figure 5.3 illustrates that when the firm already has high inventory turns, the impact from improved turns on profits and cash flow will be relatively small, with a modest decline in earnings and a modest improvement in cash flow. On the other hand, in industries characterized by low levels of inventory turns, i.e., five turns or less, a swift and successful Lean conversion may result in a significant unfavorable impact to profits and a favorable impact to cash flow.

As depicted by the IndustryWeek report in Figure 5.4, inventory turns can be quite different across and within industries. Benchmarking your firm's current level of inventory turns against other firms should help clarify how much of an improvement in turns can be expected, and therefore, provide the foundation for calculating your firm's potential financial impact.

INDUSTRYWEEK	PRODUCTION SCORECARD				
Value Chain	**Raw Material Turns** (COGS / Average Raw Material)	**Work-In-Process Turns** (COGS/ Average Value WIP)	**Finished Goods Turns** (COGS/ Average Value Finished Goods)	**Total Inventory Turns** (COGS/ Average Value Of Total Inventory)	**Asset Turn Ratio** (COGS/ Average Assets)
Aerospace	6.8 13.0	10.0 20.0	8.5 15.0	6.0 10.0	3.5 4.0
Automotive	16.2 30.0	20.0 40.0	19.0 30.0	12.0 22.0	2.4 5.0
Chemicals	12.0 24.0	20.0 55.0	12.0 30.0	8.0 20.0	1.6 3.0
Construction	8.5 15.5	20.0 51.2	11.0 27.5	6.4 12.0	3.0 7.4
Consumer packaged goods/nondurables	15.0 45.0	24.0 81.5	13.0 38.0	10.0 23.0	2.0 4.0
Consumer durables	10.0 20.0	20.0 38.4	12.5 24.0	8.0 17.3	3.0 5.0
High tech	8.0 22.0	12.0 30.0	10.0 24.0	7.0 10.0	2.0 3.8
Industrial equipment and machinery	8.0 13.0	12.0 20.0	10.0 12.0	6.0 10.0	2.3 4.0

Median   Upper Quartile   COGS=cost of goods sold

IndustryWeek, January, 2004[2]

Figure 5.4: Inventory Turns by Selected Industries

As Figure 5.4 illustrates, there is a considerable difference between median and upper quartile total inventory turns for firms in the same industry sector. Certainly, the difference between the best-in-class and average firms can be enormous. Dell Computer, renowned for its inventory turns, reports around one-hundred turns in its 2005 Form 10 - K.[3] World class divisions of a number of heavy industrial companies have inventory turns of twenty, thirty, or even forty turns. Achieving such performance across an entire company, however, is a long-term endeavor.

Even though this discussion has focused on the negative earnings impact created by improving inventory turns, we must remember that we are primarily in business to generate cash and achieve a satisfactory return on investment. Improving inventory turns is an excellent cash generator. In the preceding example, direct labor and overhead expenses were incurred during the period even though there was no production. But what about the material portion of product costs? Since the entire year's inventory requirements were already on the shelf at the beginning of the year, no further purchases of material will be required for the entire year. The company in this example will avoid the cash outflow for material. Since material is often the largest cost component for manufacturing firms, this is a tremendous cash-flow benefit.

While there will be considerable angst about the impact of improved inventory turns on the profit-and-loss statement, management and Lean leaders can (and should) initially focus on the balance sheet benefits to better understand the power of Lean.

We have demonstrated how improving inventory turns may negatively affect a company's reported profits. We also have discussed how improved inventory turns will likely be the outcome during a successful Lean journey. Therefore, one might conclude that Lean is generally detrimental to the all important "bottom line." However, there is a distinction to be made regarding Lean's role in this whole process. It is the improvement of inventory management that is causing the temporary earnings decline, not Lean. Lean simply facilitates the management of inventory. Because of accounting rules (not due to poor management or inefficient processes), profitability will fall when inventory turns increase, regardless of the production methods used to facilitate the inventory change. It just so happens that Lean tools, particularly the combination of setup reduction, TPM, single piece flow, and kanbans are the most effective production tools for reducing inventory and improving velocity through the plant. Remember that the negative profitability effects will evaporate as inventories stabilize. Further, it is expected that Lean will grow other aspects of the business that can offset the additional costs released from inventory.

Secondary Effects of Improving Inventory Turns

It is also important to understand the ripple effects from a successful Lean implementation. A company utilizing asset-based lending must project the impact of lower inventories on its borrowing capacity. A discussion with a company's creditors related to the financial ramifications from implementing Lean should take place early in the Lean journey. Of course, the freed up cash from reduced spending will allow for the repayment of debt, but the exact timing must be determined.

ASSET-BASED LENDING

Asset-based lending is a secured business loan whereby the assets of the business are pledged as collateral. Inventory is often used as collateral in such loan agreements. The creditor advances the company funds based on a percentage of raw materials, work-in-process, and finished goods. These percentages will vary by company and for each inventory classification. As inventories decline, the amount of loan proceeds also will decline.

In addition to the impact on possible funding sources, a firm's loan covenants may be affected by changes in inventory and earnings because of the changes in debt/asset ratios. The larger the company, the less immediate impact local Lean initiatives will have on the overall business, but having a working knowledge of the relationships among all of the factors will help eliminate any surprises.

Another concern is related to the incentive or bonus programs most firms have that are typically tied to profitability at either the local or company-wide level. Consider the ramifications of a successful Lean implementation that rapidly improves inventory turns, but also temporarily depresses profits, leading to greatly reduced incentive payouts. It is easy to understand why it is difficult to garner associate (and shareholder) support for such a strategy. To avoid these negative, confusing associations, companies are strongly encouraged to isolate the results from improved inventory turns and determine profitability exclusive of these temporary effects. This becomes relatively easy once a firm adopts "Plain English" profit-and-loss statements, which will be discussed in Chapter 7.

Part 2: Reduced Lead Times

In Part 1 of this chapter, the first of three situations where a successful Lean journey can depress earnings was discussed. Part 2 presents the second of these three scenarios. Improving inventory turns and the flow of product through a plant leads to much better customer service. This improved service can manifest itself in shortened product lead times, which will allow your customers to postpone purchases of your product.

The impact of shortened lead times was experienced by the first author while working for an electronics company that sold through a worldwide distribution chain. When the company first began its Lean journey, its published lead times for the entire product line were eight weeks. As throughput speed improved, published lead times were reduced from eight weeks to six weeks. At first there were no discernable differences in customer order patterns. After a couple of months, however, customers began to delay their orders, as they became confident in the company's ability to meet its new, improved lead times. It makes sense that if distributors could now get their product in six weeks instead of eight weeks, they would prefer to delay their purchases by two weeks in order to improve their own inventory turns and associated cash flows.

The following year this same electronics company was able to reduce its published lead times another two weeks—from six weeks to four weeks. As before, after a couple of months, the distributors became confident in the company's ability to meet its new published lead times and delayed their ordering for another two weeks in order to coincide with the new schedule. This exercise was repeated one more time the following year when the company reduced its lead times to only two weeks, resulting in the same distributor response.

Providing the opportunity for distributors to delay their orders for two weeks each year in three consecutive years would likely substantially affect the performance of any business. These distributors were able to lower their inventories by placing orders for fifty weeks worth of product instead of fifty-two weeks of product for each business year. The effect on the electronics company was to lower sales by about four percent per annum for three years in a row. The corresponding impact on the profit-and-loss statement from such a situation would be significant, assuming all other relationships were kept status quo.

Fortunately, in an example such as this, other relationships will likely change. Unless your competitors are making similar improvements, your company will likely gain a competitive advantage by reducing its lead times. The electronics company referred to here utilized its Lean successes to illustrate to its distributors the benefits derived from improving their own inventory turns and their corresponding returns on investment, which led to improved market share for everyone in the supply chain.

Improving customer lead times should improve a firm's competitive position. Thus, it is possible that improvements in market share will be sufficient to offset the negative earnings impact of order pattern changes. If not, the reduction in sales orders will result in another temporary hit to the profit-and-loss statement until equilibrium is reached and lead times stabilize.

Part 3: Excess and Obsolete Inventory

The last item that can be affected by improving inventory turns and increasing throughput velocity in the plant is a firm's reserve for excess and obsolete (E & O) inventory. Virtually every company with inventory has a corresponding inventory reserve for those items that have been rendered obsolete due to design changes, discontinuance of a particular model, or market changes. Excess inventory may result from inaccurate forecasts, rapid shifts in customer demand, or technological obsolescence. Whatever the reason, inventory requires an E & O inventory reserve.

Because there is a plethora of end items, product families, and models, companies develop their own specific formulas for estimating their annual E & O inventory reserve rather than specifically identifying each particular SKU that is at risk. The methodology for estimating the inventory reserve must be consistent from year to year, and must also pass the reasonableness test imposed by the company's external auditors. With inventories in the hundreds of millions of dollars and E & O inventory reserves in the millions of dollars, any year-to-year change in the reserve can have a significant impact on a company's profitability.

As a company progresses in its Lean journey and reduces inventory, the finance team will soon painfully discover that the formula used to estimate E & O inventory is insufficient to cover the actual inventory exposure. Lowering inventory exposes more and more of those dreaded rocks in the river, including those of damaged, excess, missing, and obsolete inventory. There is no formula for E & O inventory at the macro level that typically does justice to the true level of E & O inventory at a company. This seems to be a universal rule of business and is only recognized as an issue as inventory levels decline.

It is strongly suggested that a company undergoing a Lean conversion carefully monitor the impact on E & O inventory reserves from lowering inventory. As pilot cells are created for product families, and inventory levels are reduced, any impact on the local E & O inventory reserves should be projected across similar product lines.

An Inventory Turns Primer from Everyday Life

Inventory turns is a concept that is unfamiliar to many people, especially those without finance backgrounds. It will be beneficial to go through a detailed example of the inventory turns calculation, as well as the implications of excessive inventory, by applying the concepts discussed in this chapter to an example from everyday life.

Suppose you do the grocery shopping once a week for your household. Each Sunday morning at 10 a.m. you go to the neighborhood grocery store and buy exactly enough food to last one week. Since you are an efficient shopper, you complete your shopping, return to your house, and fully load the refrigerator without any significant time elapsing. Further, assume that you eat the same amount of food every day of the week. At the end of the week, at 10 a.m. on the following Sunday, your refrigerator is empty. You faithfully follow this routine every week for a full year.

How many inventory turns will you have in our grocery example? The answer is not as obvious as you may think, so take a few more minutes to think about the answer, and refer carefully to the definition in the side box near the beginning of this chapter.

Since the shopping is done once a week, most people think the correct answer is fifty two inventory turns. However, the correct number of inventory turns is actually one hundred and four. Figure 5.5 helps to explain this concept.

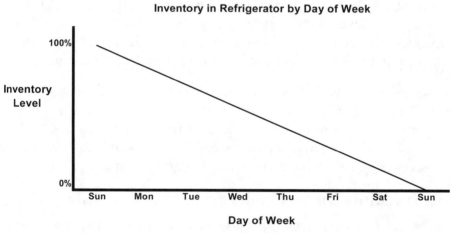

Figure 5.5: Grocery Inventory Levels During the Course of One Week

As the figure illustrates, the *average* inventory level during the course of the week is fifty percent, or three and a half days worth of groceries. Visualize the refrigerator going from full to empty evenly during the course of the week. With annual consumption (usage) of 365 days of food and an average inventory on hand of three-and-one-half days of food, the correct number is 104 inventory turns (365/3.5 = 104).

Shopping once a week results in an extremely high level of inventory turns. But you can only implement this model if all the conditions are operating according to expectations, e.g., you are confident of your dining habits in the coming week; you know the exact recipe for each dish; you are not surprised by finding spoiled ingredients; and you are confident that all of your appliances will be available and operating as intended. This is an example of a Lean operation.

Now assume you do not have a Lean kitchen, e.g., sometimes the oven does not work, so instead of making a roast, you switch to sandwiches. Also, since you never know who may stop by for drinks and dinner, you may want to purchase extra groceries to have on hand for the unexpected. Furthermore, your eating habits are such that you binge eat sometimes, and at other times you diet. With so much variability, you are not comfortable unless you have extra food in the house. You permanently stock the refrigerator with about six weeks of food and continue your weekly grocery shopping to assure a "safety stock." This contributes to an average of six-and-one-half weeks of food in the refrigerator and eight annual inventory turns (which is similar to the average turns of many of the industry sectors listed in Figure 5.4).

Think of all the issues that would arise if you really had only eight inventory turns for your groceries. First of all, you would need more refrigerators and freezers, as well as space in your house for additional storage. You would likely have needed a van or truck to initially transport the groceries. Your electric bills would increase. It would take much more of your time to keep all of the groceries neatly arranged and easily accessible. It would be virtually impossible to adopt a first-in-first-out (FIFO) loading process required to make sure your food was rotated properly. Would you really be willing to unload all of the beverages, produce, and other perishable items every week in order to load the fresh purchases in the rear? It even seems reasonable to hire a butler to keep everything organized.

Interestingly, we unreasonably expect shop workers to load from the rear and take from the front even when it is made nearly impossible by placing the shelves of materials against the walls. If we do not consistently rotate our groceries at home in this manner, why would we expect people to do it at work where it is much more difficult? The concepts are the same whether it is groceries at home or parts at work.

Next, apply the excess and obsolete inventory concepts to our grocery scenario. With so much food spread in so many refrigerators and freezers, it would be very difficult to know exactly what you have and where it is stored. The risk of spoilage (obsolescence) would increase exponentially. You would not know how bad it really was until you started to empty the refrigerators and freezers and lowered the inventory level. As you discovered all types of "surprises," you most certainly would be motivated to deploy an inventory control system in order to understand what you have, where it is stored, and how old it is.

Further, assume that on special occasions you tried to prepare gourmet dinners that required various spices and unusual ingredients. With food items scattered all over in various storage spaces, it would take a tremendous amount of time to search your inventory and either locate the items you needed or determine what additional shopping was necessary. With lower inventory levels, this information could be acquired much faster and any missing ingredients could be purchased more efficiently.

If Lean was implemented in our grocery example, inventory was maintained at only one or two weeks of supply, and shopping occurred once a week as initially discussed, a great deal of space would be freed up and electric bills would decrease. During the transitional period of lowering inventory levels, much smaller purchases would be required, resulting in significantly lower grocery bills than normal. Lower levels of inventory would result in reduced spoilage. After some training, the butler could be redeployed to work on your landscaping. Similar conceptual scenarios play out in all businesses every day during their Lean journeys.

SUMMARY

Lean is about eliminating waste, and inventory generally covers up many of the wasteful practices in a business. This chapter has reviewed three ways that improved inventory turns potentially depress earnings. The Lean journey will dramatically improve inventory turns, which in turn likely will temporarily reduce earnings (assuming cost structures and sales remain similar) due to the following:

1. The cleansing of the balance sheet of deferred capitalized labor and overhead

2. The uncovering of additional excess and obsolete inventory above normal reserve levels

3. The short-term interruption in sales resulting from improved lead times

Figure 5.6 illustrates the impact of these three factors for a one-hundred million dollar company.

Assumptions	
Sales: $100M	
Cost of Sales: $60M (65% Mat'l., 15% Labor & 20% Overhead)	
Operating Inc: $10M	
Inventory: $12M	
Inventory Turns: 5	
Customer Lead - Times: 8 Weeks	
Impact of:	**Negative OI Impact**
Inventory turns improvement from 5 to 6:	($700K), or 7.0%
Customer lead-time reduction from 8 to 6 weeks:	($2,346K), or 23.5%
Discovery of additional obsolescence:	($250K), or 2.5%
All else being equal, there can be a significant, negative OI impact, 33% in this case!	

Figure 5.6: A Simple Example of the Financial Impact of Improved Inventory Management

Figure 5.6 demonstrates the significant unfavorable Operating Income impact of improved inventory management. In this example, as inventory turns improve from five to six turns, pre-tax and after-tax income will decline by $3.296 million and $2.143 million respectfully due to the release of deferred capitalized direct labor and overhead costs, the temporary loss of sales as customers adjust their ordering patterns, and the write-off of additional excess and obsolete inventory. On the other hand, cash flow will be favorably impacted by $107,500 due to the significant inventory reduction.

	Impact on Net Income
Turns Improvement	$ (700,000)
Lead-Time Reduction	$ (2,346,154)
Excess & Osolete Inventory	$ (250,000)
Total Pre-Tax Impact	$ (3,296,154)
Taxes @ 35%	$ 1,153,654
Net Income	$ (2,142,500)
	Impact on Cash Flow
Net Income	$ (2,142,500)
Plus Change in Inventory	$ 2,000,000
Plus Excess & Obsolete Inventory	$ 250,000
Total Cash Flow	$ 107,500

**Figure 5.7: Financial Impact of Improved
Inventory Management**

The example above is based on the assumptions that sales, production, and cost structures have remained static. However, the potential for improved velocity, quality, and service from Lean initiatives should enhance a firm's competitive position. This will likely increase sales, which has the potential to offset most of the initial unfavorable earnings impact resulting from inventory reductions.

For any company undergoing a Lean transformation, it is imperative to isolate the effects of improved inventory turns in order to clearly understand the improvements made in operations.

CHAPTER 5 ENDNOTES

1. *The Web Site of The New York State Society of CPAs*, "Account Terminology Guide", http://www.nysscpa.org/prof_library/guide.htm#M (April, 2007).

2. David Drickhamer, "Tick Tock", *IndustryWeek*, http://www.industryweek.com/ReadArticle.aspx?ArticleID=1365 (January, 2004).

3. 2005 Dell Form 10 - K, *Consolidated Statements of Financial Position*, p.36, and *Consolidated Statements of Income*, p. 37.

6

Detailing the Distortions Created by Standard Cost System Metrics

As explained in Chapter 3, a traditional standard cost system cannot coexist with Lean because it motivates behavior which is actively hostile to a Lean transformation. A standard cost system is like a dinosaur: it is huge; it moves very slowly; it takes an army of people to keep pushing it forward; and it must constantly be fed work orders. In addition, a standard cost system typically reports and compares current results to the prior year's most representative "actual" costs, which include built-in allowances for scrap, yields, set-up times, waiting times, and other non-value-added activities. Is that really the type of target a firm should strive for in the upcoming year?

In particular, the intense focus placed by a standard cost system on the generation of a multitude of variances as a means of assessing operational performance is highly questionable. These variances often are extremely complex, require significant resources and associated transactions to maintain, and usually are distributed long after the activity has taken place. Very few people outside the accounting area truly understand how the variances are generated. Furthermore, since all variances are financial in nature, they distance everyone from the underlying physical activity that generated these variances, which contradicts the desired behavior in a Lean organization. A true understanding of activity can occur only in *gemba* (the place where the work is done) by observing the work, not by an end-of-the-month financial report.

The following discussion reviews the typical variances maintained by most companies as well as the difficulties encountered by their continued use during a Lean transformation.

Purchase Price Variance (PPV)

Nearly all companies routinely develop purchase price variance (PPV) reports. The PPV is perhaps the easiest variance to generate and is probably the only variance that the user community actually understands. Whether it is relevant or motivates the proper behavior is another issue. As indicated above, visiting and studying gemba is the only way to effectively identify and understand product and operational problems.

We are aware of one company that put an inordinate amount of attention on purchase price variances, awarding a quarterly prize to the senior buyer at each division who generated the largest PPV. By randomly examining open purchase orders, it was easy to ascertain that many of the favorable variances were the result of stepping up to the vendor's next larger lot size. The buyer would simply rationalize that since the company would eventually need the material, there was no harm in ordering a little extra. The motivation for lower average material costs often leads to purchasing larger lot sizes. Either purchasing or producing in larger lot sizes than required creates waste in many ways, and is the antithesis of the goals of a Lean journey.

Receiving more parts than needed might take extra time on the receiving dock, which can preclude the staff from timely receipt of those parts that are immediately needed in the shop. Gridlock on the receiving dock is a frequent occurrence and a hidden cost that is difficult to quantify. Unnecessarily loading the receiving dock will also increase errors, which likely will affect overall productivity. Lastly, purchasing one more part than needed will result in cash outflows earlier than otherwise would be the case. Once again, this cost is not captured in any PPV report.

Favorable purchase price variances are often the result of adding new suppliers to the supplier data base. Two methods are commonly utilized when adding new suppliers. One approach is to add a new supplier without undertaking a full supplier certification review. This has the potential of exposing the company to quality and service issues down the road. The alternative is to require vendor certification, which may involve significant time and resources. Regardless of the approach, significant organizational costs in adding suppliers will be incurred that are not captured in the PPV reports.

Furthermore, during a Lean transformation, the goal is to reduce the number of suppliers to facilitate long-term partnerships, whereby both companies focus all of their efforts on jointly reducing costs and lead times while simultaneously improving quality. In addition, these joint agreements can facilitate either manual or electronic kanban systems with daily or hourly milk runs for part deliveries directly to the appropriate work cells. Continually adding and changing suppliers to achieve price reductions without taking into account the additional systemic costs that will be incurred to update and modify all of the other supplier/company interactions will result in a false sense of cost savings. Finally, suppliers will lack the incentive to fully engage in a cooperative long-term improvement program if their relationship can be terminated at any moment.

Other costs incurred as a result of either purchasing materials in larger than needed lot sizes or frequently rotating suppliers to achieve favorable purchase price variances are numerous and rarely incorporated into the PPV calculation. Excess and obsolete inventory is, unfortunately, a reality for manufacturing companies. Yet, are there consistent and successful efforts to really uncover the root cause of the excess and obsolete inventory? Are the prior period favorable purchase price variances ever offset with the subsequent excess and obsolete inventory write downs? The same logic applies to purchased parts that ultimately do not meet quality standards. How often are additional costs associated with poor supplier quality that creates rework or engineering issues applied back to the original PPV?

A single metric like PPV can potentially harm a Lean transformation, as it provides incomplete information and motivates non-Lean behavior to achieve short-term gain at the expense of long-term performance.

In addition, tracking PPV is an after-the-fact measure that encourages managing by looking in the rear-view mirror. If a firm insists on tracking PPV, why not track it in advance by developing an up-front approval process for any meaningful price change. Incorporating a sign-off procedure for all price changes that have an annual impact above a specified threshold value (for both cost increases and cost decreases) will help management understand, in advance, whether or not a supplier is being changed, lot sizes are being increased, or other significant changes are being made that will affect the economics of the customer/vendor relationship. Such a procedure will promote the necessary dialogue to reinforce Lean behavior, as well as help to avoid surprises by informing management of the expected PPV prior to month-end.

With material being the largest cost component for most manufacturing companies, measuring its value appropriately is a necessity. The total acquisition and lifetime cost of materials should be considered, including initial cost, quality, packaging, receiving ease, lot-size requirements, vendor terms, vendor certification costs, lead times, warranties, service support, standardization, and obsolescence policies. The PPV metric addresses only one element of total material costs.

Lean thinking prefers that actual material costs are tracked in real time against historical costs, not against an arbitrary standard. Simple charts tracking key material costs should be developed and visible, so all associates know exactly what the company is spending for materials. The focus changes from simply looking at deviations from a preset standard to an understanding of the total material costs and their related trends. It is amazing how many suggestions will be generated from a workforce that clearly understands what a company is spending for critical items. Variances do not motivate or empower a workforce, whereas, tracking total real costs in an easily understood and visible chart both educates and motivates. Regardless of whether one is in manufacturing or product development, line of sight to actual material costs improves decision making. Easily understood charts of real total costs are easier to comprehend than the combination of standard material pricing and purchase price variances.

Direct Labor Variances

Reporting variances relative to direct labor activity originated in the days when labor was the bulk of cost of goods sold, which is no longer the case for most manufacturing operations. In a Lean environment, we are interested in producing only according to demand, but the typical standard absorption cost system rewards operations for everything produced, whether or not it is needed. This often motivates "gaming" of the system by overproducing high absorption items in order to meet monthly or quarterly profit targets, and building in large lot sizes to avoid setups.

In addition, typical labor measures such as productivity, efficiency, and utilization are painstakingly prepared in detailed reports and used as levers over production managers. These measures also promote non-

Lean behavior by focusing on individual results rather than the process. It is not healthy to promote these measures during a Lean transformation, because they have very little to do with system-wide optimization. This is especially true in a discrete manufacturing environment with multiple work centers that are not balanced and are not designed to operate according to takt time. The typical measurement system can often be detrimental to schedule attainment and quality.

What advantage is there if a non-critical machine center improves local productivity when the downstream work center is not improving? In such a case, increased productivity at an upstream work center will simply increase inventories downstream, expose the system to greater quality issues, and consume cash much earlier than necessary. Yet, you will find in these circumstances, individuals operating the improved work centers are often praised for their efforts and sometimes even rewarded monetarily. This local optimization at the expense of total system performance is often standard operating procedure in traditional manufacturing environments, where processes are not connected and product flow is not understood.

Measuring individuals rather than processes generally promotes undesirable behavior. Here is a telling example of how people can game the system. During a Lean transformation in a heavy manufacturing business with an extensive machine shop, a program was implemented to eliminate many of the labor transactions. Prior to embarking on the Lean journey, every machinist would clock their time for both the setup activity as well as the run-time for each machined part. As a first step to reduce transactions, the machinists were told to clock on a job only when they started the setup, and clock off the job when the last piece was produced. The transactions associated with clocking off the end of each setup and clocking on for the start of the first good production piece for each job were eliminated. A few weeks later, the first shift machinist mentioned that he just did not understand how at the start of each morning, he always had to begin with a fresh setup. It seemed strange that the third shift machinist always managed to complete all of the pieces on his last job of the shift.

In discussing this with the third shift machinist, he explained that his behavior was affected by the new clocking system and his supervisor's single focus on productivity measures. Under the new system, no one "earned" any hours until the last piece was produced, so at the end of the machinist's shift, he made sure to select the job that would allow him time to complete both the setup and run-time before clocking out for the day. He obviously understood the new system, which motivated him to work according to a schedule that would maximize his individual productivity score. He even received reinforcement for this behavior, as his supervisor praised his steadily increasing productivity.

In a Lean environment, the focus is on system performance, one-piece flow, and adherence to schedule, not isolated productivity measures, which can undermine the goal of system optimization.

With a trained workforce, both unfavorable and favorable direct labor variances are usually the result of the process rather than any individual machinist. Unfavorable variances can result from poorly maintained machine tools, out of specification raw materials, inappropriate scheduling of jobs, poor quality tooling, poor machine programming, poor operator training, or inconvenient interruptions for "hot" jobs. Favorable variances, on the other hand, may result from successfully negotiating loose standards, batching jobs to amortize setup times over greater volumes, or moving work to different machine tools with different rates. The key question is whether time should be spent analyzing variances by reviewing out-of-date reports, or is it better to spend time each day in gemba, with the experts, working to understand the root causes and then improving the processes? Focusing on the physical processes will lead to improvements in system productivity far above any improvements resulting from analyzing variances.

Direct Labor to Indirect Labor Ratios

Some companies focus on managing direct versus indirect labor ratios, a practice which eventually becomes a significant obstacle to a successful Lean journey. A business should not be concerned with this ratio and instead should focus on input, process, and output measures (IPO). A business is trying to achieve a certain level of output with a minimum amount of resources, regardless of labor classification. If instead of utilizing ten direct associates and three indirect laborer associates to produce a given output, a firm could achieve the same level of production with five direct laborer associates and five indirect laborer associates, would anyone care? However, this operating approach may never be attempted simply because it would result in a direct to indirect labor ratio outside the norms of the business.

Another folly of tracking direct to indirect labor ratios is that most of what normally is classified as direct labor is really indirect labor, or even worse, pure waste. Time spent in gemba observing what we typically call direct labor will clarify that most of the time classified as productive time is actually spent in non-productive activities such as looking for parts, looking for the proper tools, searching for material handling equipment, or getting clarification of job instructions from a supervisor.

To gain a better perception of the depth of waste and misclassification of direct labor, it is suggested that you participate in a process improvement kaizen event. During a kaizen event, the team generally reviews a video of the process and classifies activities as either value-added or non-value-added work. It is likely that 60 to 80 percent of the work formerly classified as direct labor is really wasted time due to the lack of standard work. After participating in a few kaizen events, even cost accountants generally agree that direct labor for most activities is a misnomer.

KAIZEN EVENT

A kaizen event concentrates a team of people, for a 3 to 10 day period, on a production process or manufacturing cell in order to rapidly and dramatically improve performance. Teams will consist of both trained and untrained members in world class techniques. The improvement activities start with an analysis of the work site's performance and then moves to a rapid implementation process.[1] Kaizen's have now expanded to all areas of a company.

Another reason to eliminate any hard and fast rules regarding the mix of direct and indirect labor is that the nature of the work and the process itself will dramatically change. Once standard work is developed, productivity will rapidly increase if the correct, defect-free parts, in the right quantities, can be delivered at just the right time to the operators. (During the initial stages of a Lean journey, this is typically where the largest initial gains can be achieved.) This approach changes the focus of most discrete manufacturers from optimizing individual cycle times to optimizing internal logistics.

WATER SPIDERS

Water Spiders are employees who deliver materials exactly on demand, at the frequency requested, in the right quantity with 100% reliability.[2]

Material handling becomes critical for success, and new positions are added, such as "water spiders," which make regular milk runs throughout the plant, delivering small quantities of the right parts to the operators. Tremendous productivity gains will be realized as total labor costs decrease, even though material handling costs may increase.

In addition, inventory will decline dramatically. Such gains would be impossible in a traditional environment where maintaining a certain ratio of indirect to direct labor is expected.

Effective in-plant logistics (material handling) is the glue that keeps the Lean shop performing at high levels. Historically, businesses have viewed in-plant logistics as an afterthought and typically staffed such positions with the lowest paid and least skilled associates, which in turn led to rules regarding the level of investment in indirect versus direct labor. This approach is another obstacle that must be removed during a Lean transformation.

During the Lean journey, the nature of everyone's job will change significantly, so an individual might be alternating between direct and indirect work throughout the course of the day. Thus, the classification of people into indirect and direct categories, as well as the need to monitor labor ratios, will diminish in importance. Furthermore, trying to keep track of the time to classify work as direct versus indirect is costly and non-value added. Additionally, as we separate the man from the machine and have individuals who are cross-trained monitor multiple machines, it will become nearly impossible to assign labor costs to specific part numbers. At this stage in the Lean journey it will be necessary to change product costing to average costs for families of parts, as explained in Chapter 7, Value Stream Costing.

At the end of the day, whether a company is compensating a direct laborer or an indirect laborer, the money comes from the same checking account and is simply a cost of doing business. Since the type of labor utilized does not affect profitability, the focus should be on the total costs of the labor inputs relative to the outputs, instead of focusing on arbitrary labor classifications.

Overhead Variances

Of all the month-end variances calculated, overhead is perhaps the most meaningless, least understood, and most ignored by its intended customers—manufacturing supervisors. Many accountants believe that, in order to conform with GAAP, as well as internal and external reporting entities, it is necessary to assign every manufacturing cost to a specific end item or SKU. This may be the single biggest misconception driving much of the wasteful activity in modern-day cost accounting. In order to adhere to all reporting requirements relative to inventory valuation, businesses have to fairly state their inventories at a materially correct amount. However, there is no requirement that material, direct labor, and overhead must be stated exactly correct to the nearest penny for each SKU.[3]

During the early twentieth century, when overhead was a very small proportion of total manufacturing costs, allocating overhead costs to individual products was far less time consuming and had minimal impact on total product costs. Over the last fifty years, however, overhead costs have mushroomed. This is attributed to the growth of product complexity and variety, the advancement of sophisticated information systems and planning tools, and the replacement of direct labor with more efficient automated machines. These changes have forced the typical manufacturing company to add the following: layers of planners and expediters; sophisticated machine tools and computer systems with their associated programmers and depreciation and lease expenses; ongoing consulting expenses; and more and more warehouse and material handling personnel. In addition, non-controllable costs of facilities, safety and environmental compliance, healthcare, utilities, insurance, and property taxes have all risen dramatically relative to direct labor, adding to the pool of overhead costs.

Despite these fundamental shifts in cost structure, the majority of firms continue to allocate these overhead costs in the same manner as was done decades ago. The explanation often given is that continuing the practice protects consistency. Many companies would rather cling to their historical benchmarks and be consistently wrong, than change methods and dramatically improve accuracy and decision making.

Anecdotal conversations with hundreds of accountants about their cost accounting systems confirm that overhead allocation schemes have not changed over time in any substantial fashion for most firms. Perhaps one excuse for their adherence to age-old questionable methods is timing. The need for accounting system change analysis would logically be the greatest when accounting data are in the forefront—at year-end budget time; but this is also when accountants are the busiest. Yet, accountants need to recognize that they may be budgeting themselves into irrelevancy, as users generally discount accounting information because either they do not understand it, or they do not believe the output is accurate or meaningful.

A careful analysis of most cost accounting systems reveals that the output is often inappropriate for many decision-making activities. Most standard cost systems take the "peanut butter" approach of spreading overhead costs evenly across departments and operations as a function of direct labor, regardless of actual overhead usage patterns and prior discussions of its ineffectiveness. It is difficult to understand why the concept persists that spreading overhead based on direct labor hours reflects the actual consumption of resources.

Most companies typically assign direct labor overtime and benefits to overhead cost pools that are spread across all work centers, even though these costs are easily traceable to a specific location where they occurred. Thus, if one area of the plant is working an extensive amount of overtime, other departments will be charged a portion of this cost, which unfairly generates unfavorable overhead variances for them. The only reasonable explanation for maintaining this allocation is that it has been done this way for decades, and cost accountants have not considered it important enough to question and change.

Tooling and supplies are another example of typical overhead costs that are usually not clearly tracked to any specific machine unless elaborate reporting systems are installed, so once again, the peanut butter approach is used. Lastly, it is nearly impossible to accurately assign general plant operating costs, such as property taxes, depreciation, and staff expenses for supervision, material handling, and planning, to individual products without using broad allocation schemes. Yet, without ever observing what is actually happening on the shop floor, well intentioned cost accountants go through all types of complex charades to allocate these costs in an effort to determine "true" product costs.

Out of this morass of data, standard overhead rates are developed and monthly variances are reported. Plant supervisors realize that the more they produce, regardless of the demand or the schedule, the better the variance results appear, and so full-throttle production becomes the mantra. There is a general lack of understanding of the derivation of the numbers, and a tremendous amount of time is wasted collecting and disseminating the information.

At the same time, millions of transactions are taking place, whereby every SKU in the plant has standard material, direct labor, and overhead costs carefully assigned to it for each step of the production process. Any production cost that materially deviates from the standard in a negative direction generates a product cost variance that often requires a management review and answers from plant supervision. Since overhead variances typically are generated through a ratio tied to direct labor, the only response to "correct" the overhead variances is to change direct labor or produce more. Yet, it should be obvious that, with overhead cost ratios equaling several multiples of direct labor, changing direct labor costs really does little to address actual overhead issues.

Much of these overhead costs are incurred due to out-of-control operations, not necessarily an out-of-control labor force. This can best be understood via Figures 6.1 through 6.3.

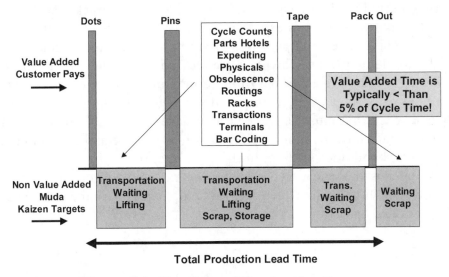

**Figure 6.1: Traditional Production Process
Spread throughout Plant**

Figure 6.1 illustrates a four-stage production process to make a finished product that requires dots, pins, tape, and final pack out. (Refer to Chapter 3 for an explanation of this process.) The four operations are scattered throughout the plant with batches of semi-completed product that are moved intermittently and subsequently in and out of inventory locations at each operation. The shaded area above the X–axis is considered value-added work. The width of these bars represents the time devoted to the four value-added operations. The shaded area below the X–axis is considered waste, as the customer would not willingly pay for any of these activities. (It does not matter how many times you move or lift or count an item, there is no value being created from the customer's perspective.) The length of the X–axis represents the total production lead time to get a product through all four operations and to the shipping dock. In most traditional assembly or machining processes, the value-added time as a percentage of the total production lead time is usually 5 percent or less. The other 95 percent of the time, the parts or semi-completed product is either waiting or being moved. One of the locations is the parts warehouse, some-times referred to as the "parts hotel," as the parts go there and liter-ally fall asleep, hoping to be used some day.

Disconnected production activities encourage careful tracking of over-head activities. There is extensive waiting time in between the four separate disconnected operations that require inventory tracking in order to identify where the parts are located in the plant at all times. Likewise, there are a number of material handlers to move the large batches of parts, as well as material handling equipment and ware-house space that must be tracked. On occasion, the company must engage material expediters to find parts in the queue and go out to the shop and hand deliver them to the next operation. All of the costs associated with these activities can dwarf the actual direct labor costs associated with the time devoted to actually performing the individual value-added operations.

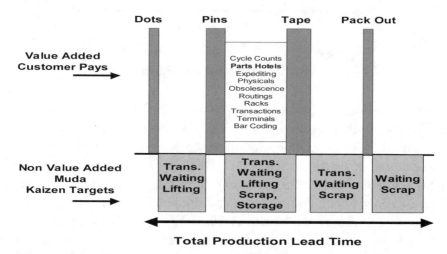

Figure 6.2: Progression to the Establishment of a Lean Cell

Figure 6.2 depicts the improvements made as the company progresses with its Lean journey. As a company begins to move operations closer and closer together, the need for various inventory locations and mate-rial moves diminishes. These operational improvements also drive the need to reduce transactions and "dismantle" some of the long estab-lished routines.

Finally, as depicted in Figure 6.3, the company moves all of the operations into one cell, produces in lot sizes of one, and produces according to demand. Standard work is established, which includes a standard amount of work-in-process throughout the production process. Moving large batches of material between operations is virtually eliminated since the batch size is one and the operators can simply hand the material to each other.

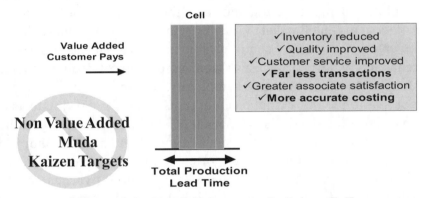

Figure 6.3: Establishment of a Lean Cell

With a Lean cell, most of the waste has been eliminated and many of the overhead requirements are no longer needed. The physical changes taking place in the production area will result in lower overhead costs. Monitoring of overhead variances is not required. In fact, the emphasis is entirely different from a traditional operation, which focuses a lot of resources on improving cycle times for the value-added activities. The big gains are achieved mainly via eliminating waste, not by speeding up a two-minute operation to one minute and fifty seconds. (Once a cell is created, there certainly is a focus on balancing the line and becoming more efficient. However, the ability to understand clearly what operations need to be improved is orders of magnitude more apparent.)

As cells are formed, costs are simply collected in total. The focus is on input, process, and output whereby average unit costs can be determined by dividing total costs by total output. There is no need to waste time deciding if someone is a direct labor person or an overhead person; they are simply all labor inputs. Likewise, all supplies and

other overhead items are charged to the cell. Over time, the cell associates graphically monitor average unit costs and the goal is simply to
lower all costs continuously. There are no pre-set standards or artifi-
cial targets at which cell associates should stop being creative or halt
the flow of suggestions. Standard overhead rates and their associated
variances are replaced with easy to understand actual costs.

Overhead costs consist of variable, semi-variable, and fixed costs.
Variable costs might include indirect labor, certain benefits, tooling,
and other items that fluctuate virtually in lock step with volume changes.
Many overhead costs are semi-variable in nature, such as supervision,
purchasing, or software leases that are the result of decisions related
to step functions in volume or complexity. These costs usually bear no
direct relation to individual product costs; therefore, trying to assign
them to individual SKU's is imprudent. Decisions relating to these
costs are often made by senior management, and holding shop floor
supervision accountable for these often uncontrollable overhead variances is counterproductive. Finally, a portion of overhead costs is
considered fixed costs, which have virtually no relationship to medium
term operational activity and might include building depreciation, insurance, property taxes, and portions of utility expenses. Unfortunately, these fixed costs are included in overhead and generate variances that only serve to confuse the rank and file.

As is evident, many components of overhead are largely unmanage-
able at the discrete product level and should be excluded from individual SKU costs and aggregated at the product family level in conjunction with the formation of cells.

Additional Standard Cost Deficiencies

There is another troubling issue regarding the irrelevance of standard
costs for decision making. In a complex, vertically integrated operation, costs throughout the production process are continually rolled up
to higher levels, whereby direct labor and overhead costs at the beginning of the production process are classified as material once the partially completed product or sub-assembly is put into another area's
work-in-process inventory (and often assigned a new part number).
Many times it is nearly impossible to segregate the underlying mate-

rial, direct labor, and overhead components throughout the value chain for critical make-buy decisions or product development cost trade-offs. With additional overhead and software development, this barrier can be overcome. But too often the day-to-day critical decisions are being made by associates who, unfortunately, do not understand the cost system.

Even in a traditional manufacturing environment, a standard cost system is difficult to maintain accurately because of the complexity of transaction recording and reporting. Trying to maintain such a level of detail in a Lean environment is no longer appropriate, because the physical activity has been modified, the workforce is cross-trained and continually moves from operation to operation, product moves through the plant at much greater velocities, and like-type products are produced in cells one at a time. The notion of achieving lower costs via larger batch sizes is no longer relevant.

Interestingly, when people who can actually make a difference in the operations have access to and understand product costs, they are more likely to work hard at searching for, recognizing, and reducing costs that have previously been hidden to them in a maze of standard costs and variances.

Figure 6.4 summarizes many of the deficiencies of traditional variances.

Variance	Non-Lean Outcomes/Behaviors
Absorption Variance	• Building of unnecessary inventory • Reluctance to change over equipment
Machine Utilization	• Reluctance to change over equipment • Reluctance to perform necessary PM procedures
Purchase Price Variance	• Promotes buying excess inventory due to quantity discounts • May compromise quality and delivery over price considerations • Promotes increase in # of suppliers
Direct/Indirect Labor Ratio	• Uses direct operators for indirect purposes • Minimizes the importance of indirect labor activities • Moves significant costs to overhead pools
Direct Labor Variance Analysis	• Use of lowest cost resource regardless of skill set • Piece rate encourages the building of unnecessary inventory, and may compromise quality
Overhead Variance Analysis	• Favorable variances interpreted as good regardless of continuous improvement trend • Encourages production regardless of demand

Figure 6.4: Non-Lean Behaviors
Resulting from Traditional Variances[4]

Budgeted Variances

The authors of this book recently were working together on a year-end budget and Lean accounting transition. One is a vice-president of operations with considerable experience in Lean thinking and the other is a professor on sabbatical who teaches and researches in this area. The company at which they were collaborating was completing its budget for the upcoming year. The professor was experiencing first-hand how budgets are prepared for a large company. She was visibly surprised to learn that the company **budgets** a multi-million-dollar variance at the division level and tens of millions of dollars on a consolidated basis. This was something that she had never considered or discussed in the classroom. She questioned why standards were not updated to better represent more accurate costs, rather than budgeting anticipated variances.

Shortly thereafter, as a speaker at the second annual Lean Accounting Summit, the vice-president of operations queried the approximately five hundred attendees to ascertain if they budgeted variances at their respective companies. A vast majority of the audience confirmed that they did indeed budget variances.

A simple Lean technique that is often used to understand and solve problems is the "5 Whys." This technique is used below to address the perplexing continued practice of budgeting variances.

5 WHYS

Lean follows a Socratic approach by asking many questions to drive down to the root cause of a problem. One very simple but effective technique is to ask "why" five times in order to uncover the root cause of a particular problem.

Let's go through the five whys:

1. Why do companies continue to budget variances, year after year, rather than adjust the standards for their expected full-absorption costs?

The simplistic answer is "because we've always done it that way."

2. Why have you always done it this way?

Year-end is stressful and the busiest time of the year already, so we don't have the necessary time to analyze and change standards to better match them with actual and expected costs.

3. Why does it take so much time to change standards?

To get the standard costs close to reality we would have to analyze our rates for every department and every cost category, as well as review production and spending forecasts. Also, we would have to review all the assumptions for allocating costs. This is very labor intensive, and it is unlikely that the result would represent our real costs anyway.

4. Then why doesn't anyone acknowledge or appear to even care that the standard costs used for decision making are outdated and incorrect?

The people who use the information on a day-to-day basis do not understand the standard cost system and therefore are in no position to challenge the process.

5. So if the only people who truly understand the system are in finance, why do they continue with a flawed system?

It is all about tradition and optics. Senior management is used to certain results and patterns. If we were to update the standard cost system and completely absorb all costs, then the variances would disappear and the costs for every product and product family would change—some dramatically. Consistency in reporting is preferred to accuracy.

CONCLUSION

As the "5 Whys" conclude, the greatest fear to changing accounting systems is the loss of optics, or the inability of senior management to maintain their internal compasses if the scorekeeping system were to change. This has been confirmed by personal experiences. Accounting leadership must be educated about the pitfalls of standard costing and the benefits of accounting changes in order to overcome these hurdles and successfully transition to accounting for Lean.

Further, the universities have a responsibility to educate their students about the failures and inaccuracies of a traditional management accounting costing system, particularly in a Lean manufacturing environment. Students should have a background in alternative accounting methods that better respond to management decision-making needs. Lean accounting champions that can lead the charge for accounting change need to be trained both in the field and in the classroom.

Chapter 6 Endnotes

1. Larry Rubrich and Mattie Watson, *Implementing World Class Manufacturing* (Fort Wayne, Indiana: WCM Associates, 2004), p.384.

2. *Business Management Systems,* Glossary, http://www.valucurve.com/glossary.html#w (April 2007).

3. Charles T. Horngren, Srikant M. Datar, and Goerge Foster, *Cost Accounting: A Managerial Emphasis, 12th Edition* (Upper Saddle River, NJ: Prentice Hall, 2006), 713.

4. Mark DeLuzio, AICPA's CFO Roundtable Series, *Real Numbers Through "Lean" Accounting,* March, 2007.

Part II

Transitioning From Traditional Accounting to Accounting for Lean

7

Preparing "Plain English" Profit-and-Loss Statements

Effective communication is critical in both our personal and professional lives, as well as in most business situations. A business organization is a human decision-making system in which the quality of the decisions is determined by the effectiveness of the communication apparatus.

If we want people to act on our decisions in the manner we would like, they need to have clear information that motivates them to respond. Motivation, or the absence of it, can often be traced back to the influence of communications upon their intended recipients. When trying to communicate, it is critical to make sure the material is easily understood. After any communication, you should ask yourself, "Did those receiving your message actually understand what you are trying to say?"[1]

Cost accountants should be particularly careful in making sure this question is answered in the affirmative. If we treat cost management reports as a product, and consider the recipients of this information as customers, then we must be certain that the customers are receiving value. Value can be realized only if customers understand the information being presented and are able to use the information to steer the company in the right direction. Unfortunately, over thirty years of manufacturing experience has proven that very little value is received from these very basic cost management reports. Operations managers simply do not understand most cost accounting information, even though it is provided to them on a regular basis.

There appears to be a real need for non-financial business people to have help in interpreting financial data. Figure 7.1 portrays a mini-industry that has developed in order to teach financial basics to managers who have not had financial training.

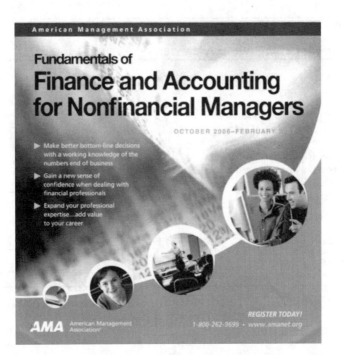

Figure 7.1: Classes on Finance for Non-Financial Managers

Are you curious as to why we need to send managers from all over the company to special finance classes in order to better understand internal financial reports that they are expected to use in their decision-making activities? After all, how many finance managers go to operations classes, such as manufacturing for non-manufacturing managers, or product development for non-product development managers? If we build financial reports in simple-to-understand formats, these training classes would not be necessary.

Figure 7.2 illustrates a common format for presenting the monthly results of a business unit, referred to here as the Traditional Company. The operating results presented for our fictitious firm are presented through the operating income line. These results could easily represent a specific business unit, product line, or entire company.

Traditional Company Profit and Loss Statement For the month ending January 31, 20XX		
	$(000)	%
Sales	1,303	100%
Cost of Sales @ Standard	787	60%
Purchase Price Variance	20	2%
Material Usage Variance	30	2%
Labor Rate Variance	10	1%
Labor Usage Variance	15	1%
Overhead Variance	50	4%
Total Cost of Sales	912	70%
Gross Margin	391	30%
Operating Expenses	250	19%
Operating Income	141	11%

**Figure 7.2: Monthly Profit-and-Loss Statement
for Traditional Company**

In this traditional format, cost of sales at standard is calculated by multiplying the quantity of each stock-keeping unit (SKU) shipped times the standard cost of each unit. The resulting product equals the cost of sales at standard. Then the period variances are added to the cost of sales at standard to arrive at total actual cost of sales. In Figure 7.2, all of the standards are unfavorable and therefore increase total period costs.

Unfortunately, the operating personnel in the plant find it difficult to decipher this information. As depicted in this typical example, the largest variance is overhead, which is the most confusing variance because its root cause is extremely difficult to understand. There is also no way to determine from this presentation exactly how much was spent in the period for material, which is likely the single largest expense. It is odd that this critical expense is invisible on the typical operating statement. In addition, it is impossible to determine if the reporting unit generated these results by building or reducing inventory. Finally, there is no measure of customer performance in the form of order fulfillment rates or lead times. The tendency for most businesses is to focus on the bottom line without regard to how the numbers were achieved.

As the physical processes are changed during a Lean transformation, the cost management practices must be changed as well. A Lean profit-and-loss statement will categorize costs in a way that is much easier for everyone to understand and take action. In the simplest of cases, the following four cost categories should be tracked by a company embarking on a Lean transformation.

1. **Material Costs:** Material costs are clearly identified on the period income statement or departmental performance report, rather than embedded in standard costs.

2. **Labor Costs:** Labor costs consist of all manufacturing expenses associated with labor and benefits, including base wages for all hourly and salaried manufacturing personnel, overtime, fringe benefits, and temporary labor. There is no distinction between direct and indirect labor; both are labor inputs to the production process.

3. **Conversion Costs:** Conversion costs consist of all costs associated with converting raw material to finished goods, exclusive of labor costs and fixed costs. Examples of conversion costs include shop supplies, tooling, equipment repairs, consulting, and shipping supplies.

4. **Fixed Costs:** Fixed costs include depreciation, property taxes, insurance, and any other items considered relatively constant in the medium term, regardless of production levels. Fixed costs can be segregated into plant level fixed costs, such as building depreciation, and value stream fixed costs, such as depreciation on equipment dedicated to a particular value stream.

Once spending is segregated into these four categories, the profit-and-loss statement is reformatted accordingly. Figure 7.3 illustrates how Traditional Company would report January's results with a "Plain English" profit-and-loss statement.

Traditional Company
"Plain English" Profit and Loss Statement
For the month ending January 31, 20XX

		$(000)	%
Sales		1,303	100%
Cost of Sales			
Material		517	40%
Shop Supplies		67	5%
Shipping & Receiving Supplies	Conversion	5	0%
Equipment Repairs	Costs	22	2%
Hardware		32	2%
Sub-Total Variable Cost of Sales		643	49%
Variable Margin		660	51%
Labor Costs		190	15%
Fixed Costs		42	3%
Cost (To)/From Inventory		37	3%
Sub-Total Fixed Costs		269	21%
Total Cost of Sales		912	70%
Gross Margin		391	30%
Operating Expenses		250	19%
Operating Income		141	11%

Figure 7.3: Monthly "Plain English" Profit-and-Loss Statement for Traditional Company – Case 1

Please note that the format of the "Plain English" profit-and-loss statement can be configured in various ways. The authors have combined labor costs, fixed costs, and cost (to)/from inventory to determine the total fixed costs for the period. The goal is to have local supervision focus on those items over which they have control, such as the variable costs in the cell and value stream, and exclude from the variable margin those items over which they have no control. In many instances, labor is relatively fixed in the short run, and therefore it is labeled here

as a fixed cost. Further, in a world class operation, the level of inventory is typically not under the control of local supervision; rather it is determined by standard work and one-piece flow according to takt time. Therefore, it is also listed below the variable margin. The exact location of these cost categories on the "Plain English" statement should be determined based on the dynamics of each particular business.

Benefits of a "Plain English" Profit-and-Loss Statement

The "Plain English" profit-and-loss statement has the same sales and operating income as the traditional statement (Figure 7.2); however, the nature of the spending is clearly identified in the monthly report at a summary level. The benefits of this report are significant and are listed below.

1. Recipients of the report are familiar with the spending categories and can track performance. Spending categories are easily understood by everyone, not just cost accountants.

2. Material spending, often the largest expenditure, can be monitored easily as a percentage of sales for quick identification of any unusual trends for further examination.

3. Trends in variable margin, the metric that operating managers have the most control over in the short term, are readily apparent. Volume fluctuations will not mask underlying performance trends.

4. Management can easily determine if overproducing has affected period results. This is, perhaps, one of the most important benefits of a "Plain English" profit-and-loss statement. The line item "Cost (To)/From Inventory" indicates whether the business unit transferred cost into inventory or whether it reduced inventory to meet shipments. Understanding how a business unit achieved its performance is critical to motivating the correct behavior.

5. The "Plain English" profit-and-loss statement eliminates the need to maintain complex allocation schemes.

6. Time-consuming variance analysis is largely eliminated.

7. Far fewer transactions are required to prepare "Plain English" profit-and-loss statements.

8. Decision making is improved.

9. The focus is on real costs, which makes improvements more readily visible.

10. Month-end closes are shorter, freeing up accounting staff time to pursue more value-added activities.

Perhaps the most significant benefit of the "Plain English" profit-and-loss statement is isolating the changes in inventory levels, as described in benefit 4 above. Figure 7.3 illustrates, in a straightforward manner, how reducing inventory also reduces income. (See the discussion in Chapter 5 related to this topic.) You can readily see from this example that decreases in inventory (costs *from* inventory) increase cost of sales and correspondingly decrease operating income. On the other hand, costs transferred *to* inventory, which reflect overproduction, improves operating income by deferring inventory expenditures.

A comparison of Figures 7.3 and 7.4 demonstrates these concepts. Figure 7.4 shows the monthly results for a companion cell that is producing nearly the same product as in Figure 7.3. Assume that two different managers are in charge of two products and each manager is pursuing different operating strategies. Please note that the top line (Sales) and the bottom line (Operating Income) are identical in both examples. At first glance one would assume that both cells are performing equally. However, a closer examination will show the fallacy of that conclusion.

Traditional Company
"Plain English" Profit and Loss Statement
For the month ending January 31, 20XX

		$(000)	%
Sales		1,303	100%
Cost of Sales			
Material		600	46%
Shop Supplies		80	6%
Shipping & Receiving Supplies	Conversion	8	1%
Equipment Repairs	Costs	25	2%
Hardware		35	3%
Sub-Total Variable Cost of Sales		748	57%
Variable Margin		555	43%
Labor Costs		222	17%
Fixed Costs		42	3%
Cost (To)/From Inventory		(100)	-8%
Sub-Total Fixed Costs		164	13%
Total Cost of Sales		912	70%
Gross Margin		391	30%
Operating Expenses		250	19%
Operating Income		141	11%

**Figure 7.4: Monthly "Plain English" Profit-and-Loss statement
for Traditional Company – Case 2**

In Case 2 (Figure 7.4), the business unit achieved an 11 percent operating income by *building* inventory, whereas the Case 1 (Figure 7.3) manager achieved the same results while *reducing* inventories. The inventory change line on the two profit-and-loss statements illustrates that the Case 1 manager reduced inventory by $37,000 and the Case 2 manager increased inventory by $100,000.

The Case 2 manager achieved the $141,000 monthly operating income by spending $137,000 more for material, conversion, and labor costs during the month. Assuming there were no seasonal requirements to build inventory, the performance by the Case 1 manager is more in line with the goals of a Lean transformation, i.e., meet customer demand while relentlessly improving productivity and inventory utilization. The Case 1 manager is achieving results the Lean way, while the Case 2 manager has had to build inventory in order to meet the targeted results of a 30 percent gross margin. Too many times we have witnessed situations where managers were rewarded for meeting income targets where the path to success was the result of large inventory buildups that will have to be reckoned with years later.

One may argue that the same conclusion could be reached by simply reviewing the balance sheet of Traditional Company. However, during a Lean journey, a company is being transformed department by department, or product line by product line. Traditional financial statements typically consolidate inventory, rather than tracking it at discrete levels. Therefore, inventory changes at the product family or departmental level are extremely difficult to decipher. Having the inventory change clearly displayed on the operating statement is a very powerful and useful metric.

"Plain English" profit-and-loss statements do not utilize misleading and confusing standard costs or absorption accounting, which are mostly irrelevant for decision making. Traditional cost accounting concepts of standard costing, labor reporting, and variance analysis are replaced with performance metrics. Many of the metrics are maintained by shop-floor employees at work cells, and form the basis of continuous improvement. The specifics of how the cost system functions in a Lean environment are addressed in Chapters 8 -10 .

Conversion Costs

Once conversion costs are reported in a simple-to-understand format, shop-floor personnel will become more interested in further understanding the drivers of these costs. Lean problem-solving tools can then be deployed to improve performance. Numerous operating teams have been observed successfully utilizing Pareto's Law to analyze conversion costs and reduce expenses. One specific example observed was in a machine shop where some of the largest conversion expenditures were related to grinding wheel expenses. Discussions with managers in this area revealed that the only criterion used to select grinding wheels was their initial cost. Once all the available options were explained to the team, the team members worked with the grinding wheel supplier and set up experiments to test costs, life expectancy, and quality of the grinding wheels.

PARETO'S LAW

In the late 1800s, economist and avid gardener Vilfredo Pareto established that 80% of the land in Italy was owned by 20% of the population. He later observed that 20% of the peapods in his garden yielded 80% of the peas. And thus was born a theory that has stood the test of time and scrutiny. The Pareto Principle, or the 80:20 Rule, has proven its validity in a number of other areas. Use of the Pareto Principle, or "Pareto Thinking," should become a way of life. Employment of the Pareto Principle improves problem-solving efficiency greatly. Rather than wasting time, energy, and money on efforts to correct everything, the experienced problem-solver will focus his attention only on those few variables which are shown to account for most of the problem.[2]

The team then tracked total grinding wheel expenses versus output for the various options. During the monthly financial reviews of the machine shop, it became apparent which grinding wheels were providing the best value. In less than six months, grinding wheel costs were reduced significantly. The key to the cost reduction was providing shop-floor personnel with financial reports they could actually understand. Surprisingly, monthly financial performance reviews became a positive experience, rather than a dreaded one. With much easier to understand financial statements, the team set forth to identify the next largest conversion expenditure and continued with the improvement process.

Like material costs, conversion costs are mostly variable in nature, and are displayed separately on performance reports to arrive at a variable margin. Generally, the variable margin is fully controlled by shop-floor personnel, and therefore provides the most accurate assessment of performance trends.

Labor Costs

Combining all labor expenses into one category and moving these expenses below the variable margin line is perhaps the most uncomfortable change for accounting and finance managers. There seems to be a fear that Lean financial statements promote labor as fixed costs that cannot be changed, which again is a misconception.

During a Lean transformation, the distinction between direct and indirect labor will disappear. People will rotate from job to job. For example, water spiders, the Lean version of material handlers, are perhaps the most knowledgeable members of the cell workforce. In addition to delivering the correct quantity of materials to the right place at just the right time, water spiders also can perform just about any activity required in the cell. A water spider can rotate temporarily into spots where workers may be absent or on breaks. Keeping track of this labor effort would be wasteful.

Likewise, the role of traditional direct labor employees will drastically change in a Lean environment once cells are properly organized, the equipment in the cell is right sized, and autonomation (jidoka) techniques are deployed. One person will likely operate multiple machines and simply load and unload material. Trying to track labor times to specific parts or products becomes next to impossible at this point. Instead, total labor is captured for the range of products produced in a given cell.

JIDOKA

Jidoka, as practiced at Toyota, has several meanings. It may mean "automation with human intelligence," also known as autonomation. Jidoka also refers to the practice of stopping a manual line or process when something goes amiss.

The purpose of Jidoka is to free equipment from the necessity of constant human attention, separate people from machines and allow workers to staff multiple operations.[3]

During a Lean transformation, it is important to promote the notion that labor is relatively fixed in the short term. Performing a kaizen on a cell and improving productivity from eight operators to four operators should not result in the dismissal of four operators. Dismissing four operators would only guarantee that future kaizen events would be unsuccessful, as operator involvement in improvement ideas would be non-existent. Instead, these freed-up resources should be deployed elsewhere in the cell, value stream, or business unit, and total labor costs may not change at all in the short term. Such a policy is consistent with the commitment to the workforce that no employees will lose their employment as a result of productivity improvements, given relatively constant volumes.

On the other hand, any business, traditional or Lean, wants to benefit from lower costs due to more productive operations. There are at least six defenses to capture the labor productivity gains made without resorting to a layoff program. These defenses are as follows:

1. Reduce the amount of overtime across the plant by redeploying freed-up personnel.

2. Reduce the number of temporary workers.

3. Eliminate the need for new hires to offset the impact of normal attrition.

4. Institute an early retirement program.

5. In-source operations and capture the margins being awarded to your suppliers.

6. Add volume without adding labor.

Proper planning will result in realizing labor efficiencies without layoffs, and productivity benefits will surely be captured in the "Plain English" profit-and-loss statements. On the other hand, if volumes permanently decline, workforce reductions will be necessary in order to maintain a sustainable business model.

Capturing all labor expenses in one area makes much more sense than assigning overtime and benefits to an overhead pool which then gets spread across many other products. At the end of the day, a Lean environment focuses on total labor inputs relative to total output and establishes an average overall labor cost per unit. The goal is to continually lower the average total labor cost.

Fixed Costs

Fixed costs are assigned to the various cells or value streams where appropriate. There are a number of techniques that can be used to motivate the desired behaviors for controlling these costs. This topic will be discussed in greater detail in Chapter 9.

Cost (To) / From Inventory

The line *Cost (To)/From Inventory* on the "Plain English" profit-and-loss statement is necessary to properly match cost of sales with shipments and also to conform to Generally Accepted Accounting Principles (GAAP). It also may be the single biggest obstacle to changing from a traditional standard cost system to a Lean cost accounting system.

Lean cost management is not a prerequisite to developing the *Cost (To)/From Inventory* line item on operating statements. In traditional operating statements, isolating the impact of inventory changes on period results is not standard practice, although such a practice would add significant insight into operating performance. The information to determine such an accounting entry is embedded in the standard cost system, but is not easily accessible, since most systems typically move product costs into and out of the inventory accounts throughout the period. If the inventory change impact was isolated and displayed on the monthly operating statements of traditional companies, management would be better informed as to the source of operating income. This perpetual updating of inventory may be important for traditional companies with large, unstable inventories, but it is not necessary when world class performance is achieved.

In a traditional environment, the inventory change entry can be calculated at the company or business unit level. However, as one drills deeper into product families or cells, it becomes nearly impossible to isolate inventory changes. Since the Lean transformation takes place in stages, it becomes necessary to develop the capability to determine inventory changes early in the journey in order to properly assess performance and motivate behaviors that lead to inventory reductions. Specific techniques on calculating the inventory change are discussed in Chapters 9 and 10. Also, in these two chapters, we will work through detailed actual case studies of the transition from traditional standard costing to accounting for Lean.

The importance of including the inventory change on the monthly operating statements cannot be overemphasized. As explained in Chapter 5, the greater the success in reducing inventory, the larger the potential negative impact on operating income. Therefore, it is critical to measure and isolate period performance into the portion arising from normal operations and the portion arising from the impact of inventory changes due to the transitional, negative financial impact of inventory reductions.

Methodology to Generate "Plain English" Profit-and-Loss Statements

Lean methodology teaches us that inventory is waste. Because of this widely accepted concept, practitioners traveling down their Lean journey try to meet the needs of their business by constantly lowering their inventory levels. Likewise, as too much inventory is waste in manufacturing, too many transactions are considered waste in Lean accounting. Most transactions are really non-valued activities that are an attempt to bring control to an out-of-control environment. For example, tracking material moves as a part or assembly travels from inventory location to inventory location is an attempt to bring order to a chaotic plant layout, and these transactions all but disappear once cells are formed and standard work is implemented.

In preparing the "Plain English" profit-and-loss statements, the number of transactions is greatly reduced. All spending is expensed to the income statement as incurred. At month end, simple routines are utilized to properly value month-end inventories of material, labor, conversion, and fixed costs at the summary level. One entry is made at month-end to "true-up" the period-ending inventory. The normal plethora of real-time transactions into and out of inventory is eliminated.

As a company improves operations and approaches world class, standard levels of inventory will be maintained. Since month-end inventory levels will be virtually unchanged, all that is required is to expense total spending to the operating statement.

SUMMARY

"Plain English" profit-and-loss statements are necessary to support the Lean transformation at any company. These statements motivate the right behavior, isolate the impact of inventory reductions, and eliminate the need for much of the wasteful clerical work currently performed in accounting departments. "Plain English" profit-and-loss statements also conform to all internal and external reporting requirements.

CHAPTER 7 ENDNOTES

1. Jim Clark, "Effective Communication," *Stress News* 15 (July 2003): No.3 http://www.isma.org.uk/stressnw/effcomm.htm.
2. "Pareto's Law, A Management Principle/Technique,"
http://home.alltel.net/mikeric/Misc/Pareto.htm (December 2006).
3. Strategies, Jidoka and Autonomation, A Pillar of The Toyota Production System, http://www.strategosinc.com/jidoka.htm (December 2007).

8

VALUE STREAM COSTING

To maximize the probability of success of a Lean transformation, it is highly recommended that companies change their cost management reporting practices in concert with their physical changes. One of the necessary changes is the adoption of "Plain English" profit-and-loss statements. Another recommended change is organizing operations by value streams and utilizing value stream costing, instead of standard costing, activity-based costing (ABC), or other more traditional costing methods.

In this chapter, we will introduce the concept of value stream costing as the preferred cost management methodology and the precursor to developing "Plain English" profit-and-loss statements. The first discussion will focus on reorganizing your company into value streams, the initial critical step in the progression to value stream costing.

Value Streams

A Lean transformation encourages companies to identify their value streams and reorganize their operations accordingly. Value streams are end-to-end processes that include everything from initial sale to final cash collection and everything in between. Ideally, they will contain all of the disciplines necessary to operate as a mini-business.

VALUE STREAMS

A "value stream" is all the actions (both value added and non-value-added) currently required to bring a product through the two main flows essential to every product: (1) the production flow from raw material into the arms of the customer, and (2) the design flow from concept to launch.[1]

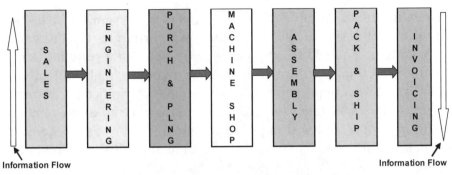

Information Flow   Information Flow

Figure 8.1: Traditional Organization

Figure 8.1 depicts a traditional company organized by departments, where work is typically "pushed" from silo to silo. Optimization occurs functionally as departmental leaders strive to meet their individual objectives rather than focus on the system goals. A silo organization has tremendous communication challenges, because information first flows up and down in the departmental silo before reaching across the organization. This is why we hear so many practitioners talk about how ideas, drawings, or designs are simply "thrown over the wall."

Value streams seek to optimize performance of the entire system, unlike silos, which attempt to optimize performance by functional area, e.g., engineering, manufacturing, or sales. Figure 8.2 illustrates a value stream organization.

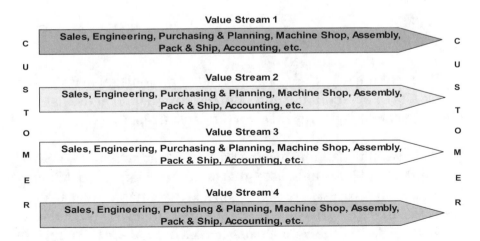

Figure 8.2: Value Stream Organization

In a value stream organization, the focus is always on the customer. To the extent possible, each value stream incorporates the full gamut of resources required to complete the process for a product family from start to finish. Information flows horizontally. The objective is to meet customer requirements, as well as pre-determined performance targets. The ideal state in a value stream is to have all of the requisite resources contained within the value stream. However, because of the many challenges that must be overcome, this ideal state is seldom achieved. Generally, every company has certain monuments that are shared by several value streams, such as massive paint booths, central machine shops, or other specialized equipment and processes. In addition, it is often impossible, inefficient, and/or illogical to permanently assign support personnel from areas like human resources and accounting to a specific value stream. These monuments and scarce resources are excluded from individual value streams and accounted for differently, as discussed later in this chapter.

Value Stream Mapping

Value stream mapping is a critical Lean tool which provides a deep understanding of almost any process. Value stream maps can be prepared for physical transformation processes, such as the production of a particular product or product family. They can be used also for idea transformation processes, such as new product development.

VALUE STREAM MAPPING

Value stream mapping is a pencil and paper tool that helps you see and understand the flow of material and information as a product makes its way through the value stream.[2]

Value stream mapping is a "picture" of all the activities—both physical and informational—that occur in a company, product family, or process, from the time a customer (internal or external) places an order, to the shipment and cash collection for a product or the completion of an intellectual work product.

Value stream mapping events are usually undertaken by cross-functional teams. It would be virtually impossible for a single person to have the requisite breadth and depth of knowledge to understand all the nuances associated with successfully completing a product or process from start to finish.

Value stream maps can be used at a global business level to improve the understanding of the entire business or at a local level in the pursuit of continuous improvement. For example, value stream mapping can be utilized in the accounting department to improve stand-alone processes, such as month-end closings, accounts payables processing, travel expense reimbursements, and account collections.

Figure 8.3 lists the significant benefits of using value stream mapping for gaining a better understanding of business processes.

Why Value Stream Mapping is an Essential Tool[3]

1. It helps you visualize more than just the single-process level, for instance, assembly, welding, production, etc. You can see the flow.

2. It helps you see more than waste. Mapping helps you see the sources of waste in your value stream.

3. It provides a common language for talking about manufacturing processes.

4. It makes decisions about the flow apparent, so you can discuss them. Otherwise, many details and decisions just happen by default.

5. It ties together Lean concepts and techniques, which helps avoid "cherry picking".

6. It forms the basis of an implementation plan. By helping you design how the whole door-to-door flow should operate - a missing piece in so many Lean efforts - value stream maps become a blueprint for Lean implementation. Imagine trying to build a house

7. It shows the linkage between the information flow and the material flow. No other tool does this.

8. It is much more useful than quantitiative tools and layout diagrams that produce a tally of non-value-added steps, lead time, distance travelled, the amount of inventory, and so on. Value stream mapping is a qualitative tool by which you describe in detail how your facility should operate in order to create flow. Numbers are good for either creating a sense of urgency or using as before/after measures. Value stream mapping is good for describing what you are actually going to do to affect those numbers.

Figure 8.3: Benefits of Value Stream Mapping

The benefits listed in Figure 8.3 focus on visualizing the entire picture of an operation as well as developing a common language and understanding for a process. Value stream mapping events also identify improvement opportunities that can be prioritized and addressed in subsequent kaizen events.

The identification and formation of value streams is the requisite precursor to developing value stream costing. Value stream mapping also provides the vision for value stream costing. First, the activities required to complete a process are co-located and sequentially laid out, whereby pull, flow, and standard work are in place. The next logical step is the adoption of value stream costing.

Value Stream Costing

The subsequent discussion of value stream costing will be confined to the manufacturing activities located within the value stream. Value streams are typically comprised of a group of products that have similar features and characteristics. A group of production cells might comprise one value stream, while a group of value streams might comprise a total business unit. Total performance is the sum of the value stream profit-and-loss statements, plus any un-assignable plant level costs, as depicted in Figure 8.4.

	Value Stream 1	Value Stream 2	Value Stream 3	Value Stream 4	Support & Unassigned Costs	Plant or Business Unit Totals
Sales	100	125	450	375	-	1,050
Cost of Sales						
Material	50	45	225	200	-	520
Conversion	20	25	50	15	-	110
Sub-Total Variable Cost of Sales	70	70	275	215		630
Variable Margin	30	55	175	160	-	420
Labor Costs	10	15	25	30	10	90
Fixed Costs	10	15	5	20	5	55
Cost (To)/From Inventory	-	-	-	-	-	-
Sub-Total Fixed Costs	20	30	30	50	15	145
Total Cost of Sales	90	100	305	265	15	775
Gross Margin	10	25	145	110	(15)	275
Operating Expenses	5	10	75	50	10	150
Operating Income	5	15	70	60	(25)	125

Figure 8.4: Business Unit or Plant Profit-and-Loss Statement

Costing of the value stream is straightforward and utilizes the same cost components as the "Plain English" profit-and-loss statement (refer to Chapter 7). The overall premise to determine product costs within a value stream is that of an input/output model. It is necessary to first collect and add all of the value stream inputs together, including labor, conversion, fixed, and material costs. To determine an average unit cost, total value stream costs are divided by the total value stream outputs in units.

Average Product Cost = <u>Total Value Stream Inputs (Costs)</u>
Units Produced

The greater the similarity of products in the value stream, the easier the costing process. As product variety increases, additional steps will be required to account for the various product features and benefits. Figure 8.5 illustrates the concept of value stream costing.

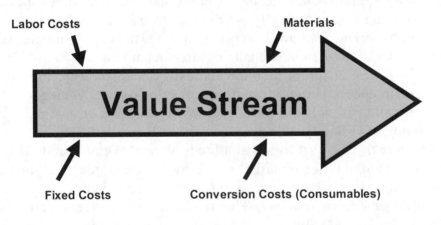

Allocated Costs are Excluded

Figure 8.5: Value Stream Costing Model

One major objective in value stream costing is to minimize the amount of allocated costs in any given value stream. Each value stream in a value stream organization will contain its own engineering, purchasing, planning, sales, and service teams. If the value stream truly acts like a "mini-business" unit, support functions such as human resources, information technology, and finance also may be included. All of these expenses linked to the value stream are charged as direct costs of the value stream.

In value stream costing, overhead costs, which are traditionally allocated throughout a manufacturing facility per a standard labor rate, are charged to specific value streams where possible. For example, depreciation for machines located in a specific value stream would be charged to that value stream; however, depreciation for a factory may not be specifically related to a single value stream, and would not be included in any individual value stream. Similarly, property taxes and insurance, which are company-wide expenses, would not be charged directly to a value stream. Treatment options for shared resources and overall plant-wide fixed costs will be discussed later.

The use of average costs rather than standard costs is a key difference between Lean accounting and traditional cost systems. However, the two approaches are more similar than they may first appear, since standard costs typically are developed from a combination of average historical costs and cost projections for the various inputs. In any standard cost system, actual costs for each unit or production lot are often quite different than the standard costs. In order to track these differences, there is an endless collection of data leading to the dissemination of multiple variances. With value stream costing, the collection of cost data is done at the work cell where the experts can track, in real time, cost trends and focus on improvement activities. There is no standard cost target to achieve; instead, the much more critical objective of continuous improvement is pursued, which is an important change in mindset. This fundamental difference between standard costs and value stream costs provides the associates, those people who are actually involved in the process and who are familiar with every nuance, with immediate and easily understood feedback on cell performance.

Figure 8.6 provides a fictitious example of value stream costing. The focus is on average costs per unit, which in this case is $560. Assuming the mix of products is fairly uniform, there is no need to waste resources tracking actual activity via real-time transactions.

Value Stream Costing - Widgets January, 2007		
Units Produced	1,000	
	Period Costs	Avg. Cost per Unit
Material Costs	$ 305,000	$ 305
Labor Costs	$ 140,000	$ 140
Conversion Costs	$ 75,000	$ 75
Fixed Costs	$ 40,000	$ 40
Totals	$ 560,000	$ 560

Figure 8.6: Value Stream Costing – Widgets

As shown in Figure 8.6, a summary value stream cost analysis lists only the major categories of costs: material, labor, conversion, and fixed costs. (Fixed costs can further be divided into fixed and occupancy costs and will be discussed in greater detail in Chapter 9.)

Detailed conversion costs are still collected via expenditure charges to various general ledger accounts. It is important to maintain drill-down capability for in-depth analysis. Cell associates should collect the detailed value stream data of their individual cells. The larger their role in data collection, the more likely they will understand the information, take ownership of performance, and ultimately reduce costs, improve throughput, and increase quality.

One of the major differences of value stream costing is that all costs are directly expensed to the value stream on an actual cost basis. This is in contrast to a standard cost system, whereby costs initially flow into inventory on a standard cost basis, and upon shipment, are relieved from inventory at the same standard cost basis. All actual cost versus standard cost differences are aggregated on month-end financial statements in the form of variances. The following concepts drive the methodological differences between standard costing and value stream costing.

1. In a Lean environment, transactions are considered wasteful activities and symptomatic of out-of-control processes, and are therefore minimized.

2. It is preferable to have associates become familiar with the actual expenditures they are creating, even to the point of assigning them the responsibility of tracking their daily expenditures, where possible.

3. A simple measurement system is much easier to understand and improve.

4. Accuracy is improved as real-time data is utilized.

5. In an ideal Lean environment, with single piece flow and instantaneous replenishment, there are miniscule changes in inventory from one period to the next. This makes it possible to simplify the preparation of financial statements by immediately expensing all costs to the value stream in the period in which they occur.

Expensing all costs immediately to the value stream is perhaps a difficult concept to grasp, especially if you are not familiar with Lean production. One of the tenets of Lean is standard work, and one component of standard work is standard work-in-process (SWIP). If a cell or value stream is Lean, then there is minimal change in inventory levels. Consequently, constant recording of material, labor, and product costs into and out of the inventory account is unnecessary and wasteful. Further, with SWIP and pull production, quantities and locations of work-in-process are always known, visible, and easily calculated, so tracking inventory through every step of the process is redundant.

(Author's note: Unfortunately, companies do not go from traditional batch and queue production to Lean overnight. During the initial transition period, which can last many years, inventory levels will fluctuate due to the combination of changing business climates and the continual improvement in inventory turns. As explained in Chapter 7, during this time period, as inventory balances fluctuate, a correcting entry entitled "Cost to/(from) Inventory" must be made at the end of each reporting period to comply with all accounting regulations. Fortunately, there are a number of techniques that greatly simplify this process. The simplest technique is to perform a monthly or quarterly physical inventory in each cell or value stream. While the thought of a physical inventory sounds onerous, remember that in a Lean environment, with far less inventory and standard quantities in easy-to-count storage containers, only one hour might be required to count inventory at month-end. A case study will be presented in Chapter 10 to review these techniques.)

Fixed Costs

One of the objectives of value stream costing is to motivate Lean behavior. Historically, assigning a portion of property taxes or plant depreciation to individual departments in the form of an overhead allocation has served only to confuse shop-floor management. In order to motivate value stream leaders to continuously reduce floor space, companies utilizing value stream costing often implement an occupancy charge based on square foot usage as a proxy for these fixed costs. These companies will determine the total cost of depreciation, property taxes, insurance, and utilities to derive a cost per square foot. This square-footage rate is charged to each value stream according to the floor space it occupies for production and inventory storage. This simple change in reporting convention motivates a more intense focus on the efficient use of space. An added bonus is that space reductions resulting from 5S activities no longer slowly fade away over time, as so often happens during Lean transformations with traditional measurement systems.

Naturally, as the value streams reduce the amount of space they occupy, the occupancy charges assigned to each value stream will decline, and correspondingly the sum of all of the value stream occupancy charges will be less than the total amount incurred by the company. The resulting shortfall should be charged to the miscellaneous cost center where all other unassigned costs are recorded. It is strongly suggested that adjustments in occupancy charges only occur quarterly and only if a threshold improvement level is reached. The intent is to motivate the right behavior, not create additional accounting entries.

It is recognized that total occupancy costs will remain unchanged even though individual value streams are making more efficient use of their space. However, if a company experiences a spike in business, relocates a recently acquired company into the same facility, or recognizes an opportunity for the marketing of a new product, enormous savings will result from having available capacity and avoiding potential investments in bricks and mortar. This is a likely scenario during a Lean transformation, as business expansion often occurs due to improved customer service, quality, and product development efforts.

Metrics in a Lean Environment

A Lean environment replaces traditional metrics and variance analysis with timely and actionable local measures. These measures differ depending on whether one is reporting at the cell, value stream, or focus factory/plant level.

At the lowest reporting level—the individual work cell—the measures are localized, collected by the cell associates, and tracked hourly. A typical cell report is illustrated in Figure 8.7.

Work Cell:	Family A	Product:	A1/A2	Date:
Takt Time:	3 Mins.	Operators:	4	4/1/2007
Time Block	Plan Units	Actual Units	Cum. Var.	Explanation
7:00- 8:00 AM	20	18	(2)	
8:00- 9:00 AM	20	21	(1)	
9:00-10:00 AM	20	15	(6)	Fixture
10:00-11:00 AM	20	10	(16)	
11:30-12:30 PM	20	18	(18)	
12:30-1:30 PM	20	22	(16)	
1:30- 2:30 PM	20	23	(13)	
2:30- 3:30 PM	20	20	(13)	
Totals	160	147		
Daily Action Plan: Redesign Fixture # 123				
Responsibility: John Doe To be Completed by 4/4/2006				

Figure 8.7: Daily Cell Performance Chart

As is evident in Figure 8.7, there is no need to wait for any month-end report to review variances. Local leadership can easily determine the problems, what needs to be corrected, and the impact on daily production. In addition, average labor costs are simple to calculate given that the cell has four people and actual production is recorded daily. The data is accumulated and maintained by the cell leader and graphically displayed. Material and conversion costs are also aggregated to determine average costs of production. Cost accounting periodically collects the information and maintains centralized records where necessary.

Measures for cells, value streams, and focus factories are illustrated in Figure 8.8. Aggregated measures are utilized to a greater degree as you move up the organizational hierarchy.

Measurement	Performance Metrics by Reporting Sector		
	Cell	Value Stream	Focus Factory or Plant
Safety	Number of Lost Time Accidents	Number of Lost Time Accidents	Number of Lost Time Accidents
	Number of Near Misses		Workers Compensation
Quality	First Pass Yield	First Pass Yield	Defects per Million Parts
	Scrap		
Cost/ Productivity	Minutes per Unit	Sales per Employee	Sales per Employee
	Hourly Performance versus Takt Time	Inventory Turns	Inventory Turns
	Standard Work-in-Process	Average Cost per Unit	Return on Assets
	Number of Line Stoppages		EBITDA
	Trends in Set-up Times	Overall Equipment Effectiveness	% Sales from New Products
Delivery		On Time Performance	On Time Performance
		Lead-Times	Lead-Times
Climate	Presenteeism	Presenteeism	Presenteeism
	Suggestions per Associate	Suggestions per Associate	Suggestions per Associate
			Turnover

Figure 8.8: Performance Metrics

Value Stream Costing of Differentiated Products

Oftentimes a cell or value stream will contain families of products that have a variety of distinguishing features or characteristics that result in different average costs by model or SKU. These various features can be easily captured in the value stream costing model, as previously explained.

One of the biggest cost differentiators in any product family is the material component. Assume a particular cell produces silver, gold, and platinum widgets. The material cost differences are captured in the bills of material for each of the different SKUs. If a similar production process occurs for each variety of widgets, the average cost of each SKU is simply the average of the labor, conversion, and fixed costs, plus the discrete material costs for each SKU. Accurate bills of material are a prerequisite for any cost system and would capture these material differences.

At the end of the day, week, or chosen reporting period, a cell records the amount of material used in both dollars and physical units of measure. This amount is compared to the number of units produced in order to determine average material costs. This information is displayed in the cell to track performance trends. Sophisticated scrap reporting is not required, as discrepant material is identified immediately and root-cause analysis and correction activities are implemented. The cell has no choice but to be proactive if it is truly operating with single-piece flow.

Another cost differentiator typically encountered in a cell is labor costs required to produce the various SKUs. This is particularly true in mixed model assembly cells where each product is produced daily or hourly in accordance with customer demand. To determine average labor costs per silver, gold, or platinum widget, the value stream leader should lay out the production sequence and associated standard manpower levels. If the difference in labor times among the various SKUs occurs in non-bottleneck operations, then the average labor cost is the same for all product types. If on the other hand, labor times in the bottleneck operation have different manpower requirements, then a labor adjustment factor would have to be applied for each SKU.

More often than not, the standard staffing of a particular cell results in significant idle time for a portion of the workforce. This idle time can be utilized to produce a large variety of products with little to no real change in average labor costs. As a company progresses in its Lean journey and begins to properly balance and staff cells, it becomes obvious which SKUs in any given product family require adjustments to the work force and demand a greater proportion of the cell's labor capacity. An example of a daily performance chart for a mixed model cell is illustrated in Figure 8.9. This information would be used to develop the costing model for the various products produced in this work cell.

Work Cell:		Widgets		Product:	SKU's 123, 124, 125		Date:
	Silver	Gold	Platinum				
Takt Time:	3 Mins.	6 Mins.	12 Mins.	Operators:	12		4/1/2007
	Plan	Plan	Plan	Plan	Actual	Cum.	
Time Block	Units	Units	Units	Total	Units	Var.	Explanation
7:00-8:00 AM	20			20	18	(2)	Material defect
8:00-9:00 AM		10		10	11	1	
9:00-10:00 AM			5	5	5	-	
10:00-11:00 AM	20			20	21	1	
11:30-12:30 PM		10		10	10	-	
12:30-1:30 PM			5	5	5	-	
1:30-2:30 PM	20			20	20	-	
2:30-3:30 PM		10		10	9	(1)	
3:30-4:30 PM			5	5	5	-	
Totals	60	30	15	105	104	(1)	
Daily Action Plan: Discuss with vendor							
Responsibility: John Doe To be Completed by 4/4/2007							

Figure 8.9: Daily Cell Performance Chart
Widgets – Mixed Model Cell

The combination of cell staffing of twelve operators and the production capability of twenty, ten, and five units per hour for silver, gold, and platinum widgets, respectively, enables the value stream leader or accountant to easily determine labor costs per SKU. Assuming cell labor costs of $300 per hour, the unit labor costs for silver, gold, and platinum widgets are $15, $30, and $60 respectively. In addition, the cost of material by type and size of widget is available from the bills of material. Following the same logic, Figure 8.10 is provided as an example of a family costing table that has been prepared for the silver, gold, and platinum widgets.

Family Costing - Widgets

Widget Product Family	Dimensions	Material	Labor Costs	Conversion Costs	Fixed Costs	Total Unit Costs
Silver - Small	10 x 10 x 5	$ 200.00	$ 15.00	$ 6.00	$ 1.00	$ 222.00
Silver - Medium	10 x 15 x 5	$ 250.00	$ 15.00	$ 6.00	$ 1.00	$ 272.00
Silver - Large	10 x 20 x 5	$ 300.00	$ 15.00	$ 6.00	$ 1.00	$ 322.00
Gold - Small	10 x 10 x 5	$ 400.00	$ 30.00	$ 6.00	$ 1.00	$ 437.00
Gold - Medium	10 x 15 x 5	$ 500.00	$ 30.00	$ 6.00	$ 1.00	$ 537.00
Gold - Large	10 x 20 x 5	$ 600.00	$ 30.00	$ 6.00	$ 1.00	$ 637.00
Platinum - Small	10 x 10 x 5	$ 700.00	$ 60.00	$ 6.00	$ 1.00	$ 767.00
Platinum - Medium	10 x 15 x 5	$ 800.00	$ 60.00	$ 6.00	$ 1.00	$ 867.00
Platinum - Large	10 x 20 x 5	$ 900.00	$ 60.00	$ 6.00	$ 1.00	$ 967.00

**Figure 8.10: Value Stream Costing
Widgets – Mixed Model Cell**

Labor and conversion cost differences between SKUs should be determined where it makes good business sense. Many times, the real differences in non-material costs within a product family are insignificant, making the cost to collect and maintain those costs much greater than the benefits received.

Box Scores

An effective performance-monitoring tool for managing value streams is the "Box Score." The box score is an operating report that contains both financial and non-financial metrics that are identified as critical to the successful operation of a value stream. Continuous improvement efforts focused on these few, but vital metrics found on the box score, are key to accelerating the Lean journey.

The box score is generally divided into three sections: 1) operational performance, 2) capacity information, and 3) financial information. Specific measures tracked in each of these sections are often identified from value stream maps. The typical box score reports 12 months of activity, a 12-month objective, and a long-term goal. Figure 8.11 provides an example of an actual box score.

		Baseline	Jan	Feb	Mar	12/20XX Goal	Long Term Goal
OPERATIONAL	Customer Satisfaction - On Time Performance	65%	68%	68%	75%	95%	100%
	Inventory Turns (6 month average)	4.0	5.0	6.0	6.5	7	10
	OFLT: Order Fulfillment Lead Time (# of weeks)	30	14	12	11	6	4
	Vendor On Time Shipments	75%	70%	80%	85%	95%	100%
	Engr. & Admin. Order Backlog (# of orders)	80	65	30	0	0	0
	Equipment Availability for Grinders (E.A.)	65%	67%	70%	80%	85%	90%
	First Pass Yield	85%	88%	92%	90%	95%	99%
CAPACITY	Productive	65%	65%	65%	62%	60%	55%
	Non-Productive	35%	35%	35%	33%	30%	25%
	Available	0%	0%	0%	5%	10%	20%
FINANCIAL	Revenue ($000)	600	625	700	850	650	700
	Variable Margin %	45%	45%	47%	50%	50%	50%
	Gross Margin %	15%	20%	22%	24%	26%	30%
	Operating Income %	0%	5%	8%	12%	15%	18%
	Cash Flow ($000)	-50	-40	0	60	60	80
	Backlog ($000)	5,000	4,500	4,000	3,750	3,250	1,400
	Inventory ($000)	1,500	1,400	1,250	1,150	825	600
	A/R Over 60 Days Past Due ($000)	500	525	475	425	250	150

Figure 8.11: Box Score of a Value Stream

The baseline metrics on Figure 8.11 are for a value stream at the beginning of a Lean conversion. The operational metrics were lifted from the targeted improvement areas identified during a value stream mapping event. The value stream goals for both the current year and the three-year planning horizon are displayed on the right hand side of the box score.

The business related to this value stream was characterized by very long lead times, poor customer satisfaction, low inventory turns, and breakeven results. The main product for this value stream was a highly-engineered assembly that spent almost as much time in administrative backlog as it did on the production floor. Therefore, a key metric was the number of orders in engineering backlog. The production process was constrained by a grinding operation that was beset with long set-ups, poor quality, and significant down-time. Equipment availability of the grinder became a main focus of kaizen activity.

This value stream consisted of a three-shift operation. Before its Lean conversion, the value stream was perceived to be operating at capacity. After completing a value stream map, opportunities to eliminate waste and free up capacity became evident. The box score helped track this excess capacity, which led to soliciting more business by the sales force.

The financial section of this box score contains selected metrics from the value stream's "Plain English" profit-and-loss statement, as well as additional financial measures, such as cash flow, backlog, inventory, and past due accounts receivable. These metrics were deemed as the most critical for the value stream.

The particular items in a box score will vary by value stream and be a function of the leverage points for the business. Targeted measures identified as important in one year may change the following year, as improvement efforts focus on new opportunities. It is vital to engage the entire value stream team in the collection of box score data and the monthly reviews, so that everyone can analyze the metrics and determine if improvement activities are achieving the desired results.

Managing the Value Stream

Value stream leaders monitor, control, and improve the activities within the value stream. These leaders have the knowledge and capability to improve overall value stream performance, with an emphasis on profitably delighting customers. Cell leaders have the information to make critical decisions in real time.

While proceeding through a Lean transformation, it is essential to develop capable value stream leaders who become the most knowledgeable members of the team. From a financial perspective, the leaders will have the clearest understanding of average product costs, make/buy decision economics, inventory turns, and the effect on cost, capacity, and overall profitability of new business opportunities. The availability of local measures, value stream costs, and easy-to-understand "Plain English" profit-and-loss statements will facilitate the development of a capable corps of general managers.

SUMMARY

Rather than going through the painstaking process of trying to calculate costs for every operation, in Lean cost management, average product costs are collected by value stream and cell. All value stream costs are considered direct costs and are posted to the appropriate general ledger value stream department or profit center. Any costs that can not be assigned to a particular value stream are excluded and captured in a "catch-all" cost center. Average value stream costs are used as the critical performance metrics that aid in the overall continuous improvement objective. Box scores also assist in monitoring key metrics and data trends that help control Lean initiatives and operational improvements.

CHAPTER 8 ENDNOTES

1. Mike Rother and John Shook, *Learning to See* (Brookline, MA: Lean Enterprise Institute, Inc., 1999), .3.

2. Ibid, 4.

3. Ibid.

9

ACCOUNTING FOR LEAN IN A LOW VOLUME, HIGH VARIETY JOB SHOP

O ne of the most valuable ways to learn is to observe the efforts, successes, and failures of others who have similar experiences, motivations, and resources. This chapter will follow the authors' experiences in facilitating the transformation of the accounting system of a low-volume, high-variety, vertically integrated business, which will be referred to as PackCo. This company transitioned from a very traditional, standard costing system to accounting for Lean, with a focus on the adoption of new inventory valuation methods and the utilization of new performance metrics. The actual data used to present PackCo information is disguised to avoid disclosure of proprietary information.

Company Description

PackCo, a division of a one billion dollar global packaging company, manufactures customized packaging equipment that sells for in excess of one million dollars per machine. Each machine is unique, having from 10,000 to 15,000 total parts. The production cycle of each machine takes two to three months to complete. PackCo has an extensive machine shop and assembly operation, and relies on a network of approximately 350 suppliers for raw materials and purchased components, such as bearings and motors. The machine shop operates as a large job shop, processing thousands of unique parts each year. The company has been in business for decades, and the machine shop has been traditionally organized, with machine tools co-located with similar equipment. With the adoption of Lean, PackCo is now organized into three value streams, although the location of the machine tools has not moved and remains a monument at the current time.

Current Traditional Accounting System

Historically, PackCo has used a standard costing system where all financial reporting for inventory and cost of goods sold is initially recorded at the pre-set standards for material, direct labor, and overhead. At the end of the month, the activity and price variances are reported per the differences between the standard and the actual quantities and costs for materials and direct labor. Overhead standard rates are developed per a relationship to direct labor hours. "Actual" overhead absorption, which is a product of standard work-center overhead rates multiplied by actual direct labor hours, is compared to the standard overhead applied, and the overhead variances are recorded.

PackCo calculates and reports twelve different variances each month. It is important to note that there is a budgeted overhead variance due to the acknowledged inaccuracy of the standard overhead rates.

A detailed examination of most of the elements of PackCo's traditional cost system reveals that its standards are generally inaccurate at the discrete level. Most standard overhead rates are several years old, and are rarely updated. Items included in overhead are direct and indirect labor benefits, overtime, depreciation, property taxes, supplies, and other incidental expenses. These overhead items are allocated to each area of the business based on outdated historical relationships to direct labor, even though this approach bears little resemblance to actual current operating conditions. Additionally, floor stock material that is not included in bills of material is also included in the overhead pools, contributing to further discrete item-level costing inaccuracies. PackCo maintains the standard overhead/direct labor ratio constant in order to have year-to-year reporting consistency.

Direct costs, such as material and direct labor standards, reflect the most recent year-end prices for each item. The standard material price is kept generally constant for the ensuing year, and all differences are recorded as purchase price variances. Direct labor processing times are reported for all machining activities, and these processing times are used to develop average hourly rates for each part. These times are then frozen and incorporated into the standards.

The following items describe the numerous challenges PackCo faces with the current costing methodology.

1. Users do not understand the cost accounting reports.

2. Inaccurate and outdated overhead standards contribute to poor make/buy and product development decisions.

3. Product-line margins are misrepresented, as large variances are aggregated into the summary account, "Other Cost of Sales." These variances are never traced back to individual product lines.

4. A tremendous amount of time is devoted to account for and review variances, with very little benefit derived.

5. Month-end close activity is stressful and consumed by work order close-outs and variance analyses.

6. Accountants spend the majority of their time acting as historians.

7. True manufacturing improvements are virtually impossible to assess from the financial reports.

8. Errors are often hidden in work-orders and are difficult to find.

9. There is little communication between shop-floor associates and the cost accounting associates.

10. Only unfavorable variances are typically reviewed.

More importantly, the current cost accounting system does not support the Lean transformation currently in progress, does not support value stream reporting, and does not motivate Lean behavior.

While the current system has a number of deficiencies, remarkably, the results appear to consistently reflect total performance. The large number of parts required for assembling each machine tends to mask the incorrect costs at the individual part level, allowing the over and under part cost assignments to generally cancel each other out. Total assembled machine costs appear to be representative of actual activity in this zero-sum system. Over the years, PackCo has had relatively level volumes and generated consistent standard product margins and comparatively constant variances.

PackCo has three distinct product lines, which are referred to as value streams under the Lean system: new machines, parts, and field upgrades. A primary concern is that it is currently impossible to correctly determine the profitability of each business segment under the existing accounting system.

If PackCo remained a traditional manufacturer, it may not be necessary to change its accounting practices. However, as the company changes its production philosophy from large batches to single piece flow, and obliterates the distinctions between direct and indirect labor, its current costing practices will become irrelevant to the user community. Work centers will be rearranged as machines are moved to cells, and current overhead rates will become even more meaningless. Direct labor measures will no longer be appropriate as the workforce constantly moves around the shop, balancing the workflow. Standard costs with embedded scrap, yield, and setup factors will hide opportunities for continuous improvement. Freed-up capacity will need to be identified and filled by in-sourcing work, which in turn will require accurate data in order to make sound business decisions.

The management of PackCo recognized that the manufacturing changes being implemented were further hindering the traditional accounting system's ability to provide accurate and timely information. Therefore, it decided to make some dramatic changes. The first objective of PackCo's accounting for Lean transformation was to implement "Plain English" profit-and-loss statements. This chapter devotes considerable effort in describing how this was accomplished at PackCo.

Material Flows at PackCo

PackCo buys raw materials and purchased parts from its vendors. The raw materials flow directly to the machine shop to be processed, while purchased parts go directly to the Stores warehouse. After processing, all completed machined parts are initially recorded as Stores inventory, even though some of them are delivered directly to the final assembly area from the machine shop. Under the current system, the journal entries for those parts that go directly to assembly are recorded virtually simultaneously in and out of the Stores inventory account for inventory tracking purposes. As Lean principles become more widespread, this "transaction waste" will change. The remaining completed machined parts and externally purchased parts are issued to assembly as they are used. Actual material flows are depicted in Figure 9.1

Pictorial of Inventory Flows

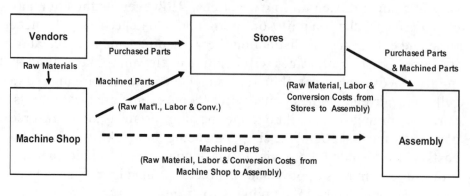

Figure 9.1: Material flow at PackCo.

PHASE I

Implementation of Accounting for Lean–Machine Shop

The first objective of the initial phase of the accounting transformation in support of Lean operations was to eliminate all financial recording of direct labor and overhead in the machine shop. Capturing detailed costs by every end item was recognized as a non-value added activity. Reduced batch sizes and correspondingly increased transactions will only escalate the cost of such activity. Further, in surveying PackCo end users of the cost system outputs, it was confirmed that the information currently generated provided no actionable information for machine shop leadership.

The critical questions that needed to be answered in the first phase of the accounting transformation were:

1. How would machine shop inventory be accurately valued without detailed tracking?

2. How would machine shop capacity be managed without labor reporting?

3. How would part costs be determined without standard costing?

4. How would machine shop monthly expenses be accurately recorded on financial statements?

5. How would machine shop costs be charged to the three value streams: new equipment, parts, and field upgrades?

While the answers to these critical questions might differ from company to company, PackCo's solutions provide a conceptual framework that can be utilized at most firms.

First Concern of Phase I : Machine Shop Inventory Valuation

The first concern that needed to be addressed by PackCo was how to accurately value machine shop inventory without detailed tracking of its part costs. An in-depth explanation for PackCo's experience in accomplishing this is provided below.

Under PackCo's traditional accounting system, all purchased raw materials for the machine shop are entered on the balance sheet as inventory at the standard raw material purchase price as soon as they are received. As the raw material meanders through the machine shop work-centers, direct labor and overhead are applied until the final machined part is completed. At every point in the machine shop production process, inventory valuation is maintained with detailed tracking of each completed machining process, including the additional direct labor and overhead that is added to the part. The constant recording of costs into inventory results in continual updating of the company's perpetual inventory records. Once the machined part is completed, it is issued a new part number and transferred to the Stores warehouse. These completed machined parts are recorded into the perpetual inventory records at their total value and reclassified with their new part numbers as material costs only. Unfortunately, PackCo usually loses visibility to the component costs (material, direct labor, and overhead) for each machined part after these parts are transferred to Stores inventory.

In a Lean machine shop organized with machining cells, the constant tracking of direct labor and overhead for each step of the operation is viewed as waste and is no longer required. Instead, the goal is to simplify inventory valuation by developing alternative valuation methods that require less effort and result in the same or improved accuracy. Lean companies typically value total labor and overhead in the aggregate, per value stream or cell, rather than at the individual part level.

Understanding the historical relationships among the various cost components is helpful for developing new inventory valuation and costing formulas. PackCo's first step in the inventory valuation transformation process was to determine the historical machine shop inventory levels separately by material, direct labor, and overhead. The restated traditional month-end machine shop inventory for PackCo, with the individual cost components segregated, is illustrated in Figure 9.2. The information was obtained by collecting the standard cost components through an analysis of all the shop orders generated each month during 2006.

2006 Machine Shop WIP Inventory Traditional Reporting Method				
Month	Raw Material	Direct Labor	Overhead	Total WIP
Jan-06	$ 680,000	$ 95,000	$ 300,000	$ 1,075,000
Feb-06	$ 780,000	$ 100,000	$ 300,000	$ 1,180,000
Mar-06	$ 730,000	$ 100,000	$ 275,000	$ 1,105,000
Apr-06	$ 765,000	$ 95,000	$ 295,000	$ 1,155,000
May-06	$ 750,000	$ 90,000	$ 290,000	$ 1,130,000
Jun-06	$ 740,000	$ 95,000	$ 290,000	$ 1,125,000
Jul-06	$ 815,000	$ 105,000	$ 315,000	$ 1,235,000
Aug-06	$ 850,000	$ 110,000	$ 300,000	$ 1,260,000
Sep-06	$ 775,000	$ 95,000	$ 290,000	$ 1,160,000
Oct-06	$ 785,000	$ 100,000	$ 305,000	$ 1,190,000
Nov-06	$ 810,000	$ 95,000	$ 295,000	$ 1,200,000
Dec-06	$ 765,000	$ 95,000	$ 290,000	$ 1,150,000
FY '06 Avgs	$ 770,417	$ 97,917	$ 295,417	$ 1,163,750
% of Material		12.7%	38.3%	

Figure 9.2: PackCo Machine Shop Inventory Month-End

Restating PackCo's historical machine shop inventory into its components provided added visibility to the physical flow of operations for the machine shop. In Figure 9.2, note that the average ratio of overhead to direct labor is approximately 3:1 ($295,417/$97,917).

Figures 9.3 and 9.4 illustrate the machine shop month-end inventory relationships among the traditional cost components: material, direct labor, and overhead. As depicted in Figure 9.3, the average monthly balance of direct labor and overhead as a percentage of total machine shop work-in-process inventories is 8.4 and 25.5 percent, respectively. These relationships remained fairly constant throughout the year, regardless of actual inventory levels, as evidenced by the low standard deviation for these cost categories.

Proportion of Machine Shop Inventory by Cost Component				
Month	Raw Material	Direct Labor	Overhead	Total
Jan-06	63.3%	8.8%	27.9%	100.0%
Feb-06	66.1%	8.5%	25.4%	100.0%
Mar-06	66.1%	9.0%	24.9%	100.0%
Apr-06	66.2%	8.2%	25.5%	100.0%
May-06	66.4%	8.0%	25.7%	100.0%
Jun-06	65.8%	8.4%	25.8%	100.0%
Jul-06	66.0%	8.5%	25.5%	100.0%
Aug-06	67.5%	8.7%	23.8%	100.0%
Sep-06	66.8%	8.2%	25.0%	100.0%
Oct-06	66.0%	8.4%	25.6%	100.0%
Nov-06	67.5%	7.9%	24.6%	100.0%
Dec-06	66.5%	8.3%	25.2%	100.0%
Averages	66.2%	8.4%	25.5%	
Standard Deviation		0%	1%	

Figure 9.3: PackCo Machine Shop Traditional Inventory

Figure 9.4 illustrates the same data graphically. Using the full-year averages we can determine that direct labor and overhead are 13 percent ($97,917/$770,417) and 38 percent ($295,417/$770,417) of material costs, respectively.

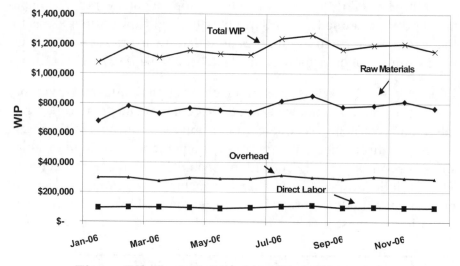

**Figure 9.4: PackCo Machine Shop Inventory
Traditional Reporting Method**

The historical inventory chart of the various cost components resulted in a much greater understanding of the dynamics of the machine shop inventory. The month-end inventory fluctuation of direct labor and overhead was $20K and $40K respectively. More significantly, raw material inventory levels varied by as much as $170K. Smaller fluctuations in month-end direct labor and overhead inventory levels were logical for a number of reasons: (1) Staffing levels were relatively constant for the machine shop as peaks in demand were addressed with overtime or increased outsourcing, while slower periods resulted in a shorter workweek. (2) Regardless of the operating profile, once work was launched in the machine shop, it proceeded through all of the operations (not necessarily in a smooth fashion) and was then transferred to the Stores warehouse. (3) The only place where there could be a build-up of inventory in the machine shop was in the raw materials receiving area. However, a kanban replenishment system at PackCo has minimized this occurrence. (4) The area around each machining center had limited space for work to pile up. As the pull system improves over time, spikes in raw material will be virtually eliminated.

Further review of the historical month-end inventory levels by cost component revealed that the relationships between the various cost categories were relatively constant. Since raw materials represented 66% of total machine shop inventory value, accurate reporting of material was critical. On the other hand, the tracking of direct labor and overhead is viewed as a non-value added activity, and therefore, in its Lean transformation, PackCo decided to track only raw materials at the detail part level. All non-material costs would be expensed directly as period costs, rather than charged to work-orders, as in the past. Since material reporting would not change as a result of the transition from traditional cost accounting to Lean cost management (at this stage in the Lean journey), there would be no loss in inventory accuracy if the relationship between the other cost components (direct labor and overhead) relative to material could be accurately determined in the aggregate. This is precisely what PackCo was determined to do.

The next step in the process to convert costing methodologies and properly value inventory was to capture the summary machine shop spending by traditional classification. "Spending" refers to the total annual machine shop expenditures (purchases) for all product costs, including all classifications of labor and associated benefits, supplies, tooling, depreciation, taxes, and insurance. Spending is differentiated from cost of goods sold because it consists of all purchases during the year, whether or not they are still in inventory. Figure 9.5 illustrates a full year of actual spending for PackCo.

2006 Machine Shop Spending Traditional Reporting Method				
Month	Raw Material Spending	Direct Labor Spending	Overhead Spending	Total Machine Shop Spending
Jan-06	$ 800,000	$ 140,000	$ 475,000	$ 1,415,000
Feb-06	$ 950,000	$ 155,000	$ 525,000	$ 1,630,000
Mar-06	$ 750,000	$ 150,000	$ 500,000	$ 1,400,000
Apr-06	$ 850,000	$ 165,000	$ 475,000	$ 1,490,000
May-06	$ 1,050,000	$ 175,000	$ 475,000	$ 1,700,000
Jun-06	$ 850,000	$ 160,000	$ 500,000	$ 1,510,000
Jul-06	$ 700,000	$ 145,000	$ 500,000	$ 1,345,000
Aug-06	$ 775,000	$ 150,000	$ 475,000	$ 1,400,000
Sep-06	$ 700,000	$ 150,000	$ 450,000	$ 1,300,000
Oct-06	$ 700,000	$ 155,000	$ 475,000	$ 1,330,000
Nov-06	$ 875,000	$ 165,000	$ 500,000	$ 1,540,000
Dec-06	$ 850,000	$ 160,000	$ 525,000	$ 1,535,000
Totals - FY '06	$ 9,850,000	$ 1,870,000	$ 5,875,000	$17,595,000
Avgs - FY '06	$ 820,833	$ 155,833	$ 489,583	$ 1,466,250
	% of Material	19.0%	59.6%	

Standard Deviation	$ 107,044	$ 9,731	$ 22,508	

**Figure 9.5: PackCo Machine Shop
Traditional Spending by Month**

Monthly spending fluctuated the most for material and the least for direct labor, as indicated by the standard deviations for each spending category. This result is expected, because material is the largest variable cost component for PackCo, while direct labor and overhead are relatively fixed in the short term.

Figure 9.5 also illustrates that overhead spending is 3.1 times that of direct labor ($5,875,000/$1,870,000), which approximates the average traditional overhead ratio PackCo used at the detailed part level. The 3:1 overhead to direct labor ratio for *spending* is similar to the overhead to direct labor ratio for *inventory,* as shown in Figure 9.2. Because the overhead ratio is based on the traditional standard overhead relationship with direct labor, there is no reason to expect different spending and inventory ratios, as long as the mix of parts does not dramatically change.

On the other hand, the relationships of direct labor and overhead to raw materials are quite different for inventory than for annual spending, as expected and as shown in Figure 9.6.

PackCo Inventory & Spending by Cost Component				
Category	Raw Material	Direct Labor	Overhead	Total Machine Shop
Inventory - Trad'l	66.2%	8.4%	25.4%	100%
Spending - Trad'l	56.0%	10.6%	33.4%	100%

Figure 9.6: Chart of PackCo Machine Shop Traditional Spending by Month

The difference in the proportions of the various cost components for machine shop inventory and machine shop annual spending occurs because parts in inventory have completed only a portion of the machining process. Inventory captures a snapshot of the production process at a single point in time. During this snapshot, there will be a certain level of machine shop raw materials that have not begun the production process and are valued in inventory at 100% of material value. As these parts wind their way through each machine shop work-center, the appropriate levels of direct labor and overhead are added to the part cost. Not until the end of the machining process does the completed part contain the "normal" proportions of material, direct labor, and overhead in its total cost. Therefore, PackCo's total month-end work-in-process machine shop inventory will contain a weighting of raw materials, partially completed parts, and finished parts. As a result, it will have a higher proportion of raw materials content to total inventory value than the corresponding ratios for annual spending.

It is important for accountants to understand the differences in the cost make-up of inventory, spending, and cost of goods sold. These differences will depend on the speed of the production process, the levels of inventory, and the proportions of each cost component in the finished product. Annual spending for the various cost components is usually more representative of the true proportion of costs, provided there are no significant changes in raw material inventories.

Ratios of cost components in inventory will differ from these same ratios for annual expenditures, as inventory balances will usually have a higher proportion of material costs. For this reason, it is not recommended to simply use spending cost ratios to estimate inventory cost ratios as a firm switches from traditional inventory valuation methods to Lean methods.

Inventory turns is also a useful metric for providing a greater understanding of machine shop performance. With the inventory and total spending levels determined for each of the individual cost components, separate inventory turns can easily be calculated by dividing total annual spending by the average annual inventory level. It is important to note that total annual spending may not generally equal annual production due to year-to-year inventory changes. However, in the case of PackCo's machine shop, it is usually very close. This example assumes that PackCo's year-to-year average inventory change was immaterial. Figure 9.7 illustrates the inventory turns for PackCo.

PackCo Inventory Turns				
	Raw Material	Direct Labor	Overhead	Total
Inventory Turns	12.8	19.1	19.9	15.1
Days of Inventory on Hand	28.5	19.1	18.4	24.1

Figure 9.7: Chart of PackCo Machine Shop Inventory Turns and Days on Hand

PackCo has approximately a month of raw materials on hand at all times. Because direct labor and overhead costs are in the production process for a shorter period of time, they are turning faster than raw materials. While it is important to identify how long it takes to turn actual product, it is also helpful for understanding the flow of the business to analyze the turns per the separate cost components.

To understand the historical component of product costs, it was necessary initially to look at inventory and spending as materials, direct labor, and overhead under the traditional cost system. For PackCo to convert to a Lean cost system and construct "Plain English" profit-

and-loss statements (as described in Chapter 7), the annual spending costs of direct labor and overhead in the departmental expense reports were reconfigured into total labor costs, conversion costs (which represents all other direct product costs), and fixed costs (which includes general factory costs such as property tax, depreciation, and insurance). Figure 9.8 presents the reconfigured 2006 machine shop spending costs for PackCo.

2006 Machine Shop Spending - P&L Lean Reporting Method					
Historical Traditional Information Reconfigured for Labor, Conversion, & Fixed Costs					
Month	Raw Material	Labor Costs	Conversion Costs	Fixed Costs	Total MS Spending
Jan-05	$ 800,000	$ 410,000	$ 125,000	$ 90,000	$ 1,425,000
Feb-05	$ 950,000	$ 455,000	$ 135,000	$ 90,000	$ 1,630,000
Mar-05	$ 750,000	$ 430,000	$ 130,000	$ 90,000	$ 1,400,000
Apr-05	$ 850,000	$ 420,000	$ 125,000	$ 90,000	$ 1,485,000
May-05	$ 1,050,000	$ 435,000	$ 125,000	$ 90,000	$ 1,700,000
Jun-05	$ 850,000	$ 435,000	$ 135,000	$ 90,000	$ 1,510,000
Jul-05	$ 700,000	$ 430,000	$ 125,000	$ 90,000	$ 1,345,000
Aug-05	$ 775,000	$ 410,000	$ 125,000	$ 90,000	$ 1,400,000
Sep-05	$ 700,000	$ 390,000	$ 120,000	$ 90,000	$ 1,300,000
Oct-05	$ 700,000	$ 410,000	$ 125,000	$ 90,000	$ 1,325,000
Nov-05	$ 875,000	$ 440,000	$ 135,000	$ 90,000	$ 1,540,000
Dec-06	$ 850,000	$ 455,000	$ 140,000	$ 90,000	$ 1,535,000
Totals - FY '06	$ 9,850,000	$ 5,120,000	$1,545,000	$ 1,080,000	$17,595,000
Avgs - FY '06	$ 820,833	$ 426,667	$ 128,750	$ 90,000	$ 1,466,250
	% of Material	52.0%	15.7%	11.0%	
Standard Deviation	$ 107,044	$ 19,462	$ 6,077	$ -	

Figure 9.8: Restated PackCo Machine Shop Monthly Spending in Conformance with Lean Cost Categories

PackCo's raw material and total machine shop spending for both traditional and Lean reporting methods are identical. The reclassification illustrates that $5,120,000 of annual spending is devoted to all labor-related activities. The reclassification of labor-related costs into one cost pool is much more revealing than the $1,870,000 identified in Figure 9.5 as direct labor. The total labor costs shown here more clearly illustrate the actual employee effort to produce the parts and manage this portion of the business. Much of this labor expense in the traditional method is hidden in overhead costs.

In order to build the foundation for the Lean inventory and costing methodology, it is necessary to restate historical month-end inventory using the Lean cost components (labor, conversion, and fixed costs). It is not feasible to restate PackCo's historical month-end inventory into their separate components, because the data was only available in the general traditional classifications of direct labor and overhead. Therefore, proxies have to be developed to estimate these values. In order to do this, we will first examine spending ratios for both traditional and Lean cost accounting. These ratios are shown in Figure 9.9

Traditional Ratios - Annual Spending				
Direct Labor	Direct Labor Spending FY '06	$ 1,870,000	19.0%	Sum
	Raw Materials Spending FY '06 = $ 9,850,000 =			78.6%
Overhead	Overhead Spending FY '06	$ 5,875,000	59.6%	
	Raw Materials Spending FY '06 = $ 9,850,000 =			
Lean Cost Management Ratios - Annual Spending				
Labor	Labor Spending FY '06	$ 5,120,000	52.0%	
	Raw Materials Spending FY '06 = $ 9,850,000 =			
Conversion	Conversion Spending FY '06	$ 1,545,000	15.7%	Sum
	Raw Materials Spending FY '06 = $ 9,850,000 =			78.6%
Fixed	Fixed Spending FY '06	$ 1,080,000	11.0%	
	Raw Materials Spending FY '06 = $ 9,850,000 =			

Figure 9.9: Restated PackCo Machine Shop Monthly Spending in Conformance with Lean Cost Management

The spending information available in PackCo's monthly machine shop expense reports was reclassified into the three new Lean categories. Regardless of whether total spending is divided per the traditional or the Lean cost method, the 2006 sum of the non-material costs for PackCo is equal to 78.6% of the total raw materials spending.

Figure 9.10 depicts the next step in estimating ending inventory, which requires determining the proportion of each non-material cost category.

The denominator of these ratios is total spending minus raw materials ($17,595,000 - $9,850,000).

Lean Cost Management Ratios - Split of Non-Material Costs						
Labor	Labor Spending FY '06		$ 5,120,000		66.1%	
	Non-Material Spending FY '06	=	$ 7,745,000	=		
Conversion	Conversion $ Spent FY '06		$ 1,545,000		19.9%	Sum
	Non-Material Spending FY '06	=	$ 7,745,000	=		100.0%
Fixed	Fixed $ Spent FY '06		$ 1,080,000		13.9%	
	Non-Material Spending FY '06	=	$ 7,745,000	=		

Figure 9.10: PackCo Proportion of Annual Spending by Non-Material Cost Component

The inventory data for PackCo found in Figure 9.2 can now be reconstructed to determine the month-end inventory values per the new Lean cost categories. Since the material content remains constant, and the total historical inventory value is known, the remaining inventory value previously classified as direct labor and overhead can be reapportioned into labor, conversion, and fixed cost components using the ratios provided in Figure 9.10. Figure 9.11 illustrates the historical month-end inventory estimated with the Lean cost components based on the non-material spending ratios from Figure 9.10.

PackCo Restated Machine Shop Month-End WIP Inventory Lean Reporting Historical Inventory Reconfigured for Labor, Conversion & Fixed Costs					
Month	Raw Material	Labor	Conversion	Fixed	Total Inventory Lean Method
Jan-06	$ 680,000	$ 261,123	$ 78,796	$ 55,081	$ 1,075,000
Feb-06	$ 780,000	$ 264,429	$ 79,793	$ 55,778	$ 1,180,000
Mar-06	$ 730,000	$ 247,902	$ 74,806	$ 52,292	$ 1,105,000
Apr-06	$ 765,000	$ 257,818	$ 77,799	$ 54,383	$ 1,155,000
May-06	$ 750,000	$ 251,207	$ 75,804	$ 52,989	$ 1,130,000
Jun-06	$ 740,000	$ 254,513	$ 76,801	$ 53,686	$ 1,125,000
Jul-06	$ 815,000	$ 277,650	$ 83,783	$ 58,567	$ 1,235,000
Aug-06	$ 850,000	$ 271,039	$ 81,788	$ 57,172	$ 1,260,000
Sep-06	$ 775,000	$ 254,513	$ 76,801	$ 53,686	$ 1,160,000
Oct-06	$ 785,000	$ 267,734	$ 80,791	$ 56,475	$ 1,190,000
Nov-06	$ 810,000	$ 257,818	$ 77,799	$ 54,383	$ 1,200,000
Dec-06	$ 765,000	$ 254,513	$ 76,801	$ 53,686	$ 1,150,000
FY '06 Avgs.	$ 770,417	$ 260,022	$ 78,464	$ 54,848	$ 1,163,750
% of Material		33.8%	10.2%	7.1%	

**Figure 9.11: Restated PackCo Machine Shop
Lean Month-End Inventory**

Another way to estimate inventory is to use inventory turns. For PackCo, the 2006 inventory turns for non-material costs is 19.69 ($7,745,000 annual spending/$393,333 2006 average non-material inventory). By dividing the non-material inventory turns into the individual non-material spending components, you can estimate ending inventory for those components. For example, $5,120,000/19.69 yields $260,031 for labor, $1,545,000/19.69 yields $78,466 for conversion costs, and $1,080,000/19.69 yields $54,850 for fixed costs. Using either inventory turns or cost ratios of non-material items as estimators for inventories should provide materially accurate estimated ending inventory figures. The more stable inventories are, the more reliable are the estimates. It is important, however, to periodically monitor both inventory turns and spending ratios and make adjustments if necessary.

Calculation of Machine Shop Inventory: First Month of New Year

At the start of the 2007 fiscal year, PackCo restated the 2006 year-end machine shop inventory records using the Lean approach, as shown in Figure 9.12.

	PackCo Machine Shop Inventory						
Month	Raw Material	Direct Labor	Overhead	Labor	Conversion	Fixed	Total Inventory
Dec 31, 2006 - Traditional Close	$ 765,000	$ 95,000	$ 290,000				$ 1,150,000
Jan 1, 2007 - Lean Approach	$ 765,000	$ -	$ -	$254,513	$ 76,801	$ 53,686	$ 1,150,000

Figure 9.12: Restated PackCo Machine Shop Monthly Spending in Conformance with Lean Cost Categories

During the month of January, 2007, PackCo recorded material into and out of inventory at the discrete part level, exactly like it had always done. Thus, the January ending material balance in the perpetual inventory account had the same value under the new method as it would have had under the old method. Material was valued at the month-end quantities times the standard costs for each item. (At this stage of the Lean journey, standard material costs are still used, and purchase price variances are still generated.)

In contrast to materials, at the beginning of 2007, PackCo no longer tracked direct labor and overhead at the discrete product level. Correspondingly, **all non-material** machine shop costs were expensed directly to the machine shop departmental expense reports. At the end of January, PackCo estimated the non-material inventories using the relationships determined from the Lean approach as shown in Figure 9.11. Labor, conversion, and fixed costs were determined by multiplying the 2007 January ending raw materials inventory by the Figure 9.11 ratios of 33.8 percent, 10.2 percent, and 7.1 percent, respectively. Periodically, these ratios should be monitored and updated per any significant changes. The January 2007 month-end inventory balances for PackCo's machine shop are presented in Figure 9.13.

PackCo Machine Shop Inventory							
Month	Raw Material	Direct Labor	Overhead	Labor	Conver-sion	Fixed	Total Inventory
December 31, 2006 Traditonal Close	$765,000	$ 95,000	$ 290,000	$ -	$ -	$ -	$1,150,000
January 1, 2007 Lean Approach	$765,000	$ -	$ -	$254,513	$ 76,801	$53,686	$1,150,000
January 31, 2007	$700,000	$ -	$ -	$236,255	$ 71,292	$ 49,835	$1,057,382

Figure 9.13: January 2007 PackCo Month-End Lean Inventory

The calculation for labor, conversion, and fixed cost inventory levels is extremely simple and takes just minutes to complete since it is a set percentage of each month's ending raw materials inventory. After the ending inventory amounts are determined, the non-material inventory accounts are adjusted to make them agree with the estimated inventory calculation. Adjusting entries representing decreases in inventory from the previous month, as is the case with PackCo, would move costs from the balance sheet to the profit-and-loss statement. For example, the January adjusting entry for labor costs would be as follows: debit to machine shop labor spending and credit to machine shop labor inventory of $18,258 ($254,513 - $236,255). The necessity for real-time processing of every transaction for every part is eliminated and replaced with one entry for each non-material cost category at month-end. For non-material costs, the month-end adjustments resemble a periodic inventory system, which may be problematic for firms with large inventory swings that want a more current update of inventory. As a reminder, the process for entering purchases of raw materials has not changed at PackCo; therefore, the ending materials inventory figure is already updated and requires no adjustment.

Valuing month-end fixed costs in inventory can be simplified further by maintaining a constant inventory value throughout the year. Month-to-month fluctuations for this inventory category likely will be negligible, and any necessary adjustments can be made at year-end.

Traditional accounting methodology uses real-time reporting and tracks costs at the part level via thousands and thousands of transactions. Lean methodology, on the other hand, eliminates a significant amount of transaction waste by utilizing overall ratios to estimate machine shop inventory. The Lean inventory approach also provides the information for making the monthly inventory change entry on the "Plain English" profit-and-loss statements.

Concern 2 of Phase I: Managing Machine Shop Capacity Without Labor Reporting

One of the first questions asked at PackCo during the transition from detailed tracking of costs to aggregate tracking was, "How will the company manage capacity without direct labor reporting?" This question is particularly relevant to PackCo's business because the machine shop is a critical element of the production process and direct labor reporting always has been essential to the production planning process. Throughout this discussion of cost-system changes, the focus has been on simplifying financial reporting. In order to institute these changes, PackCo simply changed all labor and overhead financial fields to zero for every part number. Direct labor hours, however, were maintained. This allowed PackCo to continue using the same historical system for reporting the physical activity (hours or minutes) of the direct labor production by part without having to maintain the financial data.

Because PackCo's machine shop is not totally configured into cells, it is still necessary to collect production times by discrete part. However, once the entire machine shop is reconfigured into cells, and the machinists are cross-trained to operate most of the machines in each cell, time reporting by discrete part will have to be eliminated. Because the machinists will be operating multiple machines simultaneously, it will be virtually impossible to continue tracking labor times at the discrete part level. Only average labor times will be available for families of parts produced in each cell. Understanding this eventuality, PackCo determined that it was more efficient to transition the cost system of the entire machine shop all at once, rather than cell by cell, which would require managing two different cost methodologies simultaneously.

The new cost system has provided PackCo management with much greater visibility into the flow of material through the machine shop. It is now much easier to graph actual material costs for the machine shop and compare them to actual production levels. Inventory turns data are now more meaningful because they relate to actual material costs.

In addition, inventory related to labor costs can be easily converted to labor hours once an overall labor cost per hour is determined. Such a measure provides a secondary check on inventory levels by monitoring the number of hours in the shop at all times. For instance, if labor costs were determined to be $25 per hour, and month-end labor inventory was estimated to be $25,000, then the machine shop should have 1,000 hours of work-in-process. This estimate of labor hours would then be compared to the actual labor hours still being recorded on open work orders. If material differences arise between the estimated hours in inventory and the actual hours, the inventory records should be "trued-up," and the ongoing relationships of labor to material should be adjusted. In addition, by comparing the level of work-in-process to daily throughput, PackCo can determine if the process is in balance, or whether too much work is being "pushed" into the system.

These added steps to check the estimated inventory level are required during the initial phase of the Lean journey. As the cells mature and single piece flow becomes a way of life, the amount of work-in-process labor, conversion, and fixed cost in inventory will become insignificant.

Concern 3 of Phase I: Determining Individual Part Costs Without Standard Costing

The next challenge posed to proponents of a Lean cost management system is how to accurately calculate the costs of individual parts for the various decisions that are made each day at any company. The basic assumption that companies incorrectly make is that their current cost system provides accurate data for these types of decisions. Since PackCo's managers realized that this assumption was flawed, they actually looked forward to changing their traditional accounting system in order to have more pertinent information for improved decision making.

To facilitate decision making, PackCo utilizes a separate variable cost file that incorporates the Lean cost information. This variable cost file contains each part number and the associated raw material, labor, and conversion costs. The labor component is 33.8 percent of material costs per the rates in Figure 9.11, adjusted downward by 25 percent, to reflect that portion of total labor that is truly insensitive to volume swings over the near term. (The 25 percent labor adjustment factor was determined after reviewing all labor costs and isolating the impact of salaried personnel, such as support staff and supervision, which do not fluctuate unless a major step function in volume occurs.)

Likewise, conversion costs of 10.2 percent of material, as illustrated in Figure 9.11, are also adjusted downward (however, not to the degree labor costs are adjusted) to reflect the variable nature of these operating costs. While reconfiguring the machine shop costs from direct labor and overhead, to labor, conversion, and fixed costs, PackCo ascertained that there were only two significant spending categories within conversion costs: maintenance and tooling. It was also determined that there were only two broad types of machines in the machine shop— manual and automatic machine tools— and the automatic machine tools utilized virtually all of the maintenance and tooling spending. The first step in determining variable conversion costs was to identify if a part was typically produced on a manual or automatic machine tool. The second step was identifying the proportion of raw material processed on automatic versus manual machines. The last step was removing the portion of conversion costs that was truly insensitive to volume swings. Following these three steps resulted in two different conversion costs for each part based on a percentage of raw materials. The sum of the raw material, labor, and conversion costs, by part number, is used for critical make/buy, new product development, and incremental business decisions.

The variable cost file will be updated quarterly for material cost changes and annually for other changes. Given the information uncovered when dissecting the previously used standard cost system, PackCo is confident that the new information will lead to much improved decision-making with far less maintenance effort required.

As PackCo's transition to full cellular production in its machine shop is realized, individual part costs will simply be the average family cost for labor and conversion plus the discrete material cost.

Concern 4 of Phase I: Accurately Reporting Machine Shop Monthly Expenses

Some have questioned Lean accounting's conformity with GAAP financial reporting. However, none of the accounting system changes made at PackCo are contrary to GAAP. In fact, we would argue that PackCo's inventories and its profit-and-loss under the new Lean system are more clearly based on actual numbers, rather than on standards, and therefore, more accurately comply with GAAP than under the traditional system.

As stated previously, by using the Lean accounting approach, all non-material machine shop spending at PackCo is expensed immediately to the appropriate value stream expense accounts. At the end of each reporting period, Lean cost techniques are utilized to calculate month-end inventory. The appropriate entries are made to debit or credit expenses, thereby transferring Costs to/from the "Plain English" profit-and-loss statement from/to the balance sheet in order to "true-up" inventory. The balances remaining in the individual expense accounts accurately reflect the monthly expenses in conformance with GAAP. On the P&L statement, the adjusting entry for inventory is captured separately in the line item "Costs (to)/from Inventory," and quickly informs the reader whether inventory has increased or decreased.

Concern 5 of Phase I: Charging Machine Shop Costs to the Various Value Streams

Many companies have monuments like the machine shop that service various value streams or departments. PackCo's machine shop is an example of such a monument that serves its three value streams: new equipment, parts, and field upgrades. Since nothing has changed for PackCo in the treatment of machine shop raw materials, its costs continue to be transferred by discrete part. Under the new Lean system, machine shop labor, conversion, and fixed costs flow across the three PackCo value streams based on their relationship to the raw materials content being transferred. This process better identifies the level of support each of the respective value streams are providing to one another, since the monthly charges for the various cost categories are now clearly identified. There have been some interesting discussions among the value stream leaders related to whether or not each one is paying its fair market value for the services rendered. Of course, allocation of any cost is the antithesis of Lean costing objectives. As PackCo continues its Lean journey, its ultimate goal is to eliminate the machine shop as a monument and create right-sized machine shops for each of the value streams.

Maintaining Accuracy in a Lean Cost System

Even more than a traditional organization, a Lean company is forever in transition. With the ongoing formation of cells, the continual elimination of waste, and the ability to produce more with the same resources, both total-cost and relative-cost ratios will continually change. The challenge, which is the same for any cost system, is to have the ability to easily maintain accurate information for valuing inventory and making well-informed decisions. We believe the Lean cost system actually aids in meeting these challenges much better than traditional cost systems.

Operational efficiency improvements will require less labor and conversion costs per dollar of material to produce a product. Such improvements should be reflected in the annual spending of each component. By monitoring both turns and the ratios of the various cost components at least quarterly, and making appropriate adjustments to those relationships, ongoing accuracy can be maintained. To maintain simplicity, adjustments to the inventory ratios should be made only if a material threshold is surpassed.

Another inventory accuracy check is to test the number of hours in the machine shop each quarter. Since labor **activity** will still be collected, it is easy to summarize total shop hours for work-in-process inventory. Given the overall processing rate per hour, a reasonable test can be performed whereby the actual shop hours are compared to the estimated shop hours in inventory. Again, simple charts that do not require the time and expense of real-time reporting can be set up and monitored to alert management of any significant deviations.

Finally, one must remember that the primary process objectives of Lean are to achieve pull and flow and operate with standard levels of work-in-process. Once pull and flow improve, total inventory levels will be significantly reduced and the materiality of labor, conversion, and fixed costs in inventory will diminish. A point will be reached where all product costs can be expensed to the period statements, with minor adjustments required quarterly via simple visual techniques.

Putting it all in Perspective with an Everyday Example:

Utilization of PackCo's Machine Shop Material Turns to Assess Performance and Provide a Roadmap for Improvements

Everyone knows that change is difficult. The longer you have performed certain routines, the more hesitant you become of accepting something different. This is generally true whether it relates to personal or business activities. It is understood also that there has to be rather strong motivation for individuals to embrace change. Thus, one must appreciate the micro benefits to them personally, as well as conceptualize the macro benefits to the organization with which they are associated. These advantages must be valued, as people are asked to move out of their comfort zone and take on what they perceive to be more risk. In a business situation, management should share their intentions for change and provide workers with enough information to reassure them about any changes that will affect their current status.

This chapter has described some of the changes that have taken place in the last year at PackCo. While the associates at PackCo have been mostly responsive to the concepts behind Lean, they have sometimes questioned the changes they observe at work. PackCo management understands that providing the work-force with a clear conceptual picture of how the Lean transformation will positively affect their work life is critical for securing their long-term commitment to the company's Lean journey. Relaying a simple object lesson to PackCo associates sparked their enthusiasm for Lean principles. A friend (who we will call Bill) made a recent trip to the doctor. His experience, which is shared below, painted a vivid picture of needed process improvements to which everyone can relate. After discussing the implications of Bill's adventure, the PackCo team concluded that if raw materials in a machine shop had human emotions, change would happen more easily.

A few weeks ago, Bill scheduled a doctor's appointment based on the recommendation of his family doctor. When calling for the appointment, the doctor's office requested all of Bill's personal information, including social security number, date of birth, address, medical history, insurance carrier, and health plan number. An appointment was scheduled for 9:15 A.M. on a Friday morning. Bill arrived at the doctor's office at 9:00 A.M., optimistic that he would not have a long wait since it was at the beginning of the doctor's day. Upon his arrival, Bill was extremely disappointed to see a waiting room packed with 12 other patients. He checked in with the receptionist and was given a number of forms to fill out, all of which asked for practically the same information that was supplied by Bill previously on the telephone. After sitting for 90 minutes in the main waiting area, Bill was escorted by a nurse into the "holding pen." The nurse did not weigh Bill or even take his pulse or blood pressure. She simply moved Bill from one waiting area to another. Moving to the examining office generally increases the patient's optimism about the real possibility of meeting with the doctor in the near future. However, Bill waited for another 30 minutes before the doctor actually arrived. The doctor spent a maximum of ten minutes examining Bill, after which Bill was directed to the check-out area. Here Bill waited for another patient to be processed before he could complete his final paperwork with the office manager. The end result of the doctor's visit was a recommendation for Bill to see another health care provider. An abbreviated value stream map of Bill's trip to the doctor is illustrated in Figure 9.14.

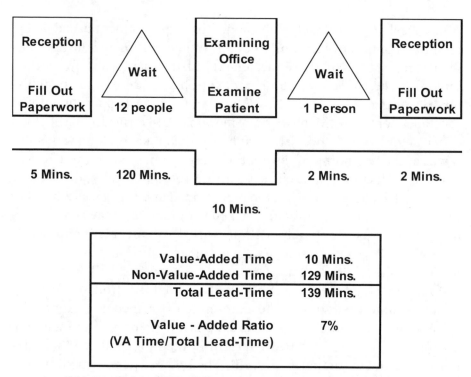

Figure 9.14: Value Stream Map of Doctor's Visit

In this value stream map, the only value-added step is the ten minutes during which the doctor actually examined Bill. The rest of the time is waste. The total waiting time was 120 minutes, with 12 patients in queue and each patient spending about ten minutes with the doctor. This includes both the general waiting room and the examining room. Upon exiting the examining room, there was one person in-process at the check-out area. Needless to say, Bill was extremely irritated to have spent 139 minutes at the doctor's office for a ten minute exam (7% value-added ratio). What inefficiency and waste! Yet this type of process exists throughout service and manufacturing industries worldwide.

You may be wondering how the activities of a medical practice are relevant to our discussion of PackCo's machine shop. Figure 9.15 answers this query by illustrating the machine shop activities that correspond to the activities in the doctor's office.

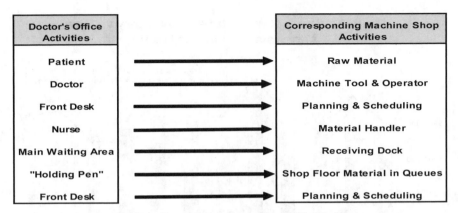

**Figure 9.15: Comparison of Activities Between
a Doctor's Office and a Machine Shop**

It is remarkable how similar the process steps are between these two radically different businesses. When this example was reviewed with PackCo's machine shop associates, many indicated that after a one-hour wait at their doctor's office, they simply leave out of frustration. They also started to make comparisons to their own work processes, and could better understand how wasteful some of their own daily work routines were.

An abbreviated value stream map of PackCo's machine shop can be drawn after determining a few critical data points. Figure 9.16 illustrates the total value of PackCo's 2006 historical monthly machine shop raw materials inventory and the total machine shop's raw materials output delivered to Stores. Figure 9.17 illustrates the same data for Stores, where the output measures the value of machine shop raw materials delivered to Assembly—Stores final internal customer.

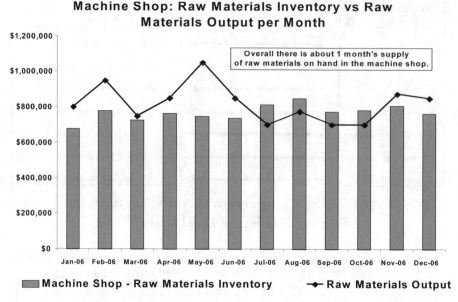

**Figure 9.16: PackCo Monthly Machine Shop
Raw Materials Inventory Vs. Output per Month**

Figure 9.16 provides a quick snapshot of machine shop inventory turns. If the solid line, which represents the raw materials value of the monthly machine shop deliveries to Stores, rested exactly on top of the monthly ending inventory columns, inventory turns would equal twelve. In this case, inventory turns equals 12.8, which means that raw materials spend approximately 29 days in PackCo's machine shop. (Refer to the information in Figure 9.7.)

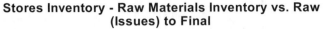

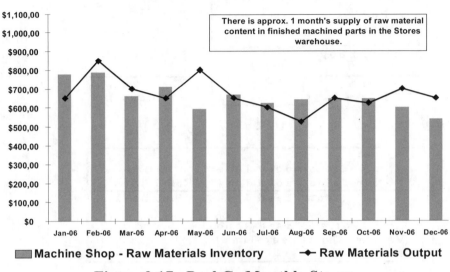

**Figure 9.17: PackCo Monthly Stores
Raw Materials Inventory and Output**

In Stores, inventory turns over 12.2 times, which means that on average, approximately 30 days worth of raw materials is in the Stores
stockroom at all times waiting to be sent to its final customer—assembly. (To clarify, these are completed machined parts that are still valued at the raw material content only, as non-material costs are no longer
maintained at the discrete part level.)

Before preparing a simplified value stream map of the machine shop
and Stores, the average processing time for a machined part must be
determined. At PackCo, the machining is estimated to take four hours
per part, equaling a half-day's work for a single-shift operation. Using the machining hours and inventory turns information, the abbreviated value stream map for PackCo's machine shop is illustrated in
Figure 9.18.

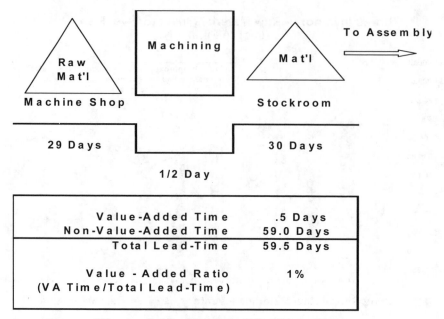

**Figure 9.18: PackCo Machine Shop
Abbreviated Value Stream Map**

As shown in Figure 9.18, the value-added time versus the total production lead time in PackCo's machine shop is only one percent, which is similar to the percentages you would find in most traditional machine shop operations. You are probably surprised and dismayed to see that the data in these examples illustrate that the medical practice is flowing product (patients) *seven times faster* than the typical machine shop. If raw material in the machine shop had emotions, it would be complaining very loudly about sitting around doing nothing for 99 percent of the time! In fact, if the material could sprout legs, it would simply get up and leave, just like some of the machinists indicated they do in the doctor's office.

The real issue is identifying why we complacently allow material to sit around idle for 99 percent of the time. Whether it is a machine shop or a doctor's office, the absence of pull and flow and the associated physical and financial systems perpetuates the current state of affairs. If the doctor's office operated at the same pace as PackCo's machine shop, Bill's wait would have been about 18 hours! Rather than spending enormous amounts of time and energy dissecting traditional direct labor reports and trying to speed up the cycle times of disconnected machines, Lean focuses on eliminating the waste in the system and establishing cells with single-piece flow to improve the overall delivery system. Like the machine shop associates at PackCo, we need to be aware of our wasteful activities and find the necessary motivation for change.

SUMMARY

In this chapter we illustrated the step-by-step process for converting a complex job shop from a traditional standard cost system with complex, detailed tracking and reporting, to a much more simplified Lean system, where costs are first expensed for the period and then adjusted by a few summary month-end entries to arrive at month-end inventory balances. As inventory turns improve, and inventory becomes a more stable and less significant portion of a firm's assets, the necessity to adjust inventory during each reporting period will slowly fade away. In the interim, it is important to instruct your associates of the benefits derived from consistently working toward Lean improvements in order to continue their progress down the Lean path. As a company approaches world class performance levels, and standard work-in-process inventory levels are maintained, no adjusting entries for inventory will be required and all non-material spending for the period can be expensed. Furthermore, with a true pull system and stable, work-in-process levels, raw materials could be accounted for in a fashion similar to other non-material cost categories. When there is no significant month-to-month change in inventory levels, simply expensing all period costs will yield accurate financial statements.

Applying Lean cost management to the machine shop at PackCo presented some unique challenges due to the diversity of the product and the sheer volume of parts. However, following the processes described in this chapter and preparing summary month-end entries appear to be sufficient for providing accurate financial statements in conformance with all internal and external requirements.

The following chapter will demonstrate how these same accounting for Lean procedures can work in an assembly operation, where all production takes place in cells.

10

LEAN COST MANAGEMENT IN LOW VOLUME/HIGH COMPLEXITY ASSEMBLY OPERATIONS

C hapter 9 focused on converting a traditional accounting system to accounting for Lean in a low volume, very high mix machine shop environment. Each individual part traveled through multiple machine centers as it was converted from raw material to a finished part. This chapter focuses on the physical process changes made in the assembly of machines at PackCo and the subsequent accounting changes made to track costs and inventory

The Build Process at PackCo

The machines built at PackCo contain 10,000 to 15,000 parts and require thousands of man-hours to complete. The entire build process spans several weeks. Historically, PackCo treated assembly as a job shop and charged all direct labor and material to individual work orders for each machine. The accuracy of final machine costs was questionable as associates juggling their work during the day often clocked their direct labor hours to the incorrect machine. Once a particular machine was completed, numerous work order variances were generated. Locating and understanding the root cause of these variances was very difficult, since the activity might have taken place weeks ago. Even if the root cause could be identified, the expiration of time diluted the potential benefits from solving it. In addition, a tremendous number of transactions were created and month-end clean-up was time consuming, with no real benefit to the user community. It definitely was time for a change.

As part of the Lean journey for assembly, PackCo developed standard work for all the build processes. Each machine was partitioned into separate sections, and specific build areas, or cells, were constructed. In this arrangement, the long build cycles were now manageable work units. The assembly process in each cell was reviewed by all the cell associates to establish the single best way to build each section of the machine. Once agreement was reached on the build sequence, the standard build process was posted in the appropriate cell on a Yamazumi board.

Yamazumi Board

A modification of *yamadzumi*, a Japanese term meaning "huge mound or heap." A Yamazumi board is a takt time/cycle time chart, used to balance a process to takt time. The board features vertical bars of varying heights, (representing relative time to complete a task), which can be moved from operation to operation in order to balance the process.

Establishing a standard build process insured that the machine sections would be built the same way every time, which is a tremendous challenge for complex equipment assembled in a three-shift operation. In addition to standardizing on the best build sequence, standard inventory was developed for each cell, and the overall build cycle was developed to meet takt time.

Discarding a 40-year-old practice and changing the haphazard process in machine assembly to standard work was a tremendous challenge. However, the concurrent cultural and organizational changes were even more challenging than the physical changes occurring on the shop floor. These efforts require strong leadership, with commitment and resolve to confront the criticisms from naysayers.

The development of standard work and the use of the Yamazumi boards were critical in several ways. First, the Yamazumi boards provided tremendous visibility to the status of each machine build. Secondly, the Yamazumi boards played a key role in simplifying the calculation of month-end inventory. Finally, these boards provided the base data to balance the work-load in each build cell. Figure 10.1 illustrates a Yamazumi board for a machine section.

Figure 10.1: Yamazumi Board at PackCo

In Figure 10.1, the vertical axis represents the hours in the day while the horizontal axis represents the days of the build process. Each build day is divided into four vertical columns; each column represents a team member working in the cell. The required activities for each team member are then broken down into exactly the number of hours required to complete each task. Finally, the tasks are identified according to color as either mechanical or electrical activities. Even in its early, partially completed stage, this particular Yamazumi board had tremendous success in directing a more visual, organized build process.

After standardizing the build process, the next step is to establish pull and flow. To facilitate the flow of parts, the build team identified, on the Yamazumi board, the exact parts required for each task. With the Yamazumi board, correct parts could be delivered in much smaller batches, exactly when needed. When a standard build process is established, the cell leader is able to timely request the needed parts for the actual required date, effectively establishing a true pull system. Not only did this new standard process help better manage inventories, but it also encouraged an immediate response to issues and problems encountered on the shop floor. For instance, under the new system, if the assembly team falls behind, the flow of material automatically shuts down, and there is no signal to deliver any more parts until production and the schedule are linked. The purpose of a pull system is to provide real-time adjustment to the needs of the customer, rather than continuing to load the shop with unnecessary parts. These physical changes laid the groundwork for the accounting changes that would follow.

Accounting for Lean in Assembly

The same inventory and spending analysis completed for the machine shop was done for assembly. Historical spending and inventory were charted and graphed for both traditional accounting classifications and the new Lean classifications, with similar results. An analysis revealed that historical direct labor and the reclassified total labor costs comprised less than ten percent of the total inventory value. Raw materials from the machine shop as well as the purchased parts issued from Stores comprised the bulk of the inventory value. Unlike the machine shop, the assembly area did not have large machine tools and the associated depreciation, tooling, and maintenance expenses. In the accounting for Lean reclassification scheme, it was discovered that assembly conversion costs were even a smaller proportion of total inventory value than labor costs. It quickly became apparent that all process time and effort expended to track direct labor costs in the traditional job-order accounting system was mostly wasteful, providing both minimal and distorted information.

The challenge for accounting was to find a replacement system to more accurately value assembly inventory in the new environment. Even though there is solid evidence of its ineffectiveness, the former traditional accounting system is steeped in a traditional system that is more difficult to change than shop-floor operations. However, accountants and managers alike were surprised at the relative ease of determining a more accurate work-in-process inventory figure with the implementation of standard work and the use of visual Yamazumi schedule boards.

Figure 10.2 illustrates a Yamazumi board for an assembly cell at month-end.

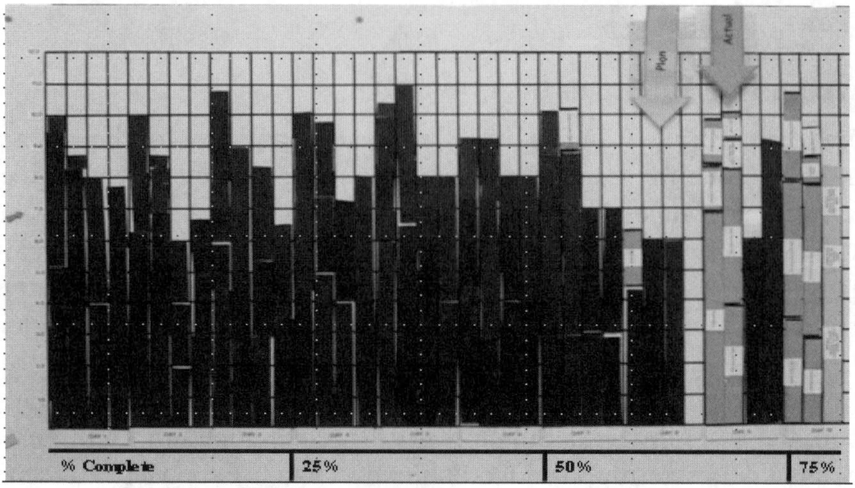

Figure 10.2: Yamazumi Board at Month-End

The vertical bars on the Yamazumi boards are magnetic. As the assembly team completes each task, it turns over the magnet so everyone can readily understand the status of the build process. In addition, the two arrows at the top indicate the goal for the day, as well as progress toward that goal. In this particular example, the team is actually ahead of the planned schedule.

At the bottom of the Yamazumi board is a simple bar indicating the percent complete for this particular section of the machine. Since the work is now relatively evenly loaded, it is a very simple matter to interpolate the actual percent complete for each section. Figure 10.2 shows a section of the machine that is approximately 60 percent complete. In a matter of minutes, a plant controller or cost accountant can go to gemba and walk the floor to ascertain the status of all assembly activity. This is the process that PackCo currently uses at month-end to determine assembly labor, conversion, and fixed costs work-in-process inventory.

The number of hours to complete each machine has been determined and entered into an Excel spreadsheet prior to the beginning of the assembly process. After the percentage complete is determined for each of the section build areas by a month-end gemba walk, the information is entered on the Excel spreadsheet to calculate the labor, conversion and fixed cost value of the assembly work-in-process inventory, as depicted in Figure 10.3. At month-end, PackCo's accountants aggregate all of the individual assembly cell inventory values to arrive at the total assembly inventory.

	PackCo Assembly Work-in-Process Inventory						
	Cell 1	Cell 2	Cell 3	Cell 4	Cell 5	Cell 6	Total
Total Hours per Unit	400	300	300	250	100	200	1,550
% Complete	60%	50%	40%	70%	85%	25%	
Labor Rate per Hour	$ 30	$ 30	$ 30	$ 30	$ 30	$ 30	
Conversion Rate per Hour	$ 15	$ 15	$ 15	$ 15	$ 15	$ 15	
Fixed Rate per Hour	$ 3	$ 3	$ 3	$ 3	$ 3	$ 3	
Labor Inventory	$ 7,200	$ 4,500	$ 3,600	$ 5,250	$ 2,550	$ 1,500	$ 24,600
Conversion Inventory	$ 3,600	$ 2,250	$ 1,800	$ 2,625	$ 1,275	$ 750	$ 12,300
Fixed Cost Inventory	$ 720	$ 450	$ 360	$ 525	$ 255	$ 150	$ 2,460
Assembly WIP ex Material	$ 11,520	$ 7,200	$ 5,760	$ 8,400	$ 4,080	$ 2,400	$ 39,360

Figure 10.3: PackCo Month-End Assembly Work-in-Process Inventory Calculation

The labor, conversion, and fixed cost hourly rates were initially determined by analyzing the prior year's total spending divided by the total hours utilized in the assembly process. No distinction was made between direct and indirect labor as PackCo is concerned with only the total costs of inputs versus the cell output. These rates are monitored throughout the year to insure that accurate inventory values are maintained.

The inventory process is simple, easily understood by everyone, and provides an opportunity for accounting to be much more engaged in the process. The first time PackCo's month-end inventory was calculated based on assessing progress in the assembly area, the Plant Controller returned from the inventory walk with a newfound understanding of the exact status of production and the implications for meeting the subsequent month's shipping schedule. The conversation was entirely different from previous month-ends, focusing on the status of production rather than a discussion on inventory calculations.

Similar to the accounting process in PackCo's machine shop, all non-material spending is initially expensed to the "Plain English" profit-and-loss statement. Once month-end inventories are determined, any adjustments required to true-up the inventory accounts are made by debiting or crediting the labor, conversion, and fixed costs (to)/from inventory account. When examining their month-end inventories, companies must individually decide what constitutes a material change that warrants a month-end entry. Once true pull and flow are in place, in conjunction with standard work and level loading, month-to-month inventory will be stable enough that inventory change entries will be unnecessary.

At this stage of the Lean journey at PackCo, there has been no change to the accounting practices for recording material because most of the equipment built is custom in nature and bills of material are different for virtually every product. All material moves into and out of inventory at standard material costs and is charged to a specific machine. When standard work-in-process, level loading, and product standardization becomes a reality at PackCo, material will be expensed in a fashion similar to labor, conversion, and fixed costs. At that time, standard, configured bills of material will provide the necessary information for accurate total product costing.

In assembly operations, most of the fixed costs are related to the facility, rather than equipment in the specific build cells. These fixed costs can be excluded entirely from the value stream and handled separately at the plant level. In order to promote Lean behavior, it is recommended that all plant fixed costs be excluded from the value streams. Instead, it is more appropriate to develop an "occupancy" charge that reflects the cost per square foot for the facility, as discussed in Chapter 9.

Accounting for Lean in Assembly – Metrics

For this new Lean cost system to be effective, cost accountants must become much more engaged in the production process and spend time out on the shop floor with the associates performing the value-added work. The cross-cultural interaction and knowledge gained by everyone will be extraordinary and will provide long-term benefits to the company.

A key component in the formation of cells is the development of real-time metrics that give clarity to the associates about the current dynamics of the business. Each day the cell team leader posts the number of hours expended by the team. In addition, data relative to quality issues, number of shortages, safety, inventory, and other critical information is recorded. At the end of the month, the data is graphed and posted to identify trends. Interpreting the data is much easier, as issues and problems are noted each day and can be correlated to overall monthly performance. Further, the implementation of these measurement tools provides the accounting team with new insight into the actual costs of the operation, a greater understanding of performance variances, and the opportunity to be an engaged change agent.

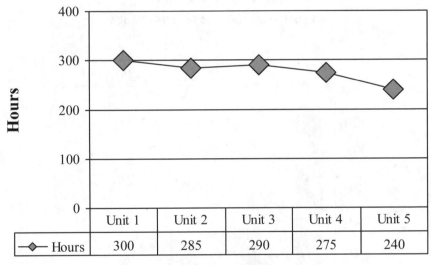

	Unit 1	Unit 2	Unit 3	Unit 4	Unit 5
Hours	300	285	290	275	240

Unit

Figure 10.4: Cell 1 Build Hours in Sequence of Build

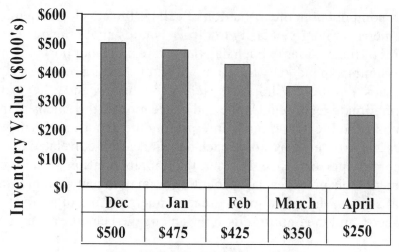

**Figure 10.5: PackCo Cell 1
Month-End Material Inventory**

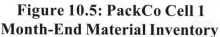

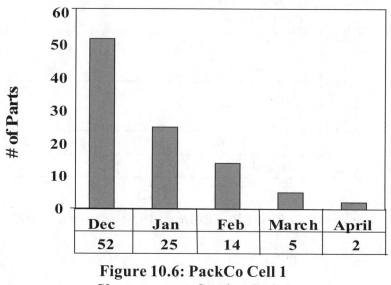

**Figure 10.6: PackCo Cell 1
Shortages per Section Build**

These three charts begin to demonstrate the impact of moving to standard work and a pull system in Cell 1, with build hours, purchased and raw materials inventory, and the number of shortages all decreasing.

Normally such data does not exist for each individual cell, and it is nearly impossible to determine the impact of improvement activities on critical performance metrics. By spending time in gemba, it is easy to understand the impact on performance of everyday shop-floor events. For example, if one went on a daily gemba walk and wanted an explanation for why the Yamazumi board indicated that the cell was behind schedule, any team member could explain the reason, such as someone new was just added to the team or quality problems surfaced. The visual performance metrics make it much easier to understand the financial impact of turnover, quality, or any other cell dynamic, whereas, assessing this information using traditional cost reports is nearly impossible.

Determining actual product costs also becomes extremely easy in this Lean environment. These charts make it simple to update labor costs in real time, particularly as total labor hours decline.

Summary

Traditional standard cost systems may be necessary when the production process is chaotic and out of control. However, as a company applies Lean techniques and brings order to the process, the cost system must change in concert with the physical changes taking place on the shop floor. This chapter demonstrates how a very complex, customized, lengthy assembly process was brought under control by implementing cellular production, standard work, visual controls, and a pull system. In addition, a new Lean cost system was implemented utilizing the visual shop floor metrics to determine non-material costs, while material was accounted for in the traditional manner.

Chapter 10 Endnotes

1. *The Northwest Lean Networks,* Lean Terms and Definitions http://www.nwlean.net/leandefs.htm#y, (April, 2007)

PART III

LEAN ACCOUNTING AND HUMAN RESOURCES APPLICATIONS

11
LEAN ACCOUNTING CASE STUDY:
THE ACCOUNTS PAYABLE PROCESS

12
LEAN BUDGETING: ELIMINATING WASTE IN THE
BUDGETING AND PLANNING PROCESS

13
USING LEAN PRINCIPLES IN HUMAN RESOURCES

11

Lean Accounting Case Study: The Accounts Payable Process at Jake Brake Division of Danaher Corporation

by Mark DeLuzio, CMA
(Former CFO of Jake Brake)

Mark DeLuzio was mentored by the originators of the Toyota Production System (TPS), and has directed the implementation of Lean principles and strategies globally for more than 15 years. Mr. DeLuzio founded Lean Horizons Consulting in 2001. A former Vice President and Corporate Officer of Danaher Corporation (NYSE: DHR), Mr. DeLuzio led the corporate-wide implementation of Lean and designed what is known today as the Danaher Business System (DBS). In 1988, as Chief Financial Officer at Danaher's Jake Brake® division, Mr. DeLuzio implemented one of the first Lean accounting processes in the USA. He was also instrumental in developing Jake's first zero-defect manufacturing process for Toyota's Hino Motors. Mr. DeLuzio, a Certified Management Accountant (CMA), holds two undergraduate degrees in business, an MBA in Operations Management, and a Certificate in Production and Inventory Management (CPIM).

Situation Analysis

Danaher's Jake Brake division was an old-line New England manufacturing company. It was plagued with inefficiencies, including low inventory turns and poor quality, delivery, and productivity. Profitability was declining, and the expiration of the company's patent on its product opened the door to competitors, many of whom were Jake Brake's angry customers. Senior management needed drastic action in order to right the ship. In response to the threatening situation, the principles of the Toyota Production System (TPS) were adopted by Jake's manufacturing operations in 1988. Over the course of the following two years, drastic improvements were made to the operations, greatly improving Jake's quality, delivery, and cost position. Correspondingly, profitability was on the rise, and this traditional manufacturing company that had been facing tremendous challenges now had a shot at survival.

The company's senior management soon realized that by focusing TPS solely on the shop floor, they were losing out on many opportunities. They recognized that many of the inefficiencies on the shop floor resonated from other areas, particularly in administration. For example, Jake Brake had a commitment to deliver product within five days from receipt of order; however, in some cases, it took seven days for the order entry department just to process a standard customer order. A new awareness of the situation triggered a Lean focus that expanded to the entire enterprise, including the accounting function. This chapter will explain the Lean changes made to Jake's accounts payable (AP) process.

Three accounting clerks were in charge of the AP department in 1988. At that time, the department was disorganized, cluttered, and fraught with inaccuracies and inefficiencies. Figure 11.1 illustrates the accounts payable department metrics prior to deploying Lean tools.

Measures	Pre-Lean Value
# of Associates	3
Productivity (Vouchers/Hour/Associate)	8.3
First Pass Defects	650,000 PPM
Duplicate Payments	25 per Month

Figure 11.1: Accounts Payable Metrics – Pre-Lean

Productivity was extremely low, with AP clerks spending inordinate amounts of time trying to solve quality issues, primarily first-pass defects. Figure 11.1 shows that 65 percent of the vouchers were deemed defective, (650,000 parts per million defective), meaning they did not pass through the AP system the first time entered without some sort of manual intervention. A Pareto analysis of the defects is shown in Figure 11.2.

PARTS PER MILLION

Parts per million (PPM) are the number of defective parts the customer receives per million parts shipped. This can be used to measure your suppliers as well as what your customers use to meaure you.[1] For clarity throughout an organization, no one needs a calculator to understand that 650,000 defective parts out of a million parts is a huge problem; whereas using percents or other measures might cause confusion.

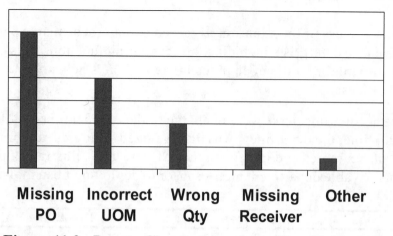

Figure 11.2: Pareto Chart of Accounts Payable Defects

As the data suggests, a majority of the quality errors were the result of two primary problems: (1) missing purchase orders (POs); and (2) incorrect units of measure (UOM) on the purchase order vs. the invoice. For example, the purchase order may have indicated that an item was to be ordered in gallons, but it was actually invoiced in pounds. It was determined that if these top two quality defect modes were resolved, productivity would improve significantly, duplicate payments would be reduced, and overall efficiency and associate satisfaction would also improve.

Kaizen Process

A cross-functional kaizen team was assembled to begin looking at the overall process. The team, representing both suppliers and customers of the process, consisted of members from accounting, purchasing, receiving, manufacturing, engineering, and marketing. It was important to involve several cross-functional representatives in this process; otherwise, the improvement event would be viewed as strictly an accounting exercise. Initially the team considered inviting some of their key external suppliers to participate in the event, as well. However, this idea was tabled until after the team could better define and examine the problem to be addressed and develop a clearer understanding of the current situation.

Before diving into the data, the team decided that the AP process first needed to be stabilized. All three AP clerks utilized different processes and procedures when processing a voucher. The pre-kaizen process is depicted in Figure 11.3.

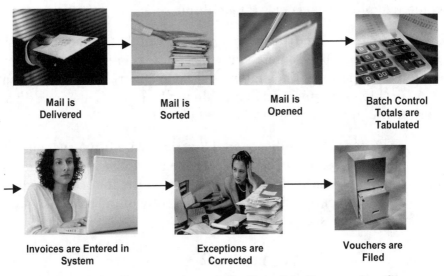

Mail is Delivered   **Mail is Sorted**   **Mail is Opened**   **Batch Control Totals are Tabulated**

Invoices are Entered in System   **Exceptions are Corrected**   **Vouchers are Filed**

Figure 11.3: Current Accounts Payable Processing Steps

A look at some of these processes revealed the following:

Mail Sorted: The responsibilities of the three AP clerks were divided based on the letters of the alphabet. For example, clerk #1 handled suppliers beginning with the letters A through H, while clerk #2 handled suppliers I through P, and clerk #3 handled suppliers Q through Z. In the kaizen event, this sorting procedure was deemed to be non-value added, as it did nothing to contribute toward the processing of an invoice. The alphabetical sorting of work had no correlation to associate workloads and also led to fairness and morale issues.

Mail Opened: Various methodologies were used to open the mail. One clerk used a manual letter opener; another clerk used an electric mail opener, while a third clerk used a ball point pen! Even though these are minor variations, they represent the inconsistent mindset that existed within the department. Once the AP personnel embarked on the kaizen process, the value of standardization became clear to all.

Batch Control Totals Tabulated: The computer system was a batch-oriented system that required invoices to be grouped together in order to tabulate batch-control totals.

Invoices Entered in System: The AP system was complicated and required duplicate data entry into multiple screens.

Exceptions Corrected: The analysis showed that 65 percent of the vouchers that had been entered into the system required manual intervention of some sort. The majority of the AP clerks' time was spent fixing problems on invoices that could not be processed correctly on the first attempt. (See Figure 11.2.)

Vouchers Filed: It was discovered that duplicate filing systems existed. For example, the receiving department, purchasing department, and accounting department each kept a manual file for every purchase order. The AP department also matched a copy of the purchase order to all of the processed vouchers.

ACTIONS TAKEN

Standard Work Developed: The processing of vouchers was standardized for all AP clerks. Standard work allowed for "one best way" to process invoices, reduced variation, and eliminated errors from the AP department. By utilizing standard work, and determining takt time, the company was able to assess appropriate staffing levels. The standard work combination sheet utilized is illustrated in Figure 10.4.

STANDARD WORK COMBINATION SHEET

A standard work combination sheet is a document showing the sequence of production steps, or office activities, assigned to a single person. It is used to illustrate the best combination of worker and machine.[1]

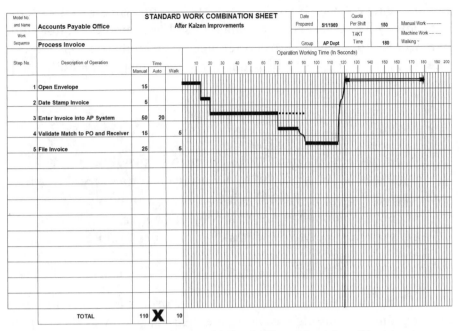

Figure 11.4: Standard Work Combination Sheet

As Figure 11.4 shows, it took only 120 seconds to process a voucher and the takt time was 180 seconds. (Total vouchers processed per day were 160, or 20 per hour, or one every three minutes.) The staffing requirement's formula based on takt time and cycle time determined that only 2/3 of a person should be required to process all of the daily vouchers for the entire company:

$$\text{Staffing Required} = \frac{\text{Sum of Cycle Time}}{\text{Takt Time}} = \frac{120 \text{ Seconds}}{180 \text{ Seconds}} = .67 \text{ People}$$

Mail Sorting Eliminated: The sorting of mail was eliminated because it was determined to be a non-value added activity for processing a voucher.

Data Entry Enhanced: An interface tool called Crosstalk® was adopted to greatly enhance the data entry process. It eliminated the need for multiple screens and duplicate entry of the same data. Additionally, data entry errors were eradicated by applying mistake proofing (poka-yoke) controls to the data fields. For example, vendor numbers were automatically cross referenced to a database to assure data integrity. These actions significantly improved the 650,000 PPM quality levels.

POKA-YOKE

Poka-Yoke is a Japanese word for mistake proofing. Literally translated it means "to avoid inadvertent errors". An inexpensive poka-yoke device prevents or eliminates the possibility of human error from affecting a machine or process and prevents operator mistakes or errors from becoming defects.[3]

Filing Discontinued: Filing of purchase orders in receiving, purchasing, and accounting was no longer necessary. It was determined that since an electronic copy of the purchase order existed within the system, paper copies were redundant.

Exceptions Corrected: The top two error defects—missing POs and incorrect units of measure—were addressed. A Pareto analysis revealed that the majority of invoices that had missing POs originated from the engineering department, as shown in Figure 11.5

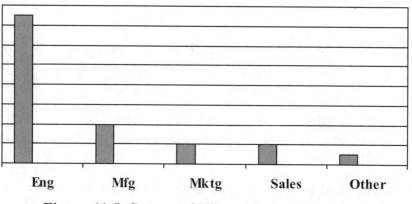

Figure 11.5: Source of Missing Purchase Orders

It was also discovered that 80 percent of the invoices that lacked POs were for amounts under $100. The costs and time associated with establishing POs for such small dollar amounts was determined to be prohibitive. Therefore, an ordering system was created called a "Special Purchase Order" (SPO). If an engineer procured anything under $100, a simple SPO was filled out and sent to the accounting department. The SPO number was required to be on all submitted invoices. The engineering group was told that without an SPO, the invoice would not be paid, and that all calls from the vendor associated with non-payment would be directed to the engineering department for resolution. The same process was instituted for all other departments. This one change alone cut down the number of vouchers with missing POs by 80 percent.

Incorrect units of measure were addressed by establishing a master UOMs list by commodity (e.g., steel and chemicals), and assuring that all purchasing personnel were trained and aware of the new procedure. In some cases, this also required some coordination with suppliers. This master list virtually eliminated the UOM defect mode.

RESULTS

The changes discussed in this chapter took place over a period of approximately 60 days. Results are summarized in Figure 11.6.

Measures	Pre-Lean Value	After Lean Event	% Improvement
# of Associates	3	2/3	78%
Productivity (Vouchers/Hour/Associate)	8.3	30	261%
First Pass Defects	650,000 PPM	50,000 PPM	92%
Duplicate Payments	25 per Month	Eliminated	100%

Figure 11.6: Results of Jake Brake Accounts Payable Improvement Efforts

The two A/P clerks freed up as a result of the Lean improvements were assigned to different roles. The remaining person was not fully utilized by the accounts payable process, so she was also given the responsibility to assist with accounts receivables. The SPO process practically eliminated duplicate payments from the system. Quality was greatly improved as first-pass defects declined by 92 percent in

60 days. At the same time, productivity improved by an amazing 261 percent.

Lessons Learned

1. Dramatic improvements were achieved in a short period of time by focusing on the few most critical issues.

2. It was important not to view this as an accounting problem alone. Therefore, getting multi-functional participation on the kaizen team was essential.

3. Principles used on the shop floor (e.g., standard work and basic problem solving) can be adapted to the office environment.

4. Improvements were made in productivity and cost by focusing on quality first.

5. ***Don't let perfect get in the way of better.*** The team knew that there were many more improvements to be made, but the greatest impact items needed to be addressed first.

It is important to note that the team did not think their work was done after the initial kaizen activity. There were many more improvements to be made. For instance, a 50,000 PPM defect rate is not considered world class. Follow-up kaizen events were held to eliminate the remaining defect modes. Additional work was done to further improve the standard work cycle time. For example, elimination of walk time and improving the data entry time were the focus of future kaizen events.

SUMMARY

The Jake Brake example describes the improvement processes made at a very progressive company almost two decades ago. Despite the passage of time and the availability of much improved technology, many of the same challenges exist in today's accounting organizations. Until the appropriate tools and disciplines are put in place, the same challenges will exist for many decades to come.

Making kaizen improvements to all aspects of the accounting function allows accountants to work "on" the business rather than "in" the business. That is, accountants can spend more time being an active part of the management team, working on accounting for Lean activities, such as value stream costing, target costing, and Lean budgeting. Additionally, they can take a more active role in working with the value stream leaders. Accountants can, and should, become navigators rather than historians.

Chapter 11 Endnotes

1. *Business Management Systems*, Value Curve, Glossary, http://www.valucurve.com/glossary.html#s (May, 2007).

2. Ibid.

3. Ibid.

12

LEAN BUDGETING: ELIMINATING WASTE IN THE BUDGETING AND PLANNING PROCESS

BY STEVE PLAYER, CPA

S teve Player, the Managing Director of the Player Group, serves as the North American Program Director for the Beyond Budgeting Roundtable, an international network focused on improving a firm's planning and control processes. He has over twenty years of experience in implementing cost and performance management tools, strategic planning, and process improvements. He is the co-author/editor of four books, including *Lessons from the ABM Battlefield*. Player served on the Board of Directors of the Consortium of Advanced Manufacturing – International (CAM-I) and provided insight for the AICPA Industry and Management Accounting Executive Committee.

Introduction

The budgeting process is alive, but not necessarily well, as companies still budget today in the same fashion in which they have performed the process for the past fifty years. For those of you involved in the budgeting process, do you consider it a high value-added activity, or is the current budgeting process fraught with waste? The planning and budgeting processes of any organization are attempts to bring better control and alignment to the business. In effect, these processes are supposed to act like the brains of the organizations, sending the signals to the far reaches of the organization and defining the expectations and actions required—in essence, detailing what the *body* of the organization should do. If our goals are to make our organizations Lean enterprises, it would seem incumbent to make sure that the brain is in sync with the body. This chapter will address the issue of how well existing budgeting practices are aligned with a firm's attempts to become a Lean enterprise.

In most organizations, the traditional budgeting practice is the antithesis of a Lean enterprise. The budget process is not about customer pull; it is about push. Senior management determines the financial objectives and targets for the firm, and pushes the organization to reach these targets. If a company that is trying to become a Lean enterprise does not fundamentally change its traditional push budgeting process, it will be extremely difficult to change the culture and become a Lean organization. The way a firm measures, directs, and motivates people sends signals about the organization's culture, and the existing budgeting process, unfortunately, sends all the wrong signals.

The Beyond Budgeting Roundtable was started in 1998 and initially attempted to find ways of budgeting more effectively. The problem is making a poorly designed process a little "better" can really hurt a company. You wind up doing the wrong things a little faster, or you generate waste more quickly. Ultimately, the biggest waste is to do very efficiently what should not be done at all. With this in mind, the objective of the Beyond Budgeting Roundtable was to create a high value-added budgeting and planning process. This requires a total re-design of the existing methodology at most organizations.

During the Beyond Budgeting Roundtable's search for a better budgeting process, we discovered companies so good at budgeting, that they could effectively forecast without traditional budgets and consequently eliminated their budgeting process altogether. For example, the roundtable uncovered Guardian Industries, one of the world's largest manufacturers of float glass and fabricated glass products. Guardian is headquartered in Auburn Hills, Michigan, and has over 19,000 employees worldwide, representing 21 countries on five continents. It has never had a budget. The company is extremely proud of its management structure, which is specifically designed to avoid bureaucratic nonsense and allow the individual to flourish.[1]

If you are employed at a publicly held company, you may doubt whether such a dramatic change could ever take place at your company. In the fall of 2005, American Express eliminated its budget. Other companies, such as Time Warner Telecom, Charles Schwab, Millipore, and Unilever are in the process of redesigning their budgeting and planning processes.

Traditional Budgeting Pitfalls

There are many problems that can be identified with the traditional budgeting process. I have identified and discussed six particularly egregious pitfalls below.

Pitfall #1: Work harder! Do it more often!

So what is wrong with budgeting as we know it? We refer to it as "Do right and the seven dwarfs." Most people think they can fix budgeting if they just do it right. Just do more—more detail, more frequency, more of everything. If we just do it right, we can get the results we need. Nothing is wrong with the process; if we just get everybody to operate this way, work a little harder, and go through the budget one more time, it will eventually come out all right. This is a Newtonian, or mechanistic view of the world.

Pitfall #2: Budgets are costly.

Even with all of our concerted, conscientious efforts to resolve issues through budgeting, the problems still remain. Budgets cost too much and take too long to prepare. Hackett estimates that it requires an amazing 25,000 man-hours per billion dollars of revenue to prepare the annual budget.[2] While companies spend a tremendous amount of energy preparing budgets, how much real value does the budgeting process add? Studies repeatedly show that most people do not think budgeting adds any value.[3] Do companies ever honestly evaluate the return on this investment, or do their budgeting efforts continue mainly out of tradition?

Pitfall #3: Budgets do not add value.

If you disparage the concept that budgeting is mainly a wasteful activity, ask your co-workers in January how much value they attribute to budgets. Ask the same question of your co-workers again in March, May, or July, and see how long the relevant shelf-life of the budget really is. Budgets are often of limited value, because they are built on assumptions that are often out of date even before they are published.

Pitfall #4: Budgets can stifle performance.

Ideally, when a firm attains true Beyond Budgeting status, performance will begin to exceed the old budgeted numbers. This is in contrast to the traditional budgeting process, where the budget is generally considered the ultimate objective—the upper performance limit. When the budget is perceived as the hurdle for achievement, people have a natural tendency to quit after it is accomplished.

Pitfall #5: Budgets slow response time.

Budgets slow a firm's response time and limit creativity and innovation. Many times I have worked with a client company that became very excited about a new initiative or program, but was incapable of funding it due to the budget process. As the idea was routed through the corporate hierarchy, the typical response was, "That's a great idea, I just wish you would've submitted it last month." When I asked what happened last month, the typical response was, "Last month we could've gotten that project into the budget. I can't ask for that money now. If we wait nine months, and it's still a good idea, we can put it in next year's budget." My response has always been, "I'm sorry. I didn't know you were only open to innovation three months out of the year!" That is the problem with budgets; they can stifle potentially good programs. I can recall many stories of managers who sacrificed known profitable business opportunities because they did not want to go to corporate and ask for more capital. Budgets are known culprits for limiting a firm's responsiveness, innovation, and growth.

Pitfall #6: Budgets promote gaming and a lack of transparency.

Current budgeting practices involve intense negotiations between operating divisions and corporate staffs to arrive at minimally acceptable results. As the year unfolds, there is a reluctance to "fess up" to any pending budget shortfalls in the hope that the original budget commitment can still miraculously be achieved. This process reduces the ability of the company to address the real business issues and develop corrective action plans until long after the reality of the situation is known.

So why do companies waste significant dollars, resources, and time on a process that many people feel does not add value? The most common response is similar to answers given for other wasteful, ensconced activities: "We've always done it that way." Companies go through the same budgeting ritual year after year. Jack and Suzy Welch accurately summed up budgeting as follows:

The budgeting process at most companies has to be the most ineffective practice in management. It sucks the energy, time, fun, and big dreams out of an organization. It hides opportunity and stunts growth. It brings out the most unproductive behaviors in an organization, from sandbagging to settling for mediocrity. In fact, when companies win, in most cases it is despite their budgets, not because of them.[4]

Unfortunately, it takes a crystal ball to prepare a worthwhile budget, and such a tool has eluded all companies.

If your company has aspirations of becoming a Lean enterprise, the budgeting and planning process is another organizational change that must be part of the cultural transformation that takes place during the Lean journey.

Changing the Budget Process

It is virtually impossible to change a firm's entrenched budgeting process without changing the mindset, behavior, and score-keeping system of senior management. Remember, the CEO, COO, CFO, and other leaders of your organization reached their positions by being good at playing the game of business as it is currently defined and measured. So when we talk about changing to either Lean accounting, or Lean planning, we are changing a system that current leadership is comfortable with, excels at, and naturally wants to maintain. Leadership prefers to continue playing the game as it is currently designed, because they understand it and achieved their lofty positions by winning at it.

It is recognized that changing the budgeting and planning process can be a tremendous challenge. However, there are leaders that clearly understand the business, understand that the current budget gamesmanship can be destructive, and also understand that the current process is part of the problem. These leaders must use their leadership roles and entrepreneurial skills to become part of the solution.

The Traditional Budgeting Process

The traditional budgeting process is similar throughout most business organizations. The following discussion of the typical process is based upon personal experience and dialogue with many organizations.

Field organizations and divisions prepare for weeks for their initial budget submissions and related presentation to corporate in defense of their budget. During their presentation, field personnel often talk about how tough the environment is. They contend that by giving maximum effort and pulling out all the stops, their division just might do a little better than the prior year. For discussion purposes, assume field tells corporate that it will achieve "ten," which could represent ten million dollars of operating income.

Of course, field is selling low; it is sandbagging. Why does field feel that it is necessary to sandbag? The politically correct answer is simple: it is called expectation management. Bonus maximization could also be the reason. It is a lot easier to achieve a low target than it is to meet a stretch target. Therefore, the field organization always submits a budget as low as it thinks corporate will accept, but high enough so it does not jeopardize its position and total compensation opportunities.

Corporate, on the other hand, is also an expert at the budgeting game and understands that it has to challenge field operations. Corporate talks up the opportunities by focusing on the great market conditions, global opportunities, new products in the pipeline, and cost reduction possibilities. Corporate talks about every concept it can think of to leverage up the commitment, and correspondingly asks field to commit to "twenty," rather than its proposed "ten." Corporate feels the need to leverage up each of the field submissions, because it knows that if it allows the original submissions from all of the field operations, the total budget will be far below what corporate and the CEO have already committed to the Board of Directors and Wall Street. The individual budget submissions continue to go back and forth, trying to satisfy corporate's masked agenda. Even though corporate has a predetermined acceptable total in mind, it muddies the process with a higher proposed initial figure to each field operation, anticipating that compromises will be made on both sides until the real corporate objective is achieved.

The budget process is like a yo-yo, with extended posturing and debate. Field submits a new budget; corporate lets field know it is not good enough, so field has to do it again. Field adjusts one more time and corporate once again confirms that it is not good enough. Finally, after several rounds, field says, "Just tell me what you want the number to be; we're tired of guessing." Corporate facetiously responds, "We can't do that because then it would not be your budget. You have to own it." Field counters with, "I quit owning the budget after the first round. Now it's yours."

Do you wonder where the value-added is in this process? What a stream of wasteful activities! For three months, organizations are crippled and cannot work on other important projects because the company is preoccupied with negotiating budgets. Corporate says field needs to achieve twenty, field doggedly responds that it can only do ten. In the final meeting, they settle somewhere in the middle, e.g., fifteen. The field team contentedly leaves the final meeting with corporate, clears the building, and high-fives each other. They believe that fifteen will be tough, but achievable. Likewise, corporate leaves the meeting with satisfaction and high-fives. They are relieved because field raised its commitment from its initial submission of ten all the way to fifteen. Corporate thought it would be more difficult than it actually was to move field that far.

If you were a shareholder of this company, how good would you feel about the time and resources wasted on this annual charade? There were no customers involved in the process. All the innovation, all the big ideas, and all the energy of the management team has been depleted during the budget period and replaced with ineffective negotiations. This budgeting process and corresponding behavior are driven by the current management system, and must change. In their book, *Straight from the Gut*, Welch and Byrne call this an enervating exercise in minimization. This game is played because everyone knows that if you make the budget, corporate will give you a little pat on the back. But what happens if you miss the budget? If you miss the budget, you get a stick in the eye.[5] If you have aspirations of becoming a Lean company, it is important to overcome the reward/punishment environment related to making the budget.

Once a negotiated budget is finalized, it is neatly packaged into an impressive binder and distributed to the associates. When the extended field team initially reviews the budget, it makes sense as all of the math works. Most of the team members are not conversant enough with the details to understand the real traps that might be present, or the opportunities that may be lost. Accordingly, the field team pushes out the individual objectives, sets individual targets and timelines, and incorporates incentive plans for local leadership. Progress is reviewed monthly with the team, and it all appears quite logical.

However, as field operations proceed through the year, what happens when they start to fall short of the budget? Field typically argues for relief by explaining the extenuating circumstances, the tough competition, the tough economic environment, the new competitor, and any other excuse it can construe. Corporate still wants to achieve the original budget and requests an updated forecast, to which field responds with a new set of numbers that magically agrees with the original budget. Field temporarily satisfies corporate with reassurances that it will make up the budget shortfalls in the ensuing months.

As the year continues to unfold, field continues to struggle to achieve budget. After the first quarter is completed there might be a significant shortfall; yet field still submits a new forecast to achieve budget by year-end. After the second quarter is completed, field may still be significantly behind budget, but it will again submit an updated full-year forecast that somehow moves the division back to budget. Even if field continues its deficit at the end of the third quarter, it projects unfounded optimism by continuing to forecast budget achievement by year-end. This whole process, referred to as "forecasting to the wall," is depicted in Figure 12.1.

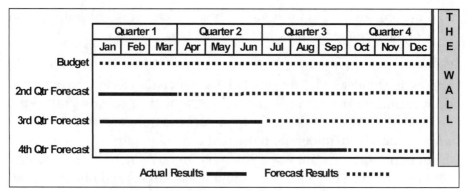

Figure 12.1: Forecasting to the Wall

The wall is field's current year-end number—the budget they have to achieve. After the first quarter of the fiscal year, the company forecasts the remaining nine months. At the half-year point, the company forecasts the remaining six months. Finally, after three quarters are completed, the company forecasts the final quarter's results. Somewhere in this process the company "walks through the wall" by forecasting another 12 months as it prepares the budget for the following year.

Forecasting to the wall is a forecasting exercise that requires meeting the current year's expected numbers, regardless of the circumstances. Forecasting, in a Lean sense, is not about submitting plans that always indicate budget attainment; instead it is a process to project the honest outlook of the business. The objective of Lean forecasting is coordination of the entire organization. On the other hand, forecasting only to see the year-end numbers is not about where the firm is going; it is about performance evaluation and perhaps, as discussed earlier, getting the proverbial stick in the eye. Forecasting to see if the division is going to make the year-end numbers is re-validating whether or not a manager needs a stick or not. It usually proceeds as follows:

1. At the end of the first quarter, "I know I'm behind, but I'm catching up."

2. As the second quarter is completed and the updated full year forecast is submitted, the thought is, "I know we are still behind, but we will catch up."

3. With the completion of the third quarter, you either have to catch up, or fess up.

In the instance when a business unit is behind budget, why does the general manager generally submit a new forecast that indicates the division will nevertheless achieve budget? What is really going through the general manager's mind? He/she is probably thinking, I know I am behind, but we are catching up, or perhaps that job transfer will come through, or the acquisition will muddy the waters; or I know we are behind, but I surely hope that resume is stimulating some interest on Monster.com. Managers prefer to avoid the truth in this kind of a budgeting and forecasting process because they know they are going to get a stick in the eye; why would they want three of them? And who knows, they might catch up. Miracles do happen. Or maybe they can think of a better explanation later; or their division can get merged; or the job transfer will come through in the nick of time.

The traditional management system drives this dysfunctional behavior. Company behavior is a function of the culture, which in turn is driven by the management systems. When the process is all about divisions forecasting to the wall, senior management is not going to get an honest answer, because they are not asking for an honest answer. Rather, they are simply asking for validation that the divisions are committed to and will achieve the budget.

When forecasting to the wall, the end of the year is some magical thing that we just smash into. In March we forecast through December as if the business only has nine months left, then in June we only forecast for six months as if the business only has another six months left, then in September, we only forecast three months out and begin the budget process for the upcoming year. When the process of constantly forecasting to the wall (fiscal year-end) concentrates only on performance evaluation, the divisions are not going to tell the truth. The process does not ask for the truth; it merely asks, "Are you still committed to the original budget?" The divisional managers are simply trying their best to manage expectations. When they have bad news, the divisional managers are trying to judiciously "bleed it in" without alarming corporate.

> The continual forecast updates do not ask for an honest assessment of where the company is headed. The process is really asking if local leadership is still committed to the original budget!

The problem with budgeting is that all of the waste that occurs in the initial stages is often repeated at each quarterly forecast update. The focus is either on delivering the minimally acceptable negotiated number, or in the case of a potential shortfall, avoiding "fessing up" until there is absolutely no other alternative.

Companies spend millions of dollars on Sarbanes-Oxley to get external transparency. Yet, the internal planning and control system is flawed, with organizations afraid to internally communicate their expectations. If companies have a budgeting and planning process that does not allow managers to share real information, how are they going to effectively run an enterprise? Even more perplexing is how they can expect to achieve a Lean culture, which routinely and aggressively exposes problems in order to address and resolve them immediately.

The Solution to the Annual Budgeting Quagmire

You can take solace in knowing that there are several ways to address the traditional budgeting pitfalls and problems that occur from this generally wasteful process. Recommendations for doing so are discussed below.

Recommendation #1: Migrate from annual budgets to five or six quarter rolling forecasts.

Manage the business via rolling forecasts that are far enough out that makes sense for your business. In most companies, the rolling forecast period is four to eight quarters, with five being the most prevalent. For some organizations, the rolling-forecast period is as short as two quarters. Time Warner Telecom forecasts two quarters. When I talked to Nevine White, Time Warner Telecom Vice President of Financial Planning and Analysis, I said, "Nevine, I've never heard of somebody just doing two quarters. Why is that?" She responded, "Steve, we talk to the field. And the field told us they couldn't see any further than that. Everything beyond that is just math. So we decided if somebody's going to do math, we would rather do it here at corporate so we would at least know what all the assumptions are."

A company should forecast as far out as they need to plan. The question becomes: How far out does a Lean enterprise need to plan and forecast? Typically, it does not go much further than the sales and operations plan.

There are some instances where you need longer-range forecasts, such as in capital spending. If a firm is in the semiconductor industry, and it has to build fabrication plants that require four years to build, it needs to have a capital forecast that goes out four years. There will be different forecasts for different purposes.

A client with whom I am working has a strong desire to move to a true rolling forecast and the Lean budgeting methodology. Unfortunately, the CFO got a little ahead of the process and asked for a four-quarter forecast into March of the following fiscal year. When the forecast was completed, it became obvious that the organization was not going to hit the December year-end numbers. Of course, all the discussion for the next three weeks was about the December numbers. Nobody cared about the fourth-quarter-out forecast that ended in March. Every time CEO's focus on fiscal year-end numbers instead of the rolling forecast, what are they really doing? It is not about where the firm is headed; it is about the division's budget performance commitment to the CEO for the current year. A critical element of moving to Lean budgeting and rolling forecasts is getting people out of the habit of only talking about that year-end number as if it is some magical point and nothing else matters.

Recommendation #2: Do not confuse budgets or forecasts with target performance!

Budgets (referred to as rolling forecasts in a Lean environment) and targets are not the same thing. A firm's target represents where it wants to go. The budget, or forecast, is where the firm is truly heading. It is helpful if budgets and targets are in alignment, but realistically, it rarely happens. The target is the medium-term aspiration of the company, and can be the three to five year out performance goals.

As an example, imagine sailing a boat: at any given time, are you apt to be exactly on course? It is more likely that you will be behind or ahead, and constantly adjusting course to reach your ultimate destination.

What happens when a firm blends budgets and targets, as in the case where a division submits a budget to achieve 10 percent operating income and corporate asks for 15 percent? If corporate continues to request a budget that must yield a 15 percent operating income, the division will eventually submit a budget that meets corporate's request. While the budget numbers and math will be satisfactory, corporate may not understand what is really going on in the business.

The budget/forecast should be a firm's best projection of operational performance at a point in time. If reality results in budgets or forecasts that are significantly different from initial company targets, then all of the time should be devoted to understanding the situation and working together with corporate to develop the appropriate strategies and action plans to close the gap. In essence, rather than negotiating numbers, the team focuses on developing a plan to close the gap between the current outlook and the desired outlook. Leadership should engage in vigorous dialogue with the management team to help develop a workable plan that will close the performance gap in a reasonable amount of time, with clearly defined programs, milestone dates, and identified process owners. The team should understand also the new plan's risks and probability for success. This is clearly more value-added work than the typical back-and-forth negotiations on meeting an arbitrary target.

Rather than depending on budgets that are simply an extension of the prior year's performance, General Electric utilizes "stretch" goals.

> In a stretch environment, the same field team is asked to come in with 'operating plans' that reflect their dreams—the highest numbers they think they had a shot at: their 'stretch.' The discussion revolves around new directions and growth, energizing stuff. The team leaves with everyone on both sides of the table having a pretty good understanding of what the business will do and what they'll try to do. An operating plan is put together reflecting that reality. The team knows they're going to be measured against the prior year and relative

performance against competitors—not against a highly negotiated internal number. Their stretch target keeps them reaching. We've never yet made a 'stretch operating plan.' Yet we've always done a helluva lot better than we ever thought we'd do—and more than Wall Street expected.[6]

The reality approach is very different than simply telling the field units that they have to hit a certain target, with the hidden message that we really do not care how you achieve it. In the traditional approach, the motivation is just to keep reassuring corporate that you will get it done. A company is far better off if they focus on the true current state, develop action plans to achieve the desired future state, and then monitor progress relative to these achievement plans. By focusing on successfully implementing carefully designed initiatives and utilizing countermeasures when specific initiatives head off course, the numbers will begin to take care of themselves and full transparency will be achieved. This is a true Lean plan, do, check, adjust (PDCA) approach to Lean budgeting, where each subsequent rolling forecast represents the true process of checking progress and adjusting the game plan based on reality.

PDCA - Plan - Do - Check - Act (Adjust)

A methodology for improvement consisting of the following elements: Plan - A change aimed at improvement. In this phase, analyze what you intend to improve, looking for areas that hold opportunities for change. Do - Implement the change you decided on in the plan phase. Check or Study - What was learned? What went wrong? After you have implemented the change for a short time, you must determine how well it is working. Is it really leading to improvement in the way you had hoped? Act, sometimes referred to as Adjust - Adopt the change, abandon it, or run through the cycle again. After planning a change, implementing, and then monitoring it, you must decide whether it is worth continuing that particular change. If the change led to a desirable improvement, you may consider expanding the change to a different area.[7]

Recommendation #3: Create an adaptive organization so forecast accuracy is less important and budgeting is unnecessary.

From your experience, how would you evaluate the capability of companies to accurately forecast? Preparing a viable traditional budget requires accurate forecasts, and unfortunately, no one has a crystal ball. For instance, what company can predict what the price of oil will be in the coming year, month by month? Can you forecast what the price of steel will be; can you predict what your competitors will do in response to your new initiatives; and can you accurately forecast exchange rates? The answers are obvious, yet almost every budget is affected by the price of oil, steel, or exchange rates. Preparing an accurate budget is dependent upon accurately predicting the unpredictable future.

Everybody wants to forecast accurately. As a consultant, I am uncomfortable when CEOs make unrealistic demands for forecast accuracy. I do not know how to help them forecast accurately in a rapidly changing world. I imagine your business is similar to every other business—somewhat unpredictable. In Lean budgeting, the goal is to build a system that is not dependent upon predicting an unpredictable world. Instead, the goal is to focus a firm's system on making it adaptive and responsive to whatever happens. A fast, flexible, adaptive organization does not need to forecast out very far; it just needs to see what has to change before it is too late to react.

For instance, what if a company could make appropriate changes daily? With daily responsiveness, a company certainly would not need a long-range forecast. The essence of a Lean enterprise is to build a responsive system that requires little inventory and is capable of mixed model production to meet market demand. Lean budgeting is also about building a responsive and flexible company by eliminating the waste in the traditional budgeting process in order to create a more adaptive company. Why would a Lean enterprise utilize a push budgeting system instead of becoming a truly Lean organization in all respects? The logical extension of what Lean companies need to do in an evolving, ever-changing environment is to build a management planning and control system that can respond quickly.

Companies that demand forecast accuracy usually receive it in one of two ineffective methods. The first method is, unfortunately, patterned after companies such as WorldCom and Freddie Mac, which used accounting methods to manipulate results. "We've tried everything. We've sold everything. We've cut all the costs. Now we're looking for an accounting miracle."

The second, more acceptable, but stifling method for assuring budget achievement is to aim for a very conservative goal. If division leadership predicts that they can grow their business anywhere from 4% to 12%, what will they likely put in their budget? Most of the time, they will rationally submit the minimally acceptable growth rate. Even though leadership realizes they can easily surpass the lower targets that were accepted by corporate, they will generally be reluctant to exceed the budget. They want to save some "wiggle room" for the next budgeting negotiation cycle. Because they are rewarded for meeting a set target, the team may logically collapse any remaining potential as soon as achievement of the budgeted target becomes a reality. Their thoughts are that if the objective is to achieve 4% growth, then they should be satisfied as soon as it is attained. As is evident, the most insidious part of budgets is that they rob potential. Divisions meet the minimally acceptable targets by forgetting about all that is possible—all the stretch, reach, and perfection. All of those collapse on the minimally negotiated number. This perspective contradicts and thwarts what a Lean company is trying to accomplish. Even I have faced situations where I have confused my targeted budget with what is possible. The focal point of the traditional budget is the initial negotiated numbers where everything centers on minimization as opposed to maximization. On the other hand, Lean strategies concentrate on being adaptive and responsive to the customer. It is critical to build a management system that allows firms to respond to opportunities in the marketplace.

In their recent article, Lindsay and Libby introduce some pioneering budgeting concepts employed by Dr. Jan Wallander at Svenska Handelsbanken AB (Handelsbanken) in Stockholm, Sweden. Wallander was an economist for twenty years before taking the position of CEO at Svenska Handelsbanken. His job as an economist was simply to predict the future, and his only inescapable conclusion was that he was nearly always wrong. When he interviewed for the CEO position at Svenska Handelsbanken, Dr. Wallander indicated that if offered the position, he would do away with the existing budgeting process, which he subsequently did. His philosophy was "Why build a management system that's always wrong?"

> Handelsbanken began operations in 1871 with 12 employees working the Schinkel Palace located in the Old Town of Stockholm, Sweden. Through internal growth and acquisitions, Handelsbanken transformed itself from a Stockholm-based bank to a national Swedish bank.
>
> In the 1960s, the bank's objective was to be the largest bank in Scandinavia based on the strategy of increasing business volume. It operated within a traditional multi-divisional model. Senior managers created strategy, made the key decisions, and allocated resources. Middle managers communicated senior management's directives to the front line who then implemented them. Budgets were used as the primary tool to plan, coordinate, and manage capital.
>
> Costs rose significantly during the period due to a growing bureaucracy, the handling of a large number of small accounts, and increasing marketing expenditures. The bank experienced a large financial loss in the late 1960s and was in trouble with the regulatory authorities.
>
> Dr. Jan Wallander was hired as the CEO in 1970 to help the bank get through this crisis. His policies have continued to provide the foundation for the modern Svenska Handelsbanken and the three CEOs who have followed Wallander.
>
> Since Dr. Wallander joined the bank it has achieved tremendous organic growth. In 2002 Handelsbanken had 560 branches and 10,000 employees across the four Nordic countries and twenty offices in other world trade centers.[7]

While Dr. Wallander was serving as CEO, Handelsbanken was a perennial top performer from any perspective, be it Moody's rankings, key performance ratios, customer satisfaction, employee turnover, or shareholder returns. Wallander stepped down as CEO of Handelsbanken in 1991 and served as Chairman until 2002, when he became Chairman Emeritus.[8]

> In Wallander's view, the usefulness of budgets depended on the validity of the assumptions underlying the construction, which fell into two basic types: "the same weather tomorrow as today" and "different weather tomorrow." Under the former construct, the budget was prepared under the assumption that management's current knowledge was an appropriate basis on which to prepare the budget. In effect, you were telling people to work as they were doing, and that perhaps they should attempt to increase sales and be a little more efficient. However, he believed that you did not need to have an intricate budgeting system to accomplish this.

> On the other hand, if you could forecast that a very different situation was going to exist, resulting in very different trends that required major changes to operations, then budgeting would prove to be enormously useful if the forecast turned out to be accurate. However, Wallander's previous experience suggested that such an outcome was rare. "How can you forecast something for which you have no experience?" Moreover, Wallander believed that psychologically, it is difficult for humans to perceive that something new is on its way even when, in hindsight, it is difficult to comprehend how one could have missed the signs.[9]

Recommendation # 4: Stop relying on Excel spreadsheets.

Excel spreadsheets should not be relied upon for forecasting tools, because they do not explain what is actually going on in the business. Rather than preparing a quantified spreadsheet based on prior data, it is suggested that you visualize what your expectations are for your firm's immediate future. Most people use spreadsheets for historical comparisons between expected numbers and actual numbers to determine variations from expectations. The problem then becomes determining whether the variations from expectations are normal variations (noise, as Deming would call it), or anomalies that need to be investigated further. The vast majority of time spent in variance analysis represents wasteful efforts in examining normal variation. This waste of time would be more obvious if the variance data were plotted on run charts, and normal variation was better understood by everyone.

Recommendation # 5: Link compensation plans to value creation for relative and actual performance.

The budgeting process is considered a critical negotiation because incentive compensation is usually linked to the original budget commitment. A lower budget commitment leads to a greater probability of maximum bonus payouts. As the year unfolds, and budget attainment becomes difficult, management will often ask for relief, as they try to explain away the performance shortfalls. Seasoned managers will never quit negotiating incentive compensation payments until their checks have been cut. This process creates a natural incentive to lowball the budget.

Additionally, this process creates a fixed compensation target rather than a relative target, which can lead to poor business decisions. Assume that your company had a 10 percent sales and profit growth target for the coming year and ultimately realized 15 percent growth in both categories, thereby exceeding the budget commitment. In a situation such as this that had fixed budgets, incentive payouts might be maxed out at 10 percent sales and profit growth. Does this make sense? What if this company participated in the Telecom sector in 1999 when the market actually grew about 50 percent? This company would be paying out maximum bonuses at 10 percent growth in a market that grew 50 percent. Should rewards be given to management, even though their company may have experienced tremendous erosion in market share?

Roll the clock forward in this example by two years. Assume the goal again is to grow sales and profits 10 percent. At the end of the year, the company experienced only 5 percent sales and profit growth. Yet, the sales manager argues for maximum payout of bonuses or the company will risk losing a number of its sales force to the competition. Often in such a scenario, finance will simply state that because actual results did not achieve at least 80 percent of budget, there will be no incentive payments. What if this company was competing in the semiconductor industry in the year 2001 when semi-conductor sales plummeted 20 percent? How would you rate the performance of the sales force if they grow sales 5 percent in a market that is declining 20 percent? The company would likely want to retain the sales force irrespective that actual performance was lower than budgeted.

These two examples illustrate the pitfalls of fixed, negotiated budget numbers. To avoid this, we suggest changing compensation strategies by tying a portion of compensation to the value created and the actual improvements made, rather than to some negotiated budget number. Incentive compensation can be linked to a value-based measure, such as economic value added. Forget what was negotiated; evaluate and reward what is actually produced.

Because Wallander wanted people setting their own objectives, "no formalized, ex-ante goal-setting process existed at Handelsbanken." Continuous improvement was encouraged by requiring each region and branch to set their own relative performance measures. Everyone was automatically focused on future expectations, rather than centering on their annual budget preparations. Relative financial measures were used at each level of the bank. Handelsbanken compared itself to its competitors; regional company banks compared themselves to each other; and branches were compared to other branches within the region per selected performance measures.[10]

Wallander did not believe in individual financial incentives, explaining that "managers will only strive to achieve ambitious goals if they know that their 'best efforts' will be recognized and not punished if they fail to get all the way."[11]

Recommendation Summary

Business would be better served if accountants spent more time on value-added activities and future opportunities. They should chart critical data and separate normal variation from special-case variation. The focus should be on analyzing the handful of items that are key drivers of the business. The typical efforts of spending 80 percent of the time gathering data and 20 percent analyzing it need to be reversed. Accountants would be more relevant to business operations if they spent 20 percent of their time collecting and reporting data, and the remainder of their time deciphering it and providing guidance. With only a finite amount of time available, the more time spent in traditional bookkeeping responsibilities, the less time there is for critical analysis.

BUDGET CHANGE AT AMERICAN EXPRESS

American Express is a good example of successfully transitioning from a traditional budgeting system to a leaner, rolling-forecast system. The elimination of traditional budgeting at American Express was a natural progression, rather than a planned event. Gary Crittenden, CFO of American Express from 2000 to 2006 (currently CFO of Citigroup) instituted a series of initiatives under the umbrella name of Finance Transformation. Mr. Crittenden had three major objectives, one of which was to transform the planning process. His planning transformation intention was to put in a rolling forecast that would speed up the company's decision cycle. American Express wanted to better define its future objectives, identify the investments required, and determine how to accelerate achieving its objectives.

In order to focus everyone's attention on attaining these carefully defined expectations, American Express implemented rolling forecasts and eliminated any reporting of budget numbers. All reporting of results focused on comparing actual performance to the latest forecast. After following this process for a year, the company was planning for the following year's budget, and realized that it was no longer necessary, as they already had a 12-month rolling forecast in place. In September 2005, both corporate and field operations agreed that their budgets had become obsolete, since for most of the previous year they had not referred to the budgeted numbers for evaluating actual performance. In less than a three-week time span, American Express decided to eliminate their budgets because essentially nobody was using them. Management felt comfortable managing by the rolling forecast, comfortable that they had their plans in place, and comfortable that their business was under control. They were adaptively watching their expenses based on critical ratios to revenues.

American Express's confidence in eliminating its budgets was buoyed by the knowledge that if its new replacement process of rolling forecasts did not work, it could immediately revert to the traditional budgeting process. American Express never made specific plans to eliminate the annual budgeting process; it just happened soon after implementing rolling forecasts and discovering that everyone had subsequently stopped using the budgets.

In addition to rolling forecasts, American Express began using a scenario-planning process. Rather than prepare only one rolling forecast, the company identified its business risks, and planned numerous scenarios addressing these risks. This allowed the company to continuously assess the direction of its business and put in place appropriate plans in the event that certain market conditions unfolded. This sensitivity analysis was much more effective than single-point budgets.

The goal of Lean budgeting is to build an adaptive Lean system that is responsive to the customer, listens to the marketplace, and moves quickly. Lean budgeting means transforming planning from the annual, look-back process, hope to negotiate where we will go practice, into an organization that focuses on the risks they face, the countermeasures that could be used to address those risks, and the identification of key indicators that clarify the strategies and tactics that should be deployed. American Express created a play book and a host of scenarios that became an effective part of its rolling-forecast process.

SUMMARY

Traditional budgeting runs the risk of achieving goals through manipulation and collapsing potential. Lean budgeting attempts to avoid the ineffective activities of forecasting to the wall, confusing forecasting with targets, and insisting on forecast accuracy in an unpredictable world. Lean budgeting does not confuse targets with reality and requires an honest assessment of business potential at all times via rolling forecasts. Rolling forecasts should be prepared for fixed time frames, typically four to six quarters. Management should focus on critical areas by monitoring key indicators. When the rolling forecast differs from the desired outcome, the value-added effort includes vigorous debate and planning that lead to an action plan with appropriate milestones and responsibility matrices for achieving target performance.

Managers will be motivated to excel only when they feel comfortable that their best efforts will be appreciated, and that they will not be criticized or threatened when uncontrollable events preclude their achievement of some arbitrary benchmark. The essence of Lean leadership is to expose opportunities and work as a team in order to achieve results that may have been considered improbable, or even impossible.

At Handelsbanken, Wallander conceded that "trying to predict discontinuous change" was "beyond human capability." Instead, he believed that the most important task was to be able to respond promptly and appropriately to the current situation. "The use of a fixed budget was considered to be antithetical to this requirement. Thus, his dictum: A budget will thus either prove to be roughly right, and then it will be trite, or it will be disastrously wrong, in which case it will be dangerous." His conclusion was to simply scrap budgeting![12]

As previously stated, American Express never planned on eliminating its budget. My advice is that if you decide to eliminate budgeting, do not even mention it. Just stop asking questions about the budget. Stop referring to the budget on all reports. Stop preparing budget variance explanations. At American Express, they just started shifting their planning process. They started comparing performance to the last forecast, and literally, the budget process just atrophied and fell off.

Change by stealth is my number one recommendation for eliminating the budgeting process. The reason we recommend the evolutionary approach to change is that everyone becomes comfortable with the new system without even recognizing the dramatic differences. It is all about showing your team a different and better way to plan and control the business.

CHAPTER 12 ENDNOTES

1. Guardian Industries, About Guardian, http://www.guardian.com/en/about.html (April, 2007).

2. Jeremy Hope and Robin Fraser, *Beyond Budgeting: How Managers Can Break Free from the Annual Performance Trap* (Boston: Harvard Business School Press, 2003), 6.

3. Cedric Read, Hans-Dieter Scheuermann and The SAP Financials Team, *The CFO as Business Integrator* (John Wiley & Sons, 2003), 171–73.

4. Jack Welch and Suzy Welch, *Winning* (Harper Collins, 2003), 189.

5. Jack Welch and John A. Byrne, *Jack: Straight from the Gut* (New York: Warner Business Books, 2001), 385.

6. *Business Management Systems*, Value Curve, Glossary, http://www.valucurve.com/glossary.html#s (May, 2007)

7. R. Murray Lindsay and Theresa Libby, "Svenska Handelsbanken: Accomplishing Radical Decentralization Through Beyond Budgeting," 1–2.

8. Ibid., p.2.

9. Ibid., p. 6.

10. Ibid., p. 10.

11. Ibid., p. 11.

12. Ibid., pp. 6-7.

13

USING LEAN PRINCIPLES
IN HUMAN RESOURCES

T he primary purpose of this book concerns the changes required in the accounting and financial functions to accommodate and support the Lean transformation process. It is important to remember that Lean philosophies and Lean tools must be applied throughout an organization to truly achieve world class performance. Chief financial officers are often responsible for the Human Resource function, one of the support areas that benefits a great deal from the application of Lean principles. Thus, we felt it would be helpful to present a "real-world" example of how Lean principles enabled dramatic improvements in one aspect of the human resource function.

This chapter presents a case study demonstrating how Lean tools can be applied to radically improve a critical human resource practice, associate reviews. An effective associate review process is even more critical during a Lean transformation because job functions expand, pay for performance programs are implemented, the number of job descriptions and job grades are greatly reduced, and the distinction between direct and indirect labor begins to disappear. It is necessary to have a high quality, on-time, well delivered, and efficient associate review process in place to support the Lean journey.

Background

A division of a capital equipment manufacturing company, which will be referred to as MLC, had been on the Lean journey for a number of years and had instituted many Lean tools in the plant, such as 5S programs, setup reduction, total productive maintenance, work cells, and kanbans. As the Lean journey progressed, MLC felt the need to change its shop-floor associate pay practices from a traditional across-the-board annual pay increase, to a pay-for-performance system more aligned with the Lean journey.

The specific objectives of the new pay system are listed below.

1. Reward associates for acquiring new skills.

2. Encourage flexibility and mobility.

3. Promote a team-based environment.

4. Encourage use of Lean tools.

5. Promote safety awareness.

6. Achieve continuous improvement.

Figure 13.1 illustrates the pay-for-performance matrix implemented at MLC over the course of a 12-month period. (Due to space limitations, the rating matrices for quality, productivity, and continuous improvement have been excluded.)

Machine Shop Associate Assessment & Performance Matrix					
Rating	Safety	Primary Work Center 5S Score (If Applicable)	Primary Work Center Set-up Reduction Score (If Applicable)	Primary Work Center TPM Score (If Applicable)	Cross Training and Individual Flexibility
Below Expectations	Does not always follow safety procedures.	0-100	External operations are not performed in a consistent manner to minimize set-up times. Setup times recorded sporadically.	TPM books maintained sporadically.	No change, can only operate one or two machine tools and unwilling to learn new work centers or processes.
Meets Expectations	Adheres to all safety guidelines & maintains good safety record.	101-200	External operations being performed while machine is running, operator provides suggestions to reduce setup times. Setup times accurately recorded.	TPM books and schedule maintained daily.	Can run multiple machine tools, willing to learn new work centers or processes.
Exceeds Expectations	Maintains good safety record and provides suggestions to improve plant safety.	201 - 300	External operations always performed while the machine is running, all setup times accurately recorded, operator implements own suggestions supported by documented improvements.	Maintains daily TPM books & TPM tickets. Provides maintenance input on needed machine repairs. Suggests improvements.	Always willing to accept new responsibilities. Seeks opportunities to learn new machine tools and processes. Totally flexible.

Figure 13.1: Pay for Performance Matrix

Similar matrices were developed for each area of the plant, including line associates and supervision. While the new methodology was very logical, its implementation was challenging.

Recognition of the need for a radical change to MLC's review process came about by overhearing a conversation between two machinists.

While walking down the hallway, the Lean leader of MLC, who we will refer to as Jim, overheard two machinists complaining about the delays in their performance reviews and evaluating the potential amount of their retroactive pay increases. One machinist mentioned that he hoped the company would start applying interest to the retroactive pay increase he expected to receive. (As a matter of background, this conversation occurred during the time period when the Federal Reserve had just raised interest rates numerous times over the prior 18 months, and interest rates were once again becoming meaningful). The second machinist agreed with the comment, joking about the difference between the money that they deserved from the postponed pay increases and the amount that they would actually receive (the difference related to time value of money concepts).

After overhearing this conversation, Jim headed straight to the Director of Human Resources' office to inquire about the status of reviews at the company. Jim was interested in the critical metrics being used in the performance review process, namely quality, cost, and delivery. While exact metrics were not available, it became apparent that the quality of reviews was very poor; reviews were inconsistent, highly dependent on the particular reviewer, and subject to numerous rewrites. An evaluation of the costs spent on the reviews revealed that they were excessive, with too much time spent on non-value added activities. Finally, delivery, which referred to on-time performance, was well below expectations, since reviews were considerably behind schedule.

Not only was the review process failing to deliver quality and timely results to its customers, the hourly and salaried workforce, the process was also generating a lot of non-value added work for the accounting department. Each late review required accounting to painstakingly calculate retroactive pay increases. Adding the additional task of calculating interest on retroactive pay increases would only increase the amount of wasted time spent on this rework process. The correct course of action was to eliminate the root cause of the problem.

Revamping the Performance Review Process

After discussing the waste in the review process with the Human Resources Director, Jim formed a cross-functional team to organize a kaizen event with the objective of implementing an associate review process consistent with the goals of MLC. The team members developed a current state map of the review process and were shocked when they quantified the metrics. The total value-added time for a review was 5.2 hours; yet the total production lead time ranged from 144 to 174 days. For the review process, production lead time started when the Human Resources department first sent out the paperwork to initiate the review, and it concluded when the review was administered and the payroll changes were entered into the PeopleSoft software. The team discovered that on-time performance was only 25 percent, and a number of reviews were over six months past due. Given the circumstances, it was no surprise that MLC associates were beginning to question the absence of interest on their retroactive pay increases.

While the metrics helped define the opportunity, the bigger issue that MLC needed to address was respect for its people. The primary focus of the kaizen event was not the elimination of the wasted effort caused by delinquent pay increases; more importantly, the event stressed the obvious need to provide timely and effective performance reviews to all associates. It is not possible to attain a successful Lean transformation without making people the priority. Understanding this concept, the kaizen team set about utilizing the Lean tool kit to develop a more robust associate review process that demonstrated MLC truly cared about and respected its workforce.

"Just the Facts" Information

Critical information is prepared in advance of every kaizen event to insure that the kaizen team productively focuses on solutions, rather than debating facts. The actual data are part of the "Just the Facts" information-sharing portion at the start of each event. Some of the MLC historical data shared with the team are depicted in the following charts.

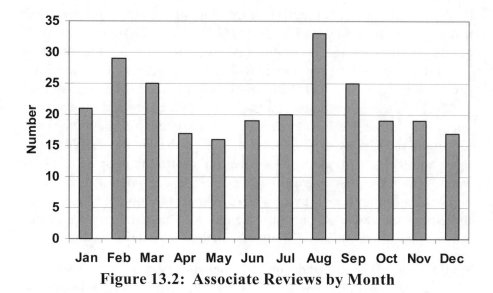

Figure 13.2: Associate Reviews by Month

Over the course of a year, each of the 260 associates at this site is scheduled to be reviewed on their anniversary hiring date. As depicted in Figure 13.2, the actual review dates are randomly distributed throughout the year. With approximately 250 workdays per annum, the takt time for each review is approximately one day. In other words, the process must be capable, on average, of completing one review each day in order to meet "customer demand" (achieve associate satisfaction) with timely associate performance reviews.

As stated at the outset, one of the objectives of this kaizen event was to achieve 100 percent on-time performance for MLC associate reviews. First, the team had to quantify the current state of on-time performance. After a thorough review of prior year activity, it was determined that on-time performance for associate reviews was only 25 percent. More revealing, however, was that reviews were much more than just slightly past due as shown in Figure 13.3.

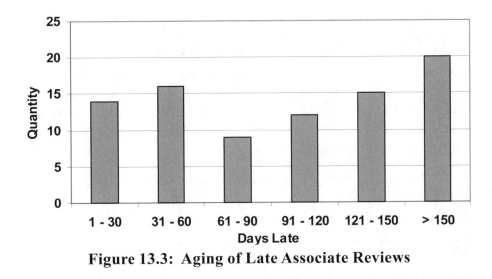

Figure 13.3: Aging of Late Associate Reviews

Of the 150 associates that were reviewed over the prior year, 86, or 57 percent were late. (Another 110 associates were not reviewed during the year.) Even more disturbing, more than half of the late reviews were over three months delinquent—evidence that the associates were justified in inquiring about interest on their retroactive raises. There is irony in examining MLC's performance of associate reviews, noting that the current process was hardly consistent with the theme of Lean and the constant pursuit of achieving perfection in quality, cost, and delivery.

In the kaizen event, late reviews were further stratified by area of the company and by individual leader to assess if there was a localized problem or a company problem. The team discovered that the problem was pervasive and symptomatic of a flawed process throughout the company.

Value Stream Mapping Results

The kaizen team's first order of business was the development of a current state value stream map of the entire associate review process. The end-to-end process, which required a team effort since no one individual truly understood every step of the process, was mapped on the walls of the meeting room. Team members simulated the performance review process by walking through the actual paperwork trail, tracing every process step, and recording the information in the various data boxes on the value stream map. The data boxes contained all of the relevant information, including the required data entry tasks and identification of the relevant software packages, the number of handoffs and queue time at each stage of the review process, the number of different forms and databases utilized, the various rework loops of reviews snaking their way through the approval process, and finally, the actual quality of the review itself.

After carefully mapping the entire review process, the team members were amazed at all of the historically "accepted" waste. Summary results of the value stream map are documented in Figure 13.4.

Value Added Time	5.2 Hours
Total Production Lead-Time	144 - 174 Days
Value Added Time to Total Production Lead-Time	0.20%

Figure 13.4: Results of Value Stream Mapping

The mapping process revealed that the entire review process, from the time Human Resources initiates the process by sending out the appropriate forms, to the time the review is actually completed and the new data are entered into the appropriate systems, should take only 5.2 hours in a waste-free world. Instead, the current process ranged from 144 to 174 days.

Production lead time includes all value-added as well as non-value added activities to complete a process. When mapping production processes, it is very common to find processes where less than 5 percent, or even less than 1 percent, is value-added. Via participation in many Lean events, manufacturing personnel have become somewhat accustomed to learning how inefficient their processes have become. However, when using the same Lean tools to reveal the waste in office processes, the initial results are often startling to teammates that have not been exposed to this type of analysis.

During the development of any current state value stream map, the "5 whys" are often used to uncover the reasons for the various wasteful activities undertaken to complete a process. During the MLC human resource event, the team members were encouraged to drill down into the data to better understand the performance review process. They repeatedly asked why certain forms were used, why multiple databases had to be updated independently, why the more difficult reviews were the longest past due, and why the Human Resources Department kept pushing more paperwork into the system despite the fact that reviews were not being filled out and returned in a timely manner. It is during this mapping process that the genesis of the future state value stream map begins to unfold, as the team uncovers the current shortcomings and starts to outline a new, improved process.

Every event usually has its critical "ah ha" moment, where the participants are, figuratively, hit on the side of the head by a two by four, and realize how a simple change would radically improve the process. In this particular event, that "ah ha" moment occurred when everyone realized that the review process did not begin until human resources handed out the paperwork 30 days in advance of the expected review completion date. One team member asked why the reviewers waited for the paperwork to start the review process when they already knew everyone's hiring anniversary date and had all of the necessary review forms available on demand. The associate review write-up should be prepared throughout the year, not batch processed right before the due date.

The kaizen team participants from manufacturing were eager to apply typical Lean metrics, such as on-time performance, quality, first pass yield, and standard work-in-process, to the associate review process. They also wanted to know how the performance review process could incorporate some of the foundational elements of Lean, such as standard work, pull, and flow. Initially, MLC office personnel were confused about identifying applications of Lean methods to their office processes. As the manufacturing team members illustrated the similarities in utilizing Lean tools in manufacturing and the office, the solutions became more obvious.

The first item the team focused on was eliminating push production and reducing work-in-process inventory. The current review process continually batched review forms and "injected" them into the system at the end of each month, regardless of the current status of reviews already in the system. The team compared this inefficiency to the traditional manufacturing process of pushing raw material into a plant regardless of potential downstream bottlenecks. In Lean manufacturing, the goal is to achieve pull and flow whereby material is pulled through the system by replacing only that which has been consumed. This insures that the material is pulled into the process only when necessary, based on actual activity, not on inaccurate forecasts. Likewise, the goal in Lean is single-piece flow, rather than batch processing. The combination of very small batches and pull production yields tremendous reductions in work-in-process inventory, as well as improvements in quality.

The MLC kaizen team discovered that there were enormous numbers of reviews pushed into the review process and not completed. Any time a process takes an extended time to complete, work-in-process inventories expand proportionally. Since the review process took months to complete, the amount of paperwork circulating in the business grew exponentially. The team estimated that about one hundred reviews were currently "in play." This scenario is analogous to work-in-process in a production environment. Exacerbating the problem, Human Resources injected more inventory into the system as each new batch of monthly hiring anniversaries approached. There was no mechanism to stop the flow of new paperwork into the system, and so it continued regardless of the late reviews still hung up in the process.

The solution to this problem was the adoption of a kanban system for performance reviews. The team first determined the maximum number of reviews that would be allowed in the system (the standard level of work-in-process) at any one time. The team then made up an equivalent number of kanban cards, and a kanban card accompanied each packet of review forms. A review form packet would only be released into the system when a completed review form and the associated kanban card were returned to Human Resources. A visual board was created to indicate the kanban cards in circulation. If these kanban cards were not returned in time, a follow-up call would be made to the appropriate manager. This simple but effective step changed the process dramatically. Figure 13.5 illustrates the associate review kanban card.

```
+--------------------------------------------------------+
|           ASSOCIATE REVIEW KANBAN CARD                 |
|                                                        |
|  Gate Keeper:                 John Doe                 |
|                                                        |
|  Kanban Replenishment:        Qty - 1 pc.              |
|                                                        |
|  Card Return Location:        John Doe's Office        |
|                                                        |
|  Card 1 of 5  Associate to be reviewed:   Jane Smith   |
|               Review due by:              March        |
+--------------------------------------------------------+
```

Figure 13.5: Associate Review Kanban Card

All managers have their own set of kanban cards to use. Managers that oversee 24 reviews a year might elect to have four kanban cards in the system at any one time (two months of activity) for their standard work-in-process. One kanban card would be attached to the paperwork for each of the four individuals. No additional reviews would be initiated until a card was returned with a completed review. This process results in a true pull system, similar to any material kanban used in the production process.

During the MLC kaizen event, the team also felt that the future state would benefit a great deal from a visual schedule board. A visual performance scorecard that is maintained in total, and by each value stream leader, was developed by the team. Figure 13.6 illustrates the visual board currently in use. (Due to space limitations, the visual board is an abridged version that only includes six months of the year.)

PERFORMANCE APPRAISAL VISUAL BOARD
FY 2007

	JAN	FEB	MAR	APR	MAY	JUN	Full Year Total
Joe Smith	●● ●● ●●	●● ●● ●●	●● ●● ●●	●● ◐● ●●	○ ○ ○ ○ ○	○ ○ ○ ○ ○ ○	65
Total	5	5	4	5	5	6	65
% On-Time	100%	100%	100%	80%			95%

1 Doe	Palm	Walter	Friedery	Fuchs	Stansbury
2 Smith	Cunningham	Luciano	Faulkner	Lin	Johanson
3 Jones	Carey	Small	Mathews	Fields	Brown
4 Wallace	Coates	Wahl	Stock	Hernandez	Pryor
5 Roberts	Koningisor		Hampton	Gobson	Levy
6					Teres

● = Complete
○ = Incomplete

Figure 13.6: Performance Visual Board

As Figure 13.6 depicts, Joe Smith, the leader of the area measured, is ultimately responsible for 65 reviews during the course of a year. Since everyone in his value stream does not report directly to him, Joe does not personally perform each review. However, he has to sign off on each review. The annual review schedule is published in advance for the entire year. Each person reviewed is represented by a blank oval on the visual board. When the review is completed on time, the oval is shaded black. If a review is late, it is shaded grey until it is completed. At that point it will be shaded half black and half white to indicate that the review was completed late.

Figure 13.6 illustrates that Joe Smith has completed 95 percent of the reviews on time through April and one late review is still open. Kanban cards for the next ten people have been injected into the system as indicated by highlighted names at the bottom of the visual board. Area leaders would typically have their own specific chart in their individual work areas. A chart for the entire company is maintained in a central hallway for all to see. Since any late review and the associated grey circles are conveniently visible to everyone in the company, area leaders take the process very seriously. It is amazing how sensitive people become to these incomplete circles next to their names.

Figure 13.7 depicts the actual Performance Appraisal Visual Board developed by the kaizen team and implemented at MLC. It shows only the first six months of the initial year of the new associate review process; however, both the horizontal and vertical totals include twelve months of data. The process changes at MLC, as described above, resulted in a steady climb of on-time performance reviews, from a low point of 13 percent to 100 percent in nine months.

PERFORMANCE APPRAISAL VISUAL BOARD
FY 2006

	JAN	FEB	MAR	APR	MAY	JUN	Total
Brown	◐	◐	◐	●		◐	7
Carlson	●		●	◐		◐	8
Herrara	◐ ◐ ◐	●	◐	●			17
Jones	◐ ◐ ◐ ◐ ●	◐ ◐	◐ ●	◐	● ◐		22
Simpson	◐ ◐ ◐ ● ◐ ◐ ◐	◐ ● ● ◐	◐ ● ◐	◐ ● ● ◐ ◐ ●	◐ ● ● ◐	● ● ◐ ● ◐ ◐	57
Total	24	18	16	22	29	25	260
% On-Time	13%	28%	38%	45%	62%	80%	70%

● = Completed On Time
◐ = Completed Late

Figure 13.7: Performance Appraisal Board – FY 2006

Because of the backlog of late reviews that had to be processed, it took nine stressful months of concerted effort to catch up and complete all performance reviews. By September of the first year of implementing the new associate review process, on-time performance at MLC reached 100 percent and remained at that level for the next few months. There were occasional late reviews due to unscheduled circumstances, such as an associate taking unexpected sick leave, but these exceptions were rare.

Achieving standard work-in-process and utilizing a pull system are well established process improvement techniques. However, the issue of quality is equally important and still needed to be addressed for the performance review process. A value stream map illuminated the number of times an individual review was recycled through the sign-off process for various levels of supervisors to edit each individual review. The percentage of times a review would proceed through the sign-off process without being returned to someone for clarification or modification—the first pass yield rate—was virtually zero. The main reasons given for these continuous rework cycles are listed below.

1. Lack of experience in writing reviews.

2. Inconsistent assessments across reviewers.

3. Incomplete guidelines for application of merit increases.

4. Reluctance of reviewers to honestly assess associates.

5. Incomplete or poorly written reviews due to batching and/or lack of adequate time commitment to the review process.

6. Short-sighted reviews that focused excessively on recent performance.

These shortcomings contributed to long production lead times, poor on-time performance, inexcusable quality deficiencies, and most importantly, frustrated associates.

With a pay-for-performance system in place at MLC, it was critical to deliver a quality review. The team developed a number of training sessions to assist managers in effectively administering associate reviews. The training focused on being honest about improvement opportunities, developing clear performance objectives and timelines, improving counseling techniques, and handling difficult situations. Application of these rather ordinary techniques that often get lost in the daily grind of a business solved many of the root-cause issues that were contributing to late performance reviews.

To eliminate the constant rework cycles, temporary human resource cells were set up to jointly evaluate reviews. After the immediate supervisor completed a review, he/she would arrange to meet with all of the other individuals involved for feedback and eventual consensus on the review and salary adjustment. After repeating this process several times, the review team settled on the standard work elements required for a high quality review as well as learned about one another's preferences and styles. More importantly, the group was able to focus on the associate being evaluated and discuss and quickly resolve differences of opinion related to the individual's performance, thereby eliminating rework loops. Eventually everyone at MLC became more comfortable with the quality of the process and performance reviews meeting certain guidelines no longer required extensive sign-offs.

Summary

Noticeable improvement of the human resource performance review process at MLC took approximately twelve months. During this time, the root causes of problems were uncovered and resolved by asking the "5 whys." Utilization of other Lean tools, such as pull, flow, kanban cards, and visual schedule boards, were essential to achieving the goals of the future state value stream map and a much improved process. Finally, tracking of critical performance metrics was critical to sustaining the new process. These metrics were similar to those used in production and included first pass yield, standard work-in-process, and on-time performance.

MLC offers frequent tours to other firms that are seeking to benchmark their Lean activities. The visitors are always given an opportunity to examine the Performance Appraisal Visual Board in MLC's main hallway, and are correspondingly asked if their own company's performance review process is satisfactory and consistently on-time. This question always elicits a good laugh from the visitors, who then relate all the shortcomings of their individual systems. It appears that most employees have learned to accept poor performance review processes. This case study reflecting what occurred at MLC demonstrates that our complacency is not warranted. The same improvement techniques that work well for production activities can also be effectively applied in a firm's support functions, such as the human resource performance review process.

It is easy to question the worth of process change and improvements in various environments. MLC consists of two facilities, one of which was previously a union shop that was decertified a few years earlier.

At the end of one of the regularly scheduled monthly plant meetings, one of the former union leaders made the following comment in front of the assembled group: "I just want to thank the leadership of MLC for getting everyone's reviews on time. It is obvious that you are now focusing on the people." It is this kind of feedback that makes change efforts worthwhile!

As you progress down your Lean journey, do not sideline one of Lean's most basic principles—respect for people. Remember this example of a rather ordinary, but critical process that is often overlooked in the Lean journey. With a cross-functional team and a disciplined improvement process, a world class associate performance review process is achievable. Your associates deserve it!

PART IV

SUMMARY

14
CONCLUDING PERSPECTIVES OF THE LEAN
JOURNEY AND ITS SUPPORTING CAST

14

CONCLUDING PERSPECTIVES OF THE LEAN JOURNEY AND ITS SUPPORTING CAST

As a world class manufacturing philosophy, Lean continues to grow in stature and popularity. While few doubt the underpinnings of this continuous improvement strategy, successful examples of truly Lean companies remain relatively scarce. One of the reasons may be the inability of management to lead significant change in all areas of the business. Your interest in this book demonstrates that you are actively pursuing a more in-depth understanding of this revolutionary enterprise paradigm and want to learn more about the involvement of accounting in making your Lean operations more competitive.

This book presents clear discussion, guidance, and examples of how the application of Lean principles can provide your business with a long-term sustainable competitive advantage. It is important to understand that Lean thinking encompasses far more than shop-floor operations. It refers to a total business strategy and a company culture that aggressively attacks waste and searches for ways to continuously improve processes. Encompassed within this Lean philosophy is the need for a performance measurement system that appropriately accounts for Lean improvements, provides suitable decision-making tools, and motivates Lean behavior. If the traditional accounting system currently used by the majority of firms implementing Lean initiatives were adequate, this book would not be necessary. However, our efforts in writing it and your interest in reading it strongly suggest that there is a need for a different, simpler accounting system that better supports the needs of a Lean environment.

Why Implement Lean?

There is ample anecdotal and empirical research that shows the value of implementing Lean practices. Toyota, arguably the premier manufacturing company over the past three decades, is the "poster-child" for demonstrating how the Lean philosophy provides a blueprint for success. Lean thinking has been used as a roadmap for excellence for many other companies as well. Some of these have been documented in this book, such as Southwest, Danaher, HNI, and Zara.

As early as 1987, Schonberger called the Toyota Production System "the most important productivity enhancing management innovation since the turn of the century."[1] However, most would agree that a true "Lean conversion" is not easy. Lean implementation can be a slow, arduous, stressful process that takes commitment, resiliency, passion, and patience. Yet, the widespread interest that continues to foster substantial growth in Lean applications is evidence that it is much more than a passing fad.

What could be the explanation for Lean's current popularity? The basic continuous improvement principles behind Lean are sensible and simple to understand. Firms are always looking for logical and meaningful ways to shore up their competitiveness, increase their market share, and sustain their profit margins. Those companies that have truly embraced Lean thinking are consistently emerging as leaders in their field. Lean makes customers' needs a primary objective and encourages respect for employees. Lean is challenging, rational, worthwhile, and proven. People at all levels of the business are involved in its implementation and can see real potential for dramatic improvements.

What Contributes to the Success of a Lean Implementation?

With the pervasive current hype about Lean, one would expect to see more examples of world class implementations. However, many firms have pigeon-holed Lean on the manufacturing floor. Further, they take piece-meal approaches, adopting one or two of the Lean tools, such as kaizen or 5S, and believe that this is sufficient to build a sustainable advantage. Too many firms do not understand that Lean is a total business strategy with a long-term focus that must permeate the whole culture of the firm. The 2006 Aberdeen study mentioned in Chapter 2 reported that there was a large performance gap between those manufacturing firms that had applied Lean practices solely on the shop floor as opposed to those that had developed a Lean culture throughout the organization.[2]

Finance and IT are critical pieces of the Lean puzzle that must be in place in order to have a successful implementation. At the most rudimentary level, finance and IT departments must embrace Lean tools in their individual areas. They should examine each report generated, determine its customer value, map its preparation and dissemination process, and work on eliminating the non-value-added activities.

Even more importantly, the finance department must provide an information system that supplies decision-making support for a Lean environment. The traditional absorption accounting system in place in the majority of manufacturing firms is no longer adequate, distributing financial reports that are too complex and difficult for most non-accountants to understand. Furthermore, the sacrosanct variances emanating from the standard costing system motivate the wrong behaviors for a Lean environment. To motivate the right behaviors and displace discouragement, performance measurements must capture the improvements and benefits of Lean, such as increased productivity and inventory turns, shortened setup and lead times, increased quality and capacity, greater flexibility, and customer responsiveness. Traditional accounting systems generally mask or distort such benefits. Guidance from this book and other materials and training seminars related to appropriate accounting systems for Lean environments are requisite for understanding the necessity of and methods for internal accounting change.

Accountants need to be involved in all aspects of Lean transitions. They should participate in kaizen events in accounting as well as on the shop floor in order to become a critical part of the cultural change and decision-making processes. They need to understand and explain to others the negative effects that can occur on the financial reports in the initial stages of Lean implementations. The following are examples of these short-term effects on earnings:

1. Improved inventory turns can negatively impact earnings as previously capitalized labor and overhead are expensed.

2. Reduced lead times may defer sales orders, as customers expect faster turnaround times and delivery dates.

3. Excess and obsolescent inventory is exposed and written off, further reducing the bottom line.

If accountants do not prepare company leadership for these results, convincing corporate of the advantages of adopting Lean may be impossible. Everyone also needs to realize that these are only temporary, short-term financial conditions, and that cash flow should actually increase, and in many instances, quite dramatically. If firms continue to focus on process improvement, the desired financial results will follow.

Too many companies are driven by meeting their budget expectations, and monthly analyses of their variance reports becomes a high priority. However, most of the rationale behind variances is contrary to desirable Lean behaviors. For example, standards that drive variances are not regularly updated. In fact, you will often find firms that have maintained the same standards for years. Thus, they are woefully outdated and inaccurate, leading firms to even budget expected variances. The objective of meeting standards and maintaining favorable variances encourages "satisficing behavior"[3] at best, and is far removed from continuous improvement.

Even if standard costs were updated per the most recent financial information available, variance reports could drive behavior contrary to Lean practices. For example, trying to meet a purchase price variance may encourage buying materials of lower quality or in larger lot sizes to obtain quantity discounts regardless of the demand. Direct labor variances may encourage workers to keep machines running continually, again disregarding demand. Further, overhead variances, which are generally tied directly to labor activity, have little relation to actually understanding and controlling overhead costs. The evidence is clear that the typical traditional costing system is not a friend to a Lean implementation. Unknowing firms may have unwarranted discouragement in their Lean efforts due to their lack of simultaneously upgrading their internal financial reporting systems.

How Can This Book Act as an Effective Tool for your Lean Conversions?

For Those Just Thinking About a Lean Journey

Whenever you are considering a radical change in business strategy, it is imperative that you gather as much information as possible about the expected benefits and risks that are involved. If you are contemplating a Lean transition, seek out and exchange information with industry leaders and experts in the field. Attend conferences and training seminars to learn about the application and implementation of specific Lean practices. Read all of the relevant materials available that will help you move towards your objectives. There is abundant literature related to Lean manufacturing, but information on how to make Lean a part of all your administrative processes, especially accounting, is limited. The discussions in this book should give you a broad perspective of Lean thinking and more specifics on the importance of including your finance department as part of any Lean implementation strategy.

In your Lean discovery period, gather reliable evidence of what others in your industry are doing related to Lean. Learn specifics about their successes, failures, roadblocks, costs, and expectations. Visit other plants that you would like to emulate who have similar processes and products and are implementing Lean practices. If feasible, benchmark your internal operations with other company plants, industry leaders, and world class firms. During benchmarking visits, inquire about the adequacy of current accounting practices and metrics. Observe operations carefully. Notice the flow of materials and discuss what changes were needed and challenges faced as velocity improved.

Share Lean thinking ideas and goals with suppliers and customers. Search out those that share your same commitment to customer value and quality. Learn what Lean tools they have in place, and volunteer to participate with them in upcoming kaizen events. Hire creative, positive workers who will lead and support change. Include all departments in Lean discovery and training. Visualize how you want your company to look in the long-term, and analyze how Lean will help you reach that objective. Always remember that it takes time, motivation, commitment, and patience to embark on a Lean journey.

For Those in the Beginning Stages of Their Lean Journey

It is important in the initial stages of Lean adoption to become comfortable with the use and implementation of the basic Lean tools. Accountants must make themselves available to participate in 5S, kaizen, setup reduction, value stream mapping, and TPM improvement events. These tools can and should be used in all areas of the business.

As defined earlier, Lean accounting (as opposed to accounting for Lean) is the application of Lean tools to improve accounting processes. Accountants should be encouraged from the initial stages of Lean to apply Lean tools for process improvement. They should focus on eliminating waste in the month-end closing process, reducing transactions, and streamlining all activities. Until the expertise is developed within accounting, Lean experts from operations should be called upon to lead the events in accounting. This internal interaction will help finance people get excited about process changes throughout the company, and will also make them more relevant and knowledgeable participants in the Lean journey.

Accountants need to also be aware of the impact Lean improvements make on inventory turns and cash flows, since these will affect their ratios and financial statements. It is important that they can clearly explain to management the possibility of and reasons for the negative results on financial performance that may initially occur from Lean improvements. Scenarios should be developed and the financial impact forecasted.

Accounting should embrace visual management techniques and clearly post the critical metrics for its various processes. First-pass yield, cost, and process times should be tracked for payroll accuracy, month-end journal entries, and accounts payable. These should be displayed with improvement targets in a prominent location, so the entire organization is aware that accounting is part of the Lean transformation effort.

During this initial stage of the journey, accounting should develop potential "defenses" that their company can use to take advantage of productivity improvements and avoid the temptation to reduce staff. They should calculate the full-time-equivalent associates consumed by overtime, outsourcing activities, and temporary hiring. In addition, the normal attrition rate and the impact of pending retirements should be ascertained. Finally, sales and marketing leadership should be engaged in this discussion to uncover areas of potential growth that would benefit from excess capacity.

This book should help remind management of the need for the accounting area to be involved in Lean changes simultaneously with the shop floor. It also gives guidance through actual case examples in how those changes can be made, beginning with accounting processes and extending to the accounting system.

For Those Making Significant Progress on Their Lean Journey

It is expected that those firms that are more mature in their Lean efforts have many of the more sophisticated Lean tools in place, such as cellular manufacturing, kanban inventory systems, poka-yokes for many of their processes, one-piece flow, and cross-trained associates. These firms have typically identified their value streams and organized their processes accordingly. As this book has carefully explained, it is critical at this juncture to have a supportive accounting system. The accounting system should be organized similar to the shop floor, and value-stream costing adopted. This requires moving, tracking, and reporting all revenues and materials, labor, and overhead costs into the relevant value stream. Inventory must also be broken down by value stream, cell, or product family, rather than remain as a single metric for the entire business. Labor tracking can be minimalized and accounting transactions reduced. Visuals should be available on the shop floor for analyzing performance and helping with inventory valuation. Financial results should be reported on "plain English" profit-and-loss statements that are simpler to prepare and easier for everyone to understand. Accountants can concentrate on business analysis, rather than transaction and variance analysis.

As accounting for Lean is implemented, be sure to discuss the methodology with your external accountants to avoid any year-end surprises. In addition, forewarn your creditors of the possible negative impact to earnings and make sure they fully understand the cash flow benefits to the company. Invite the bankers to participate in a Lean simulation so they can grasp its potential. Afterwards, take them on a tour of the company and let them experience the physical improvements for themselves.

The focus of this book is on helping you understand the need and motivation for synchronizing your accounting system with your shop-floor Lean initiatives. It is important to remember that improvements do not necessarily occur quickly, and you will never conclude your journey. The most critical and challenging characteristics are to be resilient, sustain your improvements, drive process improvements deeper and deeper, and continue forward with new Lean initiatives.

WHERE DO WE GO FROM HERE?

It is useful to recognize that while Lean is almost universally accepted as a viable manufacturing strategy, implementing Lean as a total business strategy has been accomplished by only a select handful of world class companies. To be successful, Lean must become part of a firm's culture. It must wind its way through every facet of the business. That is undeniably what has made Toyota successful. Lean is a way of life for Toyota and is the foundation of its business. Yet, cultural change is very difficult to achieve. Many Lean journeys fall short because: 1) they lack effective leadership and direction; 2) they do not adequately market the change process to all levels of the business; and/or 3) they do not fully anticipate the potential short-term consequences.

If you believe that Lean production is a valid strategy that will help your business be more competitive and profitable, it is crucial to stay committed to its principles and not waver when the waters get a little rough. Failures should provide lessons for improvements, not excuses for quick bail-outs. It is easy to let the current pull you backwards, even though you know the upstream rewards can be reached with perseverance and constant vigilance over continuous improvement. Dare to be different; the status quo is not necessarily safe or successful. In fact, generally it is quite the opposite. Lean on others' successes and learn from others' failures. Remember why you are in business, and respect, trust, and empower your associates, who will certainly help you meet your objectives if given the chance.

Encourage your accountants to actively participate in your Lean initiatives; it will be better for them and better for your business. Make your accounting systems part of the solution, rather than part of the problem. When accounting systems are carefully woven into the Lean fabric, they make it stronger and more effective. If on the other hand, finance and IT are weavers with information that misrepresents production and is out of alignment with manufacturing, the Lean fabric will unravel.

Those who understand the pitfalls of the current traditional information system in a Lean environment must assist in providing viable alternative measurement systems that unmask the benefits of continuous improvement initiatives. University professors teaching management accounting have an obligation to learn about the frailties of the traditional standard costing system in Lean environments, and share their knowledge with their students. Students need more effective educational opportunities with Lean strategies, and training in information systems that support world class manufacturing methods and environments.

More reading materials from professionals and academics, such as this book, are needed to provide a broader perspective of Lean thinking. Training seminars such as the Lean Accounting Summit and the Shingo Prize Conference are valuable for bringing companies together to learn, network, and benchmark their Lean operations. The accounting profession, including external auditors and their clients, should work jointly to assure that the accounting systems are appropriate for both external and internal reporting needs.

While opportunities for learning more about effective methods for properly reporting Lean operations are growing, the information base is still relatively small. Practitioners and professors should work together to help develop a solid framework for an accounting paradigm that will support Lean environments. More empirical research needs to be done to give credibility and legitimacy to Lean accounting. Such research will help guide and motivate others to stretch and uncover ways that will grow and sustain their own operations.

Much has been done to assist in the success and growth of the Lean paradigm, but much is still waiting for clarity, guidance, and most importantly, enlightened Lean leadership.

CHAPTER 14 ENDNOTES

1. R. J. Schonberger, *World Class Manufacturing Casebook: Implementing JIT and TQC,* (New York: The Free Press, 1987).

2. Aberdeen Group, The Lean benchmark reports: Closing the reality gap, (March, 2006), pp. 1-45.

3. Satisficing behavior represents decision making that meets one or more specified criteria, but does not necessarily seek or reach optimal preferences or objectives. (See Herbert A. Simon, "Theories of decision-making in economics and behavioral science," *American Economic Review,* (Vol. 49, 1959), pp. 253-283.) Accounting standards encourage behavior that satisfies a range of arbitrary, predefined parameters.

ABOUT THE AUTHORS

JERROLD M. SOLOMON

Jerrold Solomon has simultaneously held the positions of CFO and VP of Manufacturing at three manufacturing companies. In his dual role he was able to galvanize accounting and manufacturing to develop timely and actionable information.

While Mr. Solomon was the CFO of Vermont Castings Inc., he assumed the additional responsibility for the manufacturing operations of this heavy industrial company. He redesigned the accounting procedures and teamed with the operating folks to provide user friendly reporting that facilitated the improvement process taking place on the production floor.

As CFO and VP of Manufacturing at PACE, Inc., an electronics manufacturing firm, Mr. Solomon led the Lean transformation that resulted in customer lead time reductions of 75%, productivity improvements of 64%, space reductions of 50%, quality improvements of 100%, and a doubling of inventory turns. The cost accounting system was simplified and the use of MRP for executing the production plan was eliminated in favor of a pull system with electronic links to all suppliers. PACE, Inc. was certified as a World Class company by the Maryland World Class Manufacturing Consortium, the first and only company to be awarded this distinction in the Consortium's ten-year history.

Currently Mr. Solomon is the Vice President of Operations – Hunt Valley, for MarquipWardUnited, a division of the Barry-Wehmiller Companies Inc., the Western Hemisphere's leading packaging automation and converting group.

Mr. Solomon has a B. S. degree from Clarkson University, an M. S. degree from Michigan Technological University, and an M. B. A. degree from the University of Chicago. He has served on the Board of Directors of Vermont Castings Inc. and the Green Mountain Economic Development Corporation and currently serves on the Board of the Maryland World Class Manufacturing Consortium. He has been an instructor in Lean Accounting, a featured keynote speaker, and is the author of the Shingo Award winning book, *Who's Counting?*, a highly acclaimed business novel focusing on the interaction of the manufacturing and accounting functions during a Lean transformation, and *Leading Lean*, a novel about a three day Lean event.

ROSEMARY FULLERTON

Rosemary Fullerton, a licensed CPA in the state of Utah, is an associate professor in the College of Business School of Accountancy at Utah State University (USU).She teaches both graduate and undergraduate management and financial accounting classes. Her research has been published in top academic operations management and accounting journals, and presented at various universities and conferences throughout the U.S., and in Canada, Belgium, Finland, Italy, and The Netherlands.

Examining the relationships among cost accounting and performance measures, Lean manufacturing, and firm profitability is the focus of Dr. Fullerton's research. Currently, she is investigating the impact of cost accounting practices in world class manufacturing environments. She has presented workshops related to accounting for Lean operations to both professional and academic audiences. During her tenure at USU, she has been affiliated with the Shingo Prize, serving as a reviewer, site examiner, and team leader.

Dr. Fullerton has received several recognitions for her teaching and research. In 2004, she was awarded a Shingo Research Prize for her manuscript, "The Role of Performance Measures and Incentive Systems in Relation to the Degree of JIT Implementation," co-authored with Dr. Cheryl McWatters from the University of Alberta. In 2006, Fullerton received a Shingo Research Grant to examine the applications of management accounting systems at various manufacturing sites across the country.

Prof. Fullerton earned a PhD in accounting from the University of Utah, holds a B.S. in accounting, and a MAcc from USU, as well as a B.A. in English from Brigham Young University. She currently serves on the Business and Management Council of the Utah Association of CPAs. She is a member of the American Accounting Association, Institute of Management Accountants, and American Institute of Certified Public Accountants.

INDEX

Index

BOOKS BY JERROLD M. SOLOMON

WHO'S COUNTING?
A LEAN ACCOUNTING BUSINESS NOVEL

WINNER OF THE SHINGO PRIZE FOR EXCELLENCE IN MANUFACTURING

Who's Counting? is a business novel that for the first time explains how accounting and manufacturing personnel must develop a partnership to successfully achieve world class results. This novel takes readers on a successful "Lean Journey" and illustrates how to bring accounting practices into the 21st century in order to compete in today's global market. A must read for all those interested in successfully implementing lean accounting. 264 Pages, Hardback.

ISBN 978-9662906-2-2

LEADING LEAN
THE MAKING OF A KAIZEN EVENT

Leading Lean is the second in his series of business novels about the Lean transformation at Tricor Electronics, a fictional company. It follows the characters introduced in *Who's Counting?* and exposes the human interactions that occur during any Lean transformation. *Leading Lean* illustrates the angst people go through when asked to change, demonstrates the teamwork and leadership required, exposes the paradigms that must be changed, and lays bare the unwavering commitment required from everyone, especially the CEO. It brings to life the unending stream of interpersonal challenges as the novel chronicles the hour-by-hour progression of a three-day 5S event. *Leading Lean* demonstrates the critical role a trained facilitator plays in successfully navigating the Lean transformation and provides a road map that will enable your company to compete in the 21st century. 216 Pages, Hardback.

ISBN 978-0-9662906-9-1